SUBURBAN PLOTS

Suburban Plots

MEN AT HOME IN NINETEENTH-CENTURY
AMERICAN PRINT CULTURE

Maura D'Amore

University of Massachusetts Press
Amherst and Boston

Copyright © 2014 by Maura D'Amore

Printed in the United States of America

ISBN 978-1-62534-095-5 (paper); 094-8 (hardcover)

Designed by Sally Nichols
Set in Adobe Garamond and Trajan Pro
Printed and bound by Maple Press, Inc.

Library of Congress Cataloging-in-Publication Data

A catalog record for this book is on file at the Library of Congress.

British Library Cataloguing-in-Publication Data

A catalogue record for this book is available from the British Library.

FOR JONATHAN

CONTENTS

ILLUSTRATIONS

ACKNOWLEDGMENTS

I am indebted to the many individuals—colleagues, mentors, and friends—who read portions of this book in various stages. Philip Gura, Joy Kasson, Eliza Richards, Tim Marr, and Robert Cantwell fostered and sharpened my thinking and writing at especially formative moments. At an earlier stage, the project benefited from a summer fellowship from the Department of English and Comparative Literature at the University of North Carolina at Chapel Hill. I also received monetary support from a John R. Bittner Dissertation Fellowship in Literature and Journalism from the Department of Communication Studies at UNC. Bryan Sinche, Anne Bruder, Elizabeth Stockton, Karah Rempe, Amy McGuff, Mary Alice Kirkpatrick, and Kristina Bobo were honest critics and good friends. My time at the American Antiquarian Society, supported by the Drawn to Art Fellowship, introduced me to the pleasures of archival research and the gift of a good librarian. I extend particular thanks to Joanne Chaison, Caroline Sloat, Gigi Barnhill, and Jackie Penny for sharing their knowledge and ideas. I hope at some point to repay John Evelev's intellectual energy and generosity: he read many of these chapters in various stages over the years, and his correspondence shaped the project in important ways. I am lucky to be surrounded by lovely, supportive colleagues at Saint Michael's College, and I am particularly grateful to Christina Root and Nat Lewis for their helpful insights as I revised the work for publication.

I thank the editorial team at the University of Massachusetts Press for their work turning my manuscript into a book, especially Carol Betsch, Amanda Heller, Mary Bellino, and Bruce Wilcox. Brian Halley has been a stellar editor, shepherding me through the publication process with intelligence, wit, patience, and attention to detail. My anonymous reviewers offered suggestions that helped orient the final revisions: thank you for your engagement with my prose. Early incarnations of chapters 1, 3, 4, and 5 appeared in the *New England Quarterly, ESQ: A Journal of the American Renaissance, Studies in American Fiction,* and *Early American Studies,* respectively. In addition to the anonymous readers at each of those journals, Lynn Rhoads, Elaine Crane, Maria Farland, Duncan Faherty, and Jana Argersinger pushed me to think more deeply about these writers and nineteenth-century literary culture. Portions of chapter 6 and the afterword appeared in Monika Elbert and Marie Drews's edited collection *Culinary Aesthetics and Practices in Nineteenth-Century American Literature* (2009) and an online roundtable for the *Journal of American Studies,* respectively.

I am humbled by the love and support of my parents, Mike and Janice McKee, and my sister, Meg McKee. I am lucky to share this life in Vermont with my sweet boys, Frank and Rufus, who make every day beautiful. I am forever grateful to Jonathan, my fellow traveller and true love: thank you for the time and space to write, and for all you do to make our life together so happy.

SUBURBAN PLOTS

INTRODUCTION
Colonizing the Countryside, Plotting the Suburbs

Although we tend to associate Ralph Waldo Emerson with a Transcendental philosophy that valued nature over technology, in "The Fugitive Slave Law" he urged those in search of "the readers and thinkers of 1854" to "look into the morning trains, which, from every suburb carry the business-men into the city, to their shops, counting-rooms, work-yards, and warehouses." As they commuted, they read newspapers and periodicals that connected them to other individuals "not only virtually, but actually."[1] Emerson's commentary acknowledges that in an era of industrialization and technological change, Americans embraced print culture as a source of information about themselves and the world around them. Their reading practices, in turn, influenced the shape of the built environment, from home architecture and interior decoration to community design and social organization.

In this March 7, 1854, address at the Broadway Tabernacle in New York City, Emerson singled out a somewhat unlikely group of individuals (white-collar clerks and merchants) and a seemingly empty block of time (the commute) as worthy of attention. "Owing to the silent revolution which the newspaper has wrought," he asserted, his ideal audience of "scholars and students" had increased exponentially to become a "class [that] has come in this country to take in all classes." He urged those many "readers and thinkers" to hold themselves sacred as they deliberated on the page and in the earth. Their novel plans and "personal influence" would reverberate outward, ultimately deciding the more "public questions" of the day.[2]

Just as the proliferation, accessibility, and portability of the print medium expanded writers' and publishers' sense of audience and genre in the nineteenth century, so too did it illuminate the circular relationship between reading practices, habits of thought, and modes of living. In his impulse elsewhere to identify the domestic environment as beacon and base for those "readers and thinkers," Emerson was one of a chorus of midcentury American authors, philosophers, planners, and naturalists who sought to harness another apparently circumscribed, seemingly silent sphere in the service of larger revolutions. He and others recognized that despite its common association with women's work, the home—and its promise as ideal vision and daily reality—served as the motivating impulse for the labor and commute that took men away from it each day. In a lecture titled "Domestic Life," he maintained that a masculine engagement with the poetics and politics of home life was natural and necessary for the health of individual and nation alike:

> The Household is the home of the *man,* as well as of the child. The events that occur therein are more near and affecting to us than those which are sought in Senates and Academies. Domestic events are certainly our affair. What are called public events may or may not be ours. If a man wishes to acquaint himself with the real history of the world, with the spirit of the age, he must not go first to the statehouse or the court room. The subtle spirit of life must be sought in facts nearer. It is what is done and suffered in the house, in the constitution, in the temperament, in the personal history, that has the profoundest interest for us.[3]

Unsettling standardized demarcations between public and private life through an appeal to the regional and local, Emerson encouraged those in search of society's most powerful spheres of influence to focus their exertions in the most familiar of environments, to attempt to parse the rhythms and exigencies of oftentimes overlooked but nonetheless integral domestic intimacies.

Criticizing the status quo of home regimes governed by "prudence" and "display" as "laborious without joy," he urged American men to reform their lives by "the arrangement of the household to a higher end than those to which our dwellings are usually built and furnished" through "plain living and high thinking" achieved "in connexion with a true acceptance by each man of his vocation, not chosen by his parents or friends, but by his genius, with earnestness and love."[4] If American men felt more comfortable voicing their domestic desires and discontents, and if print culture applied itself to the task of mapping the depth and sincerity of their engagement with its geographies, he reasoned, personal and business interests would accommodate themselves to new orientations and techniques. Rather than feeling bound by systems that repeatedly refused to recognize their needs, men could bind themselves together in a playful, cathartic effort to weave a collective purpose and identity into the patterns and structures that were already in circulation.

In *Suburban Plots* I map the process whereby the text-fueled reveries of clerks transformed the terrain along the eastern seaboard from rural townships into commuter suburbs during the middle decades of the nineteenth century. From urban apartments, offices, and garrets, men were looking outward, hoping to invest in themselves at the same time that they escaped from the world of exchange. Contrasting industrialization, overcrowding, disease, and expense with the restorative effects of the natural environment on body and mind, writers, editors, architects, and reformers urged men to leave their work behind in the city at the end of each day. In leafy-bowered homes on the border between nature and civilization, they could experience the freeing sensation of a bird's-eye view of business concerns. Brooklyn, Hoboken, Chestnut Hill, Concord, and a host of other suburban towns ballooned in the 1850s and 1860s, as middle-class men constructed houses and communities from plans outlined in periodicals, pattern books, novels, and domestic treatises.

The world of print operated both as an index to geographic, cultural, social, and political developments and as a vessel for visions and desires. In their own ways, the authors at the heart of my book utilized the pen to plot opportunities for a new sort of male agency that was grounded, literarily and spatially, in a suburbanized domestic landscape. Henry David Thoreau, Henry Ward Beecher, Donald Grant Mitchell, Nathaniel Hawthorne, Nathaniel Parker Willis, Frederic Cozzens, Robert Barry Coffin, and others cultivated a masculine domesticity of self-nurture in suburban environments as an antidote to the malaise of urban life and the strictures of feminine self-sacrifice. While prominent female domestic reformers such as Lydia Maria Child, Catharine Beecher, Catharine Maria Sedgwick, and Harriet Beecher Stowe preached the virtues of labor and sympathy, viewing leisure with suspicion and allowing it only in the service of a greater good such as healthful exercise or community building, proponents of masculine domesticity mitigated service of family, God, and nation through the embrace of home-based, organic programs of self-rejuvenation and aesthetic gratification. Nineteenth-century print culture offered men relief from urban anonymity and powerlessness through experiences of quiet contemplation in the library, plant propagation in the garden, whispered intimacies at the hearth, impromptu celebrations with male friends in the dining room, and beer-making in the basement. As an illustration from Barry Gray and John Savage's *Ale: In Prose and Verse* (1866) makes clear (fig. 1), in parklike suburban settings they could defend the boundaries of personhood through domestic modes and activities that bespoke individual dreams and aspirations.

In the process of recasting a potentially tired known environment as a dramatic, even exotic locale to which men could turn for fresh perspectives and to experiment with new identities at the end of each workday and on weekends, these writers enacted a peculiar form of authorial self-promotion that utilized humorous private theatricality to deconstruct old boundaries and erect new ones with their particular needs and desires in mind. Vying for recognition in a rapidly expanding world of print, men especially appealed to domestic quirkiness in order to compete with the domestic fiction written by women which had begun to dominate the marketplace. They promised to surprise, amuse, touch, and inspire readers with unconventional narratives of their home lives outside major cities. In doing so, they asserted the possibility of resisting anonymity and mediocrity even as their prose traded in larger domestic trends and desires.

In search of a path that would allay the ennui of the nuclear family and engender a moderate response to the go-get-'em ethos of urban competition, they sought to reclaim what they viewed as endangered space for unsupervised camaraderie within a broader family of neighbors in the suburbs. In the process, they generated a politics of home life that operated as both retreat and refuge. Early suburban development offered them the opportunity to cultivate a neighborly orientation toward readers that was predicated on notions of exception. They romanced homeliness as a stage for self-fashioning at the same time that they practiced selective visibility toward the less savory implications of their own acts of appropriation and exclusion, advancement and association. Their efforts to improve quality of life by turning to home-building activities in nature were both forward- and

FIGURE I. An illustration from *Ale: In Prose and Verse* (1866). Courtesy American Antiquarian Society.

backward-looking in orientation, acts of cowardly evasion and passionate embrace.

These are fascinating plots that we don't know, gendered representations that appear to be anomalies. And yet both their proliferation and their universally breezy, conversational tone suggest otherwise. The male writers I treat here obviously relish the eccentric personae they create, but it is also clear that they assume readers will sympathize with their struggles, discoveries, and celebrations. As the titles of two of Frederic Cozzens's better-known short comedies of suburban life, "Wives and Weathercocks" and "Private

Theatricals," suggest, these men were involved in a complex process of locating a more balanced gender identity in the suburbs as well as the construction of privacy as a social space of male power, hospitality, and conviviality.[5] Their literary portrayals of domestic men reflected a rise in unfulfilled class desires for the pursuit of happiness, and the process of advertising those desires made the desperation more profound. As they performed their own class privilege through projections of alternate lives, they simultaneously admitted that they only partially controlled their fantasies and could therefore only partially fulfill them.

If it is obvious that these men recognize the parts they play in rehearsed dramas, their portrayals do not fit easily into our accounts of midcentury domesticity, which largely neglect men's relationship to the home.[6] Looking back at a genealogy of scholarship that has so radically impacted our understanding of American literature and culture, we may find it strange that such a gap remains. Efforts to deconstruct an obstinate "separate spheres" critical narrative tend to focus on men's participation in cultures of sentiment while continuing to align domesticity exclusively with women's ideological interests.[7] In doing so, scholars inadvertently reproduce the fiction of separate spheres and miss opportunities to consider the ample evidence of men's communal efforts to reshape domesticity to better suit their own needs.

This oversight appears all the more surprising given the explosion of work in queer studies and the history of masculinity in recent decades. Indeed, articulations of the ways in which men fashion selfhood in relation and in response to various anxieties appear ripe for consideration alongside our comparatively settled narratives of domesticity. By looking closely at men's representations of their domestic lives in print, I demonstrate that concepts of masculinity in the nineteenth century were not incompatible with sincere engagements with home life. In suburban America, men sought to redraw the contours of manhood as they mapped their domestic dreamscapes on the page and in the earth.

To classify a landscape as suburban rather than agricultural necessarily influences interpretations of the writings about that space. Environmental historians trace America's suburban roots to the 1820s, but the vast majority of literary scholars still fail to acknowledge the existence of suburbs until the advent of the streetcar in the 1870s, erroneously labeling all small communities on the urban periphery during the 1840s and 1850s "villages," associating authors who wrote about life there with an antitechnological, antiurban nostalgia for a preindustrial pastoral landscape, and characterizing residents as either farmers or wealthy elites who played at farming. While the term "pastoralism" may access the idealism that motivated early removals to suburban areas in the nineteenth century, it does not adequately represent the goals of those relocations. By and large, men who dreamt of houses outside the urban center did not hope to return to the land—they wanted to retain their jobs in the city and retire each evening to a more natural environment outside but within reach of it. This suburban trend marked a new orientation to home life that the field of literary studies has not yet recognized.

In addition to providing a much-needed literary corollary to the major accounts of American suburbanization, then, I reframe the terms of inquiry to examine the ways in which desires articulated in print influenced the shape of early suburban development. The formulation of a masculine aesthetics of home life by means of literary portrayals of suburbanization informs both the title and structure of *Suburban Plots*. Through the title's multivalence I seek to cast writers' play with the architectural, infrastructural nature of language itself during this period as deliberate and rehabilitative. Individual chapters follow the progression of their vision from a radical reformist impulse born out of personal and professional desperation toward an acceptance of ideological containment as business opportunity. While the first half of the book grapples with writers' responses to perceived implications of suburbanization, the second half analyzes some of the ways in which they turned geographic developments to their own literary ends.

In the opening chapters I analyze the environmental writings of two very different reformers, Henry David Thoreau and Henry Ward Beecher, to theorize the basic tenets of suburban masculine domesticity at midcentury. Although Thoreau approached the desperation of urban clerks from a Transcendentalist perspective while Beecher's faith in the restorative potential of nature was informed by the religious enthusiasms of the Second Great Awakening, both writers tapped into larger cultural trends and geographic shifts in their reflections on the state of men's lives in an increasingly urbanized, networked society. Their respective surveys of popular habits, habitats, and modes of habitation led them to insist that many seemingly indispensable cares and calculations could be abandoned without repercussion. At the same time, whether meditating on the ways in which the Fitchburg

Railroad into Boston was changing conceptions of locality or marveling at the layout of the suburban towns of Brooklyn, New York, or Norwich, Connecticut, they embraced the potential of language to inspire physical and mental domestic architectures governed by organic forms and patterns. The inescapably transitory nature of the space between city and country, both insisted, was predisposed to new ways of seeing the domestic environment for men in dire need of inner housekeeping.

I then parse the gender politics, reformist agendas, and class anxieties that undergird declarations of suburban masculinity from the period. Building on efforts to situate the self-consciously literary narratives by Thoreau and Beecher within the context of architectural pattern books, women's housekeeping manuals, and behavior guides oriented to young men, I advance the foray into popular print culture in chapters 3 and 4 with examinations of bachelor fictions and periodical articles to help highlight the fetishization of liminality as a defining characteristic of masculine domesticity. From male speakers who articulate longings for intimacy even as they reject opportunities for communion, to plots that resist closure and court unsettlement, the writings of Nathaniel Hawthorne and Donald Grant Mitchell (better known by his pen name, Ik Marvel) alternately bemoan and perpetuate what we might identify today as the hallmarks of bourgeois liberalism. Feeling under siege in an era of war, industrial expansion, massive waves of immigration, urban overcrowding, and technological innovation, and in search of a domestic order that would enable them to court romance and adventure without relinquishing the safety a protected shell, their narrators stake their claim in a landscape that geographically reproduces their middling dreamscapes.

For all the rehearsals of idealized visions of domestic life as an escape from the world of exchange, the central problem for the writers treated in this book is that, in an industrialized society, the process of what William Dean Howells refers to as "turning to account" is inevitable: business concerns always hover around the edges, even and especially for writers of fiction. In diverse ways, each of the authors in this study articulates this conundrum, a prescience that their narratives will register as being as unfinished and half exposed as the suburban plots they picture: manifestations of dreams already rehearsed and abandoned even as the structures themselves stubbornly persist in their claims to signal something precious and worth preserving precisely because it *can't* be regulated and assessed.

In the book's final chapters I explore the creation of textual suburbs by authors as innovative interventions into the landscape of print in the face of such realizations. In the ultimate embodiment of the suburban ethos, Nathaniel Parker Willis, Frederic Cozzens, Robert Barry Coffin, and William Dean Howells accept the inescapable presence of economic and class issues in any discussions of aesthetic cultivation or appreciation. In their positions as editors and writers for popular magazines, they inaugurate suburbanization of the periodical industry by marketing to the niche interests of readers. Just as the suburbs themselves declared that every individual's needs could be customized through an infinitely varied combination of set patterns, these writers turned men's greatest threat—a fear that the market would permeate every part of their existence, even insinuating itself into the space of the home—into an opportunity for investment, promulgation, and fraternity.

SKETCHING DOMESTIC MANHOOD
Early Suburbanization, Literary Celebrity, and Irving's Snuggery

A wildly popular cultural interlocutor, Washington Irving crafted the prototype of the domestic-minded man adopted by the male authors who populate my book. In addition to registering the signs and significance of early suburbanization along the eastern seaboard of the United States in the early decades of the nineteenth century, Irving's literary stylings offer compelling evidence of a nascent symbiotic relationship between celebrity culture and print culture that would flower more visibly only a few decades later. At a time when novels, periodicals, and advice manuals had begun to link bachelors with an urban sporting culture of sex, alcohol, gambling, and indolence, Irving used his sketches and authorial presence to craft an alternate vision: from his position outside the city, he presented a new model of suburban masculinity for a newly industrialized nation.[8]

Reflecting on the ways in which landscape registers new social, economic, and political realities, Irving's 1819 sketch "Rip Van Winkle" comments on the narrative attempts of men to establish domestic regimes on their own terms upon finding themselves in alien, disorienting environments. From the outset, the story troubles neat distinctions between page and landscape; in the process of figuring physical place and space as printed matter, Irving's frame casts narrative itself as an architectural construction. The narrator, Geoffrey Crayon, informs readers that the story was found among the papers of Diedrich Knickerbocker, an old New York gentleman with a penchant for researching Dutch families in the Hudson River Valley, who approached houses and their inhabitants "as a little clasped volume of black-letter, and studied it with the zeal of a bookworm."[9] The tale itself centers on the extraordinary experience of "a simple good natured fellow" (61) named Rip Van Winkle whose avoidance of any "profitable labor" (63) creates a tension between himself and his wife. The narrator describes Rip as "meek," "obedient," and "henpecked," "rendered pliant and malleable in the fiery furnace of domestic tribulation" (61–62), an emasculated man who is treated more like a wayward child than a husband.

There are hints, however, that Rip's obstinacy might be a pointed demonstration of masculine resistance. After all, he refuses to make any effort to placate Dame Van Winkle, ignoring her angry outbursts and attempting to avoid her whenever possible. A lazy disposition is not entirely to blame, either; he exercises "diligence" and "perseverance" (63) when fishing, hunting, husking corn, building stone walls, assisting other people's wives, and finishing odd jobs for neighbors. Although he claims that he does not attend to his own domestic duties because his efforts are doomed to fail, it seems just as likely that he simply does not like to be told what to do and prefers a home life that does not feel so much like work. The narrator depicts the domestic environment as a battlefield, with Dame Van Winkle announcing victory. As the supposed loser, Rip "was fain to draw off his forces, and take to the outside of the house—the only side which, in truth, belongs to a henpecked husband" (65–66). Associating the home space with tasks and criticisms, mistakes and tribulations, activities and mental states that he would rather do without, Rip appears to relinquish his hold there, searching for freedom elsewhere. He frequents the local inn for conversation and turns to the natural world for "his only alternative to escape from the labour of the farm and the clamour of his wife" (69). In the woods with his gun and his dog Wolf, his sole "domestic adherent" (66), he can forget his troubles and relax unmolested.

While it is relatively easy to see what Rip wants to escape—wife, work, and responsibility—initially his domestic designs are less clear. Not only do we lack knowledge of what occurred during the twenty-year span in which he was away, but also we are unable to access the motivations for his respite in nature, if that is indeed where he went. All we know is that, ultimately, he appears pleased with the course of events, as upon his return he no longer has to deal with "petticoat government" (92). Although the shock of discovering his house in shambles, his dog starving, and his friends long gone momentarily unnerves him, Rip's sole source of anxiety relates to the situation of finding himself "alone in the world" (86). Once he has reunited with his children and settled into the role of town storyteller, he voices no regret. Wolf may not recognize him, but he is regarded as an Odysseus of sorts by the community at large: no longer treated like a child, he is "reverenced as one of the patriarchs of the village" (91) and finds himself comfortably situated in a more organic, fraternal domestic order. For the other men of the town especially, Rip's ramble points toward the viability of an alternative to household "despotism" (92). Like Rip, they believe that the ability to be "a free citizen of the United States" has less to do with "the changes of states and empires" than with the politics of life at home (92). Although we can link his "mountain spree," as Leslie Fiedler calls it, with the impulse to free himself from stifling household regimes, Rip's true escape lies in his return, a domestic homecoming on his own terms.[10]

In the 1820s and 1830s, towns similar to the one depicted in "Rip Van Winkle" experienced massive growth spurts. As northeastern metropolitan areas expanded in response to immigration, industrialization, and transportation innovations, the shape and organization of surrounding communities changed alongside them. While Jeffersonian agrarian ideals continued to resonate for many Americans, a new business mentality had begun to leave its mark on the landscape. Trains and steamboats initiated the process of transforming sleepy villages into bustling urban satellites as they shuttled goods and people from country to city. Soon after the establishment of steam ferry access between New York and Brooklyn in 1814, for example, Brooklyn Heights became a popular residential spot for wealthy city merchants, and as early as 1836 construction began on a planned community in New Brighton on Staten Island. Designed by the British émigré architect John Haviland, the three rows of villa homes overlooked the water and boasted steamboat access to lower Manhattan throughout the day.

In language that echoes Rip's response to his own transformed village, an article from the September 1838 *Knickerbocker* commented on Long

Island's population explosion in the 1830s, as "villages enlarged their borders, and aspired to the rank of cities; wide avenues intersected the country in all directions, and the wiseacres, with pupils dilated with amazement, exclaimed, 'What a change!'" According to the article's author, new suburban trends caught the area's Dutch farmers by surprise; the town of East New York, for example, appeared almost overnight. Referring to the town's developers, the article reports:

> They laid out four-and-twenty avenues, called after all the States of the Union. They addressed a circular, couched in handsome terms, to all classes of citizens in the metropolis. They invited the artisan, the mechanic, and the manufacturer, who could there pursue their arts more easily, and be free from the exorbitant rents and charges of the town; and the man of leisure, for the site was unequalled for country-seats, and the air came pure and fresh from the bay. . . . The enterprising founders, to give an impulse to 'improvements,' built a tavern; I should have called it a hotel. They got a post-office established, which will be a great convenience to the future population. . . . The speculating spirit at last invaded all the ancient towns and villages on the island.

The piece goes on to discuss the impact of the aforementioned "rage for speculation" on plans for future railroads to transport commuters from these new towns into Manhattan.[11] Using periodicals to advertise their residential properties to a wide range of individuals, early suburban developers sought to convince city dwellers of the possibility of a better life in the surrounding countryside. In an effort to popularize and profit from a desire for urban exodus, their activities effectively reshaped the earth and erased the landscape's history. As rural America was hit particularly hard by the financial panic of 1837, that process of colonization was only accelerated, forcing farmers to relocate either farther away from metropolitan markets or, alternately, into the city as members of the dispossessed poor.

These transformed villages began to be populated by "gentlemen farmers" as early as the 1820s, men who worked in the cities and maintained their primary residence there but wanted to move their families to the surrounding countryside, at least in the hot summer months. Transportation developments during this period had the effect of emptying out the urban centers even as people continued to move to cities, whose "enormous growth to metropolitan size," writes Kenneth T. Jackson, "was accompanied by rapid population growth on the periphery, by a leveling of the density curve, by an absolute loss of population at the center, and by an increase in the average journey to work, as well as by a rise in the socioeconomic status of suburban residents."[12] Given their desire to maintain a distance from the manufacturing, dirt, overcrowding, and class diversity of the city while retaining easy access to their urban workplaces, the prospect of country life within city reach became increasingly alluring to middle- and upper-middle-class Americans. Associating nature with rest and recreation rather than labor and production, they turned to previously rural areas with new visions for the landscape.[13]

Returning in the 1830s to the Hudson River Valley he had written so much about, Irving gradually Americanized the pose of the gentleman farmer—until then largely derivative of European precedents—through his public association with his country home, Sunnyside. He had first visited Tarrytown as a teenager, when he spent a summer at his brother's house there in an effort to escape a yellow fever epidemic in New York City. After seventeen years abroad (he had written *The Sketch Book* while in Europe), he returned, like Rip, to the United States in 1832 to great acclaim. In addition to *The Sketch Book,* he had written three other popular volumes, *Knickerbocker's History of New York* (1809), *Bracebridge Hall* (1822), and *Tales of a Traveller* (1829), and New Yorkers were happy to welcome the father of American literature back to the city he had made famous. Upon learning that his nephew had recently purchased land next to a small Dutch cottage, he wrote to his sister while traveling through the West of his inclination to buy the adjoining property. By the time he settled along the Hudson River in 1835, twenty-five miles north of Manhattan, he had become one of the country's first literary celebrities, a figurehead for a rising generation of young authors. The eventual acquisition and renovation of the spot was closely followed by the press.

Although initial improvements were complete by the end of 1836, the home grew with Irving as a material compendium of his personality and interests, a respite from the world of business and an inviting habitation for friends and relatives. When Irving bought the dwelling for $1,800, it was a two-room farmhouse, and while he hoped to expand it substantially, he also wanted to retain the colonial-era elements that drew him to it in the first place. Over the next fifteen years, as steamships and trains became commonplace sights in the

Hudson River Valley, he renovated and expanded the home with the help of his artist friend George Harvey. Influenced by the picturesque style that was then in vogue, Irving made a special effort to fashion an abode that reflected a personal aesthetic. He added features—such as a weathervane—that harkened back to an earlier time in New York's history, but he also modernized the structure with indoor plumbing, an icebox, and a cast-iron stove. Each detail was the result of careful consideration, as Irving corresponded voluminously with Harvey about individual rooms as well as the surrounding grounds. He christened his "nest," or "snuggery," as he sometimes referred to the home in letters, with the name "Sunnyside" in 1841.

A. J. Downing, the domestic reformer and landscape architect who lived in nearby Newburgh, took note of Irving's plans for the house in his *Treatise on the Theory and Practice of Landscape Gardening* (1841) as an example of the "cottage ornée" and maintained that it was "even more poetical than any chapter of his *Sketch Book*."[14] The author had worked hard to facilitate such comparisons. Downplaying the typical gentleman farmer's mastery of livestock and farming in favor of forging a new domestic ethos that centered on relaxed hospitality, edifying leisure, and self-expression, Irving—an erstwhile man of leisure whose entrenched bachelorhood was supposedly a result of the untimely death of his young fiancée Matilda Hoffman in 1809 and financial troubles in early adulthood—attempted a rehabilitation and reorientation of popular understandings of men's relation to home life through his domestic flourishes. As suburban proprietor and literary celebrity, he was socially aware, community oriented, artistically informed, historically grounded, and open to possibility. At the same time, his perspective from a slight remove acted as an aid to reflection on everything from marriage to industrialization. Whether he was writing in his study, perusing his grounds, or hosting a dinner party, his lifestyle suggested that Dame Van Winkles need not hold sway over all domestic matters.

Sunnyside's location along the Hudson River contributed to its public conflation with Irving's identity toward the end of his career, even as he left in 1842 to serve as the U.S. minister to Spain for four years. It served as a welcome break from the bustle of New York City, without being inaccessibly remote. He sounded upbeat about the effects of his celebrity on the neighborhood in a letter to his sister Sarah from 1840, in which he claimed that she would "hardly recognize Tarrytown, it has undergone such changes" and

FIGURE 2. *Sunnyside from the Hudson,* oil on canvas, artist unknown (ca. 1850). Courtesy Historic Hudson Valley.

attributed them to his influence: "My residence here has attracted others; cottages and country seats have sprung up along the banks of the Tappan Sea, and Tarrytown has become the metropolis of quite a fashionable vicinity."[15] Upon his return to the United States in 1846, he commenced plans for a tower and other revisions that would better accommodate Sunnyside's growing number of inhabitants and visitors. In addition to a constant stream of tourists who viewed the property from steamboats, celebrities in their own right such as John Jacob Astor, Fitz-Greene Halleck, Edward Everett Hale, James Kirke Paulding, and Frederic S. Cozzens admired Irving's home and grounds, in many cases sharing their reflections on the place with periodical readers. He planned lavish dinners each Christmas, and his hosting abilities were touted as extraordinary. As the 1850 painting *Sunnyside from the Hudson* makes clear (fig. 2), Irving's "snuggery" was truly suburban. Recognizing itself as an object of display, a sign of success, and source of inspiration, it also communicated a belief in the democratic possibility of locating one's self in nature, the ability to mark the material environment in a powerful and lasting way, and the importance of physical and temporal space to gather one's thoughts and create something new.

In his history of the suburb, John Archer argues that in the nineteenth century, "building a house was an effort to establish a material and rhetorical apparatus that could sustain and advance the economically and politically more liberated self in a world of competitive individualism."[16] Fancying himself a "gentleman cultivator" at Sunnyside,[17] Irving modeled the process by which a home could become a life's work, a record of personhood for a generation of readers who had become captivated by his literary style and authorial persona. Downing advised that "a person of correct architectural taste will carry his feeling of artistical propriety into the interior of his house, and confer on each apartment, by expression of purpose, a kind of individuality." The "true artist," according to Downing, "breathes a life and soul, *which is beauty,* into the dead utilitarian materials, stone and wood, and they speak a language that is understood as readily as that of animate nature."[18] Writing to his sister Catherine from Madrid in June 1843 while she was house-sitting at Sunnyside in his absence, Irving invoked his own faith in the ability of humans to continue speaking through a domestic landscape long after their death: "Everything concerning dear little Sunnyside is interesting to me. My heart dwells in that blessed little spot; and I really believe that when I die I shall haunt it; but it will be a *good spirit,* that no one need be afraid of."[19] Twenty-four years earlier, Irving's Peter Vanderdonk had made a similar claim about the mountain sprites that had accosted Rip Van Winkle when he assured his audience that the Catskills "had always been haunted by strange beings" (90). Irving undoubtedly hoped that his presence would be felt by visitors to the Hudson and that he would hold vigil over later American writers just as Hendrick Hudson had over Rip.

In 1863, four years after the author's death, Christian Schussele, drawing inspiration from a sketch by Felix Darley and utilizing photographs of individual authors by Mathew Brady, conjured a gathering of popular writers at Sunnyside in an oil painting titled *Washington Irving and His Literary Friends at Sunnyside* (fig. 3). Schussele exhibited the painting in a gallery on Broadway with an accompanying booklet that textually staged the painting. The booklet states in no uncertain terms that the image is "in the truest and completest sense, a National picture . . . presenting as it does the very embodiment and central unity of native genius."[20] In a gesture that harkened back to Emerson's "Domestic Life," Schussele selected the domestic realm as the ideal setting for this evocation of American literary

FIGURE 3. *Washington Irving and His Literary Friends at Sunnyside,* Christian Schussele, oil on canvas (1863). Courtesy American Antiquarian Society.

and cultural virtuosity. Transitioning easily from historical realism to imaginative reverie, both painting and booklet invite the audience to envision the scene as actually having occurred: "Yes, here they are—the loved and lamented Geoffrey the unassuming centre of the fraternal group. They have assembled for a morning's conversation in the little Knickerbocker library at Sunnyside, a place dear to the recollection of all who have visited that classic spot. Irving sits in an easy, unaffected attitude, in his big arm chair, at once the honored host and genial companion of the distinguished party which surrounds him." Ralph Waldo Emerson, Nathaniel Parker Willis, Henry Theodore Tuckerman, Oliver Wendell Holmes, Fitz-Greene Halleck, Nathaniel Hawthorne, Henry Wadsworth Longfellow, William Cullen Bryant, James Fenimore Cooper, and others are envisioned as friends who have arrived to celebrate Irving's career in the comfort of his own home.

Characterizing the group as "the hospitable Knickerbocker's friends and intimates," however, belies the strange assemblage that confronts the viewer of this painting. The authors seem almost disembodied, posed as ghostly shells that recall Rip's encounter on the mountain with "the most melancholy party of pleasure he had ever witnessed." Irving himself, in contrast, appears dapper and ageless; plump with a cartoonish vigor and life, he looks younger than his surrounding literary inheritors. And despite any pretense of relaxation conferred through the presence of a lounging dog, the artists' postures are staid, their clothes formal. These are men of business, the portrayal admits even as it denies it, and the painting itself is doing work for the nation. In a strangely prescient way, *Washington Irving and His Literary Friends* speaks to the complexities of the pose Irving popularized and the tensions felt by the writers who surround him—the fact that, as the crumpled paper in the foreground suggests, they were still in the process of drafting a viable fantasy. As they plotted their own suburban retreats, many of them struggled to fashion something more than a Glissantian detour, to establish luminal roosts in the domestic from which they launched their literary journeys.

With the spread of railroad lines and growth of large-scale manufacturing, an explosion of suburban communities throughout the Northeast over the course of the 1840s and 1850s made isolated examples of early suburbanization in the 1820s and 1830s appear quaint in comparison. Irving's insistence on men's capacity to mediate the potentially devastating effects of the world of business by cultivating the domestic realm on their own terms seemed particularly evocative to the writers pictured in Schussele's painting as well as a host of others not represented. Because of and in spite of their qualms, midcentury male authors began the process of adapting and reinventing Irving's pose for a new generation of readers. Their desire to infuse a spirit of adventure into the home environment was tied to their belief that the guidelines and concerns that typified women's approach to the domestic sphere not only stifled the creative spirit but also acted as unnecessary, unfortunate hindrances to naturally occurring, healthy somatic impulses. Overburdened and overwhelmed with business transactions, health concerns, familial obligations, and identity crises, men united in a joint restorative effort to recoup, buttress, and enshrine an essential element of themselves within built environments in the earth and on the page.

Publicly reflecting on his pilgrimage to Sunnyside in the August 15, 1857, issue of the *Home Journal,* Nathaniel Parker Willis marveled at "the spell in [the] inner sanctuary" of Irving's home. As the old writer showed him original architectural drawings of various rooms, Willis could not help but feel as though he were in the presence of Geoffrey Crayon himself. Remarking that additions to the house were products of "gradual pleasure toil," he urged readers to think of the residence as one of Irving's "works," constructed very much as his *Sketch Book* had been, and assured them that "the playful and affectionate reciprocity between Geoffrey Crayon and his readers, is the key-note of Washington Irving's life at home."[21] For Willis and the other writers treated in *Suburban Plots,* Irving's personal and professional life offered a vision of domestic manhood that would be replicated, modified, expanded, and refined by writers engaged in a collective, if motley, effort to reshape the literary and literal space between country and city in the middle decades of the nineteenth century. That project is the subject of this book.

1

THOREAU'S UNREAL ESTATE
Playing House at Walden Pond

On January 4, 1855, under the heading "Counting-House and Country Life," *The Country Gentleman: A Journal for the Farm, the Garden, and the Fireside* carried the following letter:

New-York, Dec. 12, 1854.

Dear Eds.—It may perhaps surprise you to receive a letter for a farm journal from this modern Babel, but you little know how many clerks, who are penned up between four brick walls from one week's end to another, eagerly seize upon any book or paper that treats of green trees and blue skies.

Posted upon my stool sometimes at nine and ten o'clock at night,—a time when all decent country folks are in their beds, I take from my pocket some treatise on agriculture or its branches, and stealing still another hour from my wished-for bed, study away at plows and plowing, spades and spading,—indeed anything that will say there is a life in the open air away from ledger and ink, stores and "m'c'h'dise."

The unnamed clerk goes on to say that he has acquired "quite a little library" in the hope "that *Book Farming* will answer all purposes until I can get the practice, which will, united with the aforesaid theory, make a true farmer of me." His purpose in writing, he declares, is both to ask the editors' opinion as to where he should spend his $1,500 to $1,800 and to encourage farmers to keep their prices low if they decide to sell. In return, he promises to use his experience and rhetorical skills to dissuade country boys from "*clerking it.*"[1]

Over the course of the next year, the periodical published letters from a number of readers who had left the city to take up farming in the country-side. Recommending that the clerk abandon his plans to farm, most insisted that books could not prepare him for the labor he would face; others suggested that he limit his ambitions by purchasing one or two acres rather than twenty. Still others advised that he keep his job and buy property just a mile beyond city limits on a well-traveled street near a railroad. A kitchen garden would satisfy his rural impulses, they maintained; any larger enterprise should be overseen by a hired man, not by the clerk himself. As letters continued to stream into the office of *The Country Gentleman,* the editors began appending their own comments to those they chose to publish. Recognizing that the clerk's letter had ignited the enthusiasms of a significant portion of their readership, they invited more responses, expressing their hope that the paper's content would speak to citified young men as well as rural farmers.

The market revolution that commenced in the early decades of the nineteenth century drew young men away from their agrarian communities and into cities. Pioneering a new life about which their families could offer little advice, the young men came to depend on print culture—in forms as wide-ranging as conduct books, underground city guides, fiction, and sporting newspapers—to negotiate their new environment. In addition to easing their adaptation to city life, books and periodicals helped young men cultivate their imagined escapes. Agricultural periodicals like *The Country Gentleman* began to shift their focus from the rural farmer to the city worker who sought out the countryside for the relaxation, health, and pleasure it might afford him without requiring that he sacrifice urban amenities. At the same time, extolling the benefits to middle-class Americans of country life within reach of the city, architectural handbooks generated home designs for suburban locations. Fiction writers increasingly idealized cottage life just beyond the urban threshold, and newspapers urged young men to purchase land in the suburbs and commute instead of renting or boarding in the city.

Sitting at their work tables, the consumers of such literature dreamt of leaving the city for green fields and clean air, mentally surveying lots, building houses, choosing furniture, and planting trees. As readers took pleasure in imaginatively inhabiting the spaces the texts described, their lessons in "book farming" helped them contemplate a way of living that would be more meaningful and fulfilling. Many bachelor clerks believed that literary experiences of ownership, freedom, and responsibility would prepare them to assume control of their lives in both the public and private spheres. Within this context, Henry David Thoreau's *Walden* can be read as an attempt to demonstrate the feasibility of amalgamating "castles in the air" with the "foundations" to which young clerks like the *Country Gentleman* writer were compelled to cling for survival.[2]

While it might seem counterintuitive to open a book about the effects of print culture on early American suburbanization with the treatment of a literary figure who largely managed to remain out of the limelight during his lifetime, Thoreau's opinions about men's place in the domestic order crystallize the sense of urgency, frustration, and desire that motivated textual and physical movements toward liminal spaces by nineteenth-century writers and readers. In addition, his writings advance a fraternal, social vision of home life shared by the other authors discussed in this book, one that represents a significant departure from the model of domesticity that scholars have advanced as the era's norm. Finally, the comprehensiveness of his survey, his ability to resonate in multiple registers, makes his a particularly appealing voice for helping us locate the suburb from the standpoint of various overlapping taxonomies. Drawing from a Transcendentalist background that insisted on an organic, relational, and self-evident theory of humans' connection to nature, Thoreau constellated a domestic environment around the celebration of openness, sincerity, fellowship, and appetite. Rather than something to be feared and hidden, imagination, in Thoreau's formulation, can be an essential vehicle for the formulation and confrontation of essential natural facts, truths that turn out to be inherently domestic in the sense that they are grounded in perceptions of place which are at once known and exotic.

A self-professed jack-of-all-trades, Thoreau understood that for many young men, dreams about future homes outside the city were dreams of escape from meaningless and unending work, low social status, lack of capital, and persistent bachelorhood. In *Walden,* he insists that suburban spaces, even literary ones, promise more than escape; they offer opportunities to theorize and practice a new form of domesticity grounded in self-nurture and consciousness transformation rather than in the emphasis on Christian duty and moral inculcation of children which dominated women's experiences of nineteenth-century home life. Thoreau invites his readers—whom he identifies as poor students, New Englanders, and "the mass of men who are discontented, and idly complaining of the hardness of their lot or of the times, when they might improve them" (16)—to play house outside of town, regardless of whether they ever decide to purchase land or build homes there, much less marry or become managers or merchants. Cultivating unreal estate in *Walden,* Thoreau draws on imaginative capital to reconcile the fact of the city with a desire for the rural. Throughout his narrative, he insists that aesthetic stimulation and appreciation of the natural world matter and that printed records of such experiences can transform understandings of basic concepts such as home, work, family, and self, thus clearing space for living and dreaming within even the tiniest urban garret or office.

CONTEXTUALIZING *WALDEN*
Print Culture and Suburbanization in Mid-Nineteenth-Century America

Concord was not a country town when Thoreau decided to retire to Walden Pond in 1845. The transformation from village to suburb that had occurred there and in many other towns during the first half of the nineteenth century, in Robert Gross's words, "enabled middle-class Americans to enjoy all the exciting advantages of the city without ever having to live there."[3] The railroad reached Concord in 1844, bringing Boston within an hour's travel. Arguing that the railroad had "destroyed the old scale of distances," Thoreau appealed for access to the Harvard College library in 1849, persuading the president to extend borrowing privileges to alumni living beyond the ten-mile radius from Cambridge that had earlier been established.[4] Given new perceptions of scale, he demanded new classifications and opportunities, marveling in his journal that even though he lived in the midst of nature, "five times a day I can be whirled to Boston within an hour."[5] To ignore the evolving relationship between the community of Concord and the city of Boston is to neglect a development that Thoreau himself recognized and felt compelled to write about in *Walden.* Positioning his project in relation to a growing body of literature on the benefits of suburban living, Thoreau muses in "Economy" that "it would be some advantage to live a primitive and frontier life, though in the midst of an outward civilization, if only to learn what are the gross necessaries of life and what methods have been taken to obtain them" (11).

By the 1840s and 1850s, newspapers and periodicals were saturated with editorials about the amenities of suburban life, sample home designs, and discussions of landscape architecture, building materials, furniture choices, and decorating decisions. Architects like A. J. Downing, Calvert Vaux, Gervase Wheeler, and Lewis F. Allen quickly became famous with treatises and guidebooks such as *Cottage Residences* (1842), *The Working-Man's Cottage Architecture* (1848), *The Builder's Pocket Companion* (1850), *The American Cottage Builder* (1854), *Homes for the People, in Suburb and Country* (1855), *The Cottage Builder's Manual* (1856), *The Economic Cottage Builder* (1856), and *City and Suburban Architecture* (1859), works that, in offering patterns for houses that could be efficiently and economically constructed, met the demand from individuals who could not afford to hire their own architects but who lacked the skills and community support to build homes as their forebears had done.

Like the period's behavior manuals, home pattern books detailed the benefits that would accrue from correct choices, and toward the end of creating a home space that would shelter and protect the aspiring young businessman and his current or future family, they provided step-by-step instructions on how to fashion a well-designed and appointed home. All of the texts insisted that beauty could coexist with economy and that working-men deserved comfortable homes in desirable locations as much as, or even more than, the elite. *The Economic Cottage Builder,* for instance, which marketed itself as a democratizer, claimed to be written "for the benefit of those whose means will not allow them to procure professional assistance, and yet whose tastes are as worthy of being gratified, even in an humble manner."[6] During the antebellum anti-rent wars, books and periodicals promoted home ownership as the first step to financial freedom and social advancement. In *Homes for the People, in Suburb and Country,* Gervase Wheeler bemoaned the fact that "many a respectable mechanic, or young beginner in business, is forced to live with his family in a boarding or lodging-house, when he might, at an equal, possibly at a less expenditure, have a home of his own."[7] But there was no need to despair. In the countryside, economic downturns and rising land costs were driving farmers farther away from population centers, and "the suburbs [were] rapidly filling with rows of dwellings" intended for people of modest means.[8] To facilitate relocation to the suburbs, authors proffered procedural advice on matters such as forming associations to purchase large plots, which could then be subdivided among individual families but maintained collectively.[9]

In addition to plans and building instructions, pattern books often included guidance on how to select and purchase property as well as essays on suburban life. Resembling the era's fictional accounts of the vine-covered cottage, the descriptions were generally romanticized. *The Economic Cottage Builder* recommended that houses face east, "so that the rising sun may throw its first rays upon your cottage porch, to enliven you to your daily toil, and may leave his golden blessing with you as he sinks at evening into his purple cushion in the west."[10] Occasionally the manuals quoted notable celebrities to back up their claims, as when *The American Cottage Builder* invoked Washington Irving to argue that even bachelors should add plantings to their yards. Future pleasures were always promised, and the books offered trellises, blooming flowers, spreading grapevines, and happy hummingbirds and bees as rewards for planting and caring for the recommended vegetation.

Idealized renderings showing couples and small children conversing or walking around the grounds complemented textual portrayals (fig. 4). Although the houses were small, they were pictorially set against a natural paradise of rolling hills, streams, and trees, with paths gently curving toward viewers, inviting them to imagine themselves in the role of the people pictured in the scene. Depictions of life in the suburbs downplayed the labor involved in shaping the domestic environment. Focusing instead on completed visions, texts characterized the home as a retreat, situated in a community of like-minded individuals. *The Working-Man's Cottage Builder,* for example, argued that men should separate business from family life, since "the facilities of ferriage, and the opportunities for healthful exercise, (if desired,) are all favorable to suburban residents; while a family residence within the city is (at best) but a poor reward to citizens in active life, who might almost as well be doomed to perpetual confinement in their place of business."[11] Although authors were forthright about the materials and funds required to live comfortably in the suburbs, the emphasis was always on the home as a record of success rather than a site of production.

Thoreau conducts a rigorous investigation of these print-fueled domestic dreamscapes in *Walden,* urging readers in the midst of a changing economic and cultural landscape to reconsider and recenter the relationship between self and home. Drawing from and commenting on popular pattern-book literature, engaging with new developments in land appropriation and use,

FIGURE 4. Title page from *The Economic Cottage Builder* (1856). Courtesy American Antiquarian Society.

he seeks to address in a new way the widely published desires and concerns of the nation's city-trapped young men. In the process of staking out a literary terrain that corresponds (even in name) to a physical one, Thoreau launches an inquiry into the art of living, a domestic meditation on what it means to live well.

"Pasture Enough for My Imagination"
A New Type of Ownership for a New Type of Space

Even though *Walden* is subtitled *Life in the Woods,* Thoreau's house was not located in the wilderness; it stood about a mile and a half south of Concord's town center on land, recently cleared by loggers, that was owned by Emerson. Despite his claim that the nearest neighbor was a mile distant, Irishmen who were working on the Fitchburg Railroad, which crossed the pond on its southern edge, lived in small shanties nearby. Thoreau started building his cabin in March 1845 with boards he bought from one of those laborers, and some of his friends assisted with the framing. "Occasion[s] for neighborliness" could be had by a brief walk along the tracks into town, and Thoreau mentions performing some surveying and carpentry there as well. Even at his cabin, as he remarks from time to time in *Walden,* he entertained visitors, conversing with friends and accepting gifts of food and clean laundry from his mother and sisters (45). The community knew about his experiment; sometimes when he returned to his cabin, he found calling cards, flowers, or other evidence of townspeople's visits. Aware that he was a local curiosity, Thoreau notes that visitors of both sexes and all walks of life came "to see me and the inside of my house," asking for a glass of water as an excuse for calling (150).

Although Thoreau fashions Walden Pond as a private, natural environment, then, his narrative simultaneously registers the fact that he is not the only one looking for new experiences and opportunities on the urban periphery. He invokes popular literature associated with suburban domestic life as he considers his personal relationship to the community of Concord and the town's relationship to Boston. With the distance between his house and Concord center mirroring the suburbanite's remove from the city, he claims that he selected Walden Pond because of its unique combination of opportunities for both privacy from (an ideal place "to transact some private business with the fewest obstacles" [19–20]) and proximity to ("a good port and a good foundation" [21]) others. Although Thoreau's "business" is non-traditional—he is a surveyor of daily life as commonly as of geographical distances—he acknowledges that business is a prominent factor when people are deciding where to live.

Listening to the sound of the train passing near his cabin as it "convey[s] travellers from Boston to the country," he reflects on the changing landscape (114). The availability of regular and efficient transportation had transformed the meaning and implications of the word "business." A new class of men were sitting in offices, scheduling meetings, making deals, settling transactions—working mentally rather than physically on problems and opportunities that had not existed twenty years earlier.[12] Even the lives of farmers had been transformed as they recalibrated production to the demands of unseen markets in the wider world. "With such huge and lumbering civility the country hands a chair to the city" (115–16), Thoreau remarks, as country and city became inextricably linked in success and failure. The impact of that new relationship was felt at the micro level as well. Surveying the future of what would soon be identified, owing to its proximity to the railroad and its picturesque qualities, as valuable land, Thoreau conjures "the ornamented grounds of villas which will one day be built" where his cabin now stands (180). The pond environment had already begun to reflect the changing relationship between country and city: trees were being cut for lumber at an alarming rate and transported by rail to other locations, making it increasingly difficult to describe the area as forested at all.[13]

Thoreau did not count himself exempt from the developments he observed around him; even in his own life, the pencil factory always lurked. In an 1844 journal entry Emerson recalled Thoreau speaking of the difficulty of single-mindedness when one was faced with a daily schedule that compartmentalized certain modes of behavior and types of thinking into standardized allotments. "Henry Thoreau said, he knew but one secret, which was to do one thing at a time, and though he has his evenings for study, if he was in the day inventing machines for sawing his plumbago, he invents wheels all the evening and night also; and if this week he has some good reading and thoughts before him, his brain runs on that all day, whilst pencils pass through his hands."[14] As Thoreau's famous 1848 reply to the Harvard ten-year-alumni survey suggests, it was a problem concomitant with the age, and one that he sought to address straightforwardly in *Walden*. For all the era's emphasis on direction, professionalization, and uniformity, he found his own path to be circuitous, his occupations haphazard, and his training incomplete and irrelevant:

> I don't know whether mine is a profession, or a trade, or what not. It is not yet learned, and in every instance has been practised before being studied. The mercantile part of it was begun *here* by myself alone.
>
> —It is not one but legion, I will give you some of the monster's heads. I am a Schoolmaster—a private Tutor, a Surveyor—a Gardener, a Farmer—a Painter, I mean a House Painter, a Carpenter, a Mason, a Day-Laborer, a Pencil-Maker, a Glass-paper Maker, a Writer, and sometimes a Poetaster. If you will act the part of Iolus, and apply a hot iron to any of these heads, I shall be greatly obliged to you.
>
> My present occupation is to answer such orders as may be expected from so general an advertisement as the above. That is, if I see fit, which is not always the case, for I have found a way to live without what is commonly called employment or industry attractive or otherwise. Indeed my steadiest employment, if such it can be called, is to keep myself at the top of my condition, and ready for whatever may turn up in heaven or on the earth.[15]

The ability to fit a standard and to "see fit" are two different matters entirely, the letter implies, one an activity of accommodation and the other of discernment. While he concedes in *Walden* that "strict business habits . . . are indispensable to every man" (20), Thoreau also resists conventional wisdom by appropriating the language of business and capital for an altogether new form of reckoning. He came to believe that writers are inherently surveyors and that the discipline, calculation, and determination of the employed clerk, carpenter, or engineer might productively find application in the exigencies of the natural world—in other words, that anyone of a sound constitution could harness the tools of his trade toward the employment of plain living through open-ended discovery, a playful reacquaintance with and appreciation for the most basic domestic impulses.

And so, characterizing the longing for a home as universal, Thoreau allies himself with folks like *The Country Gentleman*'s clerk from the opening line of "Where I Lived, and What I Lived For": "At a certain season of our life we are accustomed to consider every spot as the possible site of a house" (81). Lacking careful approach, however, the domestic environment that lures a clerk or student will become, for him, a trap that ensnares rather than liberates, "a workhouse, a labyrinth without a clew, a museum, an almshouse, a prison, or a splendid mausoleum" (28). Before purchasing land or building materials, Thoreau instructs, individuals should pare down their desires to the essentials. Whereas A. J. Downing maintained that "for that species of suburban cottage or villa residence which is most frequently within the reach of persons of moderate fortunes, the environs of Boston afford the finest examples in the Union,"[16] Thoreau claims that it would take a laborer ten to fifteen years to earn enough money to buy an $800 house near Walden Pond. His point, that a prospective home owner could easily "have spent more than half his life commonly before *his* wigwam will be earned" (31), provided concrete evidence that property was not always a boon. Throughout *Walden,* Thoreau alludes to the fact that debt was common in the mid-nineteenth century and that it prevented men from living in their homes as they had originally envisioned.

The task of locating property and constructing a domicile, Thoreau warns, is more easily imagined than executed. Young men from the city are well advised to avoid rash decisions and to act with deliberation and intelligence, for the solution to urban malaise does not necessarily reside in the suburbs, as appealing as that prospect might be. As Thoreau famously states in "Economy": "The mass of men lead lives of quiet desperation. What is called resignation is confirmed desperation. From the desperate city you go into the desperate country, and have to console yourself with the bravery of minks and muskrats" (8). "Quiet desperation," in Thoreau's formulation, characterizes the day-to-day lives of thousands of young men who had abandoned their family homes for the city in search of opportunities and advancement, only to find themselves bereft of both. A space outside the city would not allay their despair, and a new house would not guarantee a fresh lease on life, "for our houses are such unwieldy property that we are often imprisoned rather than housed in them; and the bad neighborhood to be avoided is our own scurvy selves" (34). Men should attune their habits and longings to the rhythms and beauties of nature, Thoreau cautioned, before appealing to society's dictates for direction, for a thorough, situated inquiry into the landscape of inner desire would help them align their dreams with the realities of their lives.

Over the course of *Walden,* Thoreau crafts a domestic environment from words and phrases that draw inspiration from the phenomena and patterns of the natural world. His pond house is, to be sure, material, but his cabin in the woods is a confluence of his mind and his surroundings as much as of his hands. Referring to the rest cures that sent many nineteenth-century Americans in search of greener spaces, he remarks in his "Conclusion" that "to the sick the doctors wisely recommend a change in air and scenery." But, he maintains, "we should oftener look over the tafferel of our craft, like curious passengers, and not make the voyage like stupid sailors picking oakum" (320). The "craft" for Thoreau is, first, the self and, second, the vessel, and this statement highlights the common and continual slippage of mind and matter in everyday activities. His fundamental question as to "what a house is" (35)—the purpose it serves as well as its relationship to its inhabitant—seeks to collapse the ideal and the real, to eliminate the gap between an imaginative and a physical existence. The mind, Thoreau insists, is itself a home, as is the landscape, and both should be valued as much for their ability to function as conduits for inner transformation as for their service as background, setting, lot, or claim. Playing house on Walden Pond, in an urban garret, or "even in a poor-house" (328) is serious work—more serious and worthwhile, and certainly more economical, than relocating to the suburbs.

Approximating the poet's project of creating a literary incarnation of a physical landscape, Thoreau promises yet more: his unreal estate, he claims, is more valuable than property in possession. Land, he comes to realize in "Former Inhabitants," resists ownership. Though only a squatter, he declares, he "owns" more of Walden Pond than those individuals who may, in the future, build ostentatious villas on the site. Much like *The Country Gentleman*'s clerk, Thoreau admits to having mentally surveyed the landscape that surrounds him, claiming in the opening of "Where I Lived, and What I Lived For," "In imagination I have bought all the farms in succession" (81). At the same time, he recognizes that since his motivations differ from those of the farmer, so should his methods. Like the clerk, Thoreau works with his head rather than his hands, and he hopes to benefit from an aesthetic appreciation of the landscape, not from its economic appreciation. The ideal fruit of his labors is essentially intangible—he seeks happiness, contentment, and spiritual gratification—a different sort of fruit altogether.

While the farmer toils for weeks and months preparing the earth, sowing seeds, and tending the vine, Thoreau spends "an afternoon" fashioning a landscape that suits his mind's eye, leaving the fields "fallow . . . for a man is rich in proportion to the number of things which he can afford to let alone." Reworking the Jeffersonian myth of the yeoman farmer, he argues that the student who loves the farm from afar asserts ownership more palpably and powerfully than does the farmer: "When a poet has put his farm in rhyme, the most admirable kind of invisible fence, has fairly impounded it, milked it, skimmed it, and got all the cream, [he leaves] the farmer only the skimmed milk" (81–83).

At a time when new suburban residents were pushing rural farmers farther and farther away from the city as they attempted to purchase their dreams, Thoreau proposes an imaginative ownership not bound by time, space, or money. Recognizing that the growth of popular print coverage of suburbia reflects readers' desires, he gauges its allure for himself and for men in similar situations. As a liminal space that exists in readers' minds, the suburb is inherently literary, a locus for the satisfaction of unfulfilled needs and hopes in private and public life. In *Walden,* Thoreau exposes that disconnect between ideal and real, but more important, he demonstrates a way out of such binaries and distinctions. Because he does not own the land he lives on, he is able to cultivate unreal estate, all the while remaining fully grounded in his material existence. His domestic arrangements and activities at Walden Pond become conduits to worlds around and within him, as a new delineation of the purposes and possibilities of domesticity takes root.

"BEAUTIFUL HOUSEKEEPING AND BEAUTIFUL LIVING" AT WALDEN POND

Having settled into confirmed bachelorhood after Ellen Sewell refused his proposal, Thoreau, as Washington Irving had before him, sought to prove that even a less than desirable lot by society's standards could be transformed into something singularly valuable. By focusing on the needs of an individual occupant, Thoreau offers an alternative to the ordinary model of domesticity, which, he believes, is as damaging to men as it is to women. Arguing that a home's primary purpose should be to provide shelter, serving as a means rather than an end, he questions common conceptions of domestic life that associate the home with certain types of furniture, food preparation, family structure, or religious practice. In "House Warming," he claims to comprehend the effort and activity involved in taking care of a house, explaining that, as a result of his experiences living alone, "I began to see where housework commences, and whence the endeavor, which costs so much, to wear a tidy and respectable appearance each day, to keep the house sweet and free from all ill odors and sights. Having been my own butcher and scullion and cook, as well as the gentleman for whom the dishes were served up, I can speak from an unusually complete experience" (214). From that standpoint, he argues, it would be better to simplify, getting rid of furniture and objects at the very least, and perhaps the house altogether, than continually dust and take care of them.

Simplifying the domestic environment renders it not only more efficient but more beautiful as well; it minimizes the work of arranging and cleaning in favor of looking and listening. Thoreau argues that the domesticity he models in *Walden,* though seemingly without function, demonstrates the ultimate commitment to functionalism, as it operates on the premise that it is better to dust the mind than the home: "Before we can adorn our houses with beautiful objects the walls must be stripped, and our lives must be stripped, and beautiful housekeeping and beautiful living be laid for a foundation: now, a taste for the beautiful is most cultivated out of doors, where there is no house and no housekeeper" (38).

Interrogating Thoreau's proposed revisions to domestic practice and ideology, the critic Sarah Wider asks, "Who can afford to dispense with certain household amenities?—not the wife, not the mother, but the man without children."[17] Her question is as pertinent for *Walden's* nineteenth-century readers as it is for today's. While it is tempting to approach the book as the personal musings of a literary man—that is, as social commentary not directed toward an audience and existing in a vacuum—the text's shape and content suggest that Thoreau was not speaking to himself alone or about his condition only. Despite arguments to the contrary, he was no misanthrope. In the most local sense, as Wider recognizes, Thoreau was speaking to men—and to a very specific class of white, educated men at that. But although his aesthetic model is definitely the product of certain privileges—he does not have to contemplate the effects of his actions on a wife or children, and many of his basic needs are met by friends and family members—his "unusually complete experience" of housekeeping should not be discounted nor his dismissal of treatises by female domestic reformers such as Catharine Beecher and Lydia Maria Child be viewed as disdain for a female perspective.[18] He was focusing not on the limitations of female domestic practice but rather on the short-comings of traditional approaches to home life, those held by both men and women and propagated by society at large.

Similarly, while his otherwise complete reckoning fails to account adequately for the fact that his lifestyle was complicit in larger machinations that controlled ethnic others by incorporating them into the domestic economy, and that Irish laborers like John Field were preparing the land to be occupied by early suburbanites, his attention to their presence in the landscape itself is not inconsequential. Directing his attention to the unpretentious lower-class cottages nearby, homes of railroad workers and town outcasts, Thoreau muses that "equally interesting will be the citizen's suburban box, when his life shall be as simple and as agreeable to the imagination, and there is as little straining after effect in the style of his dwelling" (47). Whatever shortsightedness he displays when he writes about the Irish, Thoreau's inclination to approach their homes as models of ideal dwellings (itself an appropriation) for his materially pared-down, intuition-driven, nature-based domesticity reflects a thoughtful perceptiveness that is not nullified by the sometimes practical incompatibility of playfulness and a life of extreme hardship and labor. Although he certainly recognizes that his plight differs from that of the Irish and African Americans he observes around him, he hopes that his recommendations will find healthy application even and especially in what appear to be the most dire of circumstances.

In an early, little-known essay titled "The Landlord," Thoreau turned to the architecture of the country tavern and inn and to its proprietor, whom he alternately refers to as the "landlord" and "host," for a model of the reformed domesticity he would propose more directly in *Walden*.[19] As a place "where especially men congregate," the tavern, in Thoreau's formulation, provides welcome, camaraderie, and entertainment without succumbing to trendy ornaments or display-oriented showmanship. The space dispenses with distinctions between public and private in favor of a general, all-encompassing gesture of goodwill. At the same time, it retains an essentially domestic air of "simple and sincere" cheer and restorativeness; above all, it "warms and shelters its inhabitants." Its structure and application demonstrate that popular associations of domesticity with consistency, stability, and ownership need not define the shape of home life. Personal belongings are eschewed in favor of a sense of belonging, and transience becomes a quality to welcome rather than avoid. Not motivated by principles of philanthropic philosophy or Christian charity, and forgoing the "civilities of commerce" in favor of an unembarrassed embrace of "a vast relish or appetite," the "downright" (rather than "upright") disposition of Thoreau's ideal masculine steward originates "by a necessity of his nature" rather than his conscience.

In a conscious decision to avoid limiting activities and identities through processes of allocating, partitioning, and concealing, the tavern's open architecture enables its frequenters "free range, as not in palaces, nor cottages, nor temples." While pattern books fetishized a nested geography of private life through their architectural renderings of hallways, porches, closets, libraries, parlors, hidden kitchens, and an ever-increasing number of bedrooms, Thoreau saw that the effects would extend into social interactions, daily routines, and imaginative forays. For him, plainness would leave room for spontaneity. Just as at his cabin on Walden Pond, "all the secrets of housekeeping are exhibited to the eyes of men." Here is no "disgust at kitchens" (evidenced in pattern books by relegating them to the basement or rear of the house); instead, they are reverenced as essential elements, along with the hearth, which is truly "the heart, the left ventricle, the very vital part of the house," in the satisfaction of the most basic human needs of sustenance, shelter, and companionship.

As for the proprietor of this domestic landscape, "he knows what a man wants," Thoreau writes, "for he is a man himself." Embodying "the true house-band, and centre of the company—of greater fellowship and practical social talent than any," he is, all in all, "a good fellow—good to be associated with." In this early essay Thoreau intimates that an ability to look beyond advertised felicities would enable a man to entertain possibilities for thought and behavior that architects and reformers had overlooked in their quest for new patterns and designations. As in *Walden,* rather than theorizing an alternative to domesticity that Milette Shamir identifies as a "masculine ideal of isolationist individualism . . . an ethos of privacy, bounded self-containment, affective restraint and reticence, all at the expense of emotional expressiveness and intimacy," Thoreau heralds a man's ability to assume any number of roles in and orientations to his home environment at a time when he and others felt an acute need for such organicism.[20]

As Thoreau urges young clerks and managers to consider what they really want from their domestic lives, he reflects on the role of print culture in shaping domestic desires and transforming communities. Drawing on popular interest in the space between city and wilderness as the ideal location for the home, he suggests that precisely because young men like the letter-writing clerk are *not* settled or satisfied, they may be more likely than other individuals to ground experience in imagination, thought, and observation. For that reason, he believes, they are ideal stewards of an evolving suburban landscape. A new type of space invites new ways of living, and the unique perspectives and needs of men like the clerk promise not only to transform houses or landscapes but to reshape the lives of their inhabitants as well.

Taking note of Thoreau's 1849 lecture tour, Horace Greeley remarked in the April 2 issue of the *New York Tribune,* "There is not a young man in the land—and very few old ones—who would not profit by an attentive hearing of that lecture [on 'Life in the Woods']." Referring to Thoreau's decision to pare down material essentials in an effort to perceive more clearly the needs of his soul, Greeley continues, "If all our young men would but hear this lecture, we think some among them would feel less strongly impelled either to come to New-York or go to California." Greeley's commentary suggests that, although Thoreau's work was not popular in his day, it had the potential to change the way people thought about themselves in relation to their homes, thus allowing them to harness social, economic, and cultural trends and apply them to new ends.

In the latter decades of the nineteenth century, the proliferation of rail and streetcar lines accelerated suburbanization, and distinctions between work and home, labor and leisure became more apparent for many Americans. Commuting from urban offices to leafy-bowered cottages in planned developments and bedroom communities, businessmen adjusted their rhythms to suit different environments. Even though the prescience of his predictions about the impact of industrialization and transportation on people's conceptions of place and scale would not be fully appreciated until decades after his death, Thoreau's recommendations did resonate with contemporaries who struggled for direction in lives that often seemed dominated by endless shuttlings from one set of obligations to another. Contemplating the path he had worn between his front door and Walden Pond, Thoreau remarked, "How easily and insensibly we fall into a particular route, and make a beaten track for ourselves" (371). At the same time, however, he celebrated the imagination's capacity to forge new paths and to fashion edifices that would suit new needs and desires.

Thoreau understood that even in its earliest incarnations, suburban America was built on the promise of a better life through bigger houses, greener lawns, more capable homemakers, and heartier children. As print culture responded to readerly desires for identity and ownership, escape and rejuvenation, romanticization of the resulting vision was inevitable. Sympathetic to the dilemmas faced by clerks like the one who wrote to *The Country Gentleman* for direction, he validated their domestic longings for a space of their own, a yard, attractive furniture, happy hummingbirds, and interesting visitors. After all, even in his room at his parents' house, he clearly derived pleasure and utility from the driftwood-hewn bookshelves that he populated with displays of stones and lichens, nests and arrowheads. He consciously fashioned a room that spoke to his sensibilities, accommodated itself to seasonal rhythms, and recognized the necessity of access to wild land and water. In *Walden,* he simply advised mindfulness as his readers cast their lot textually and geographically. Though the material landscape might provide a foundation for a new way of living, his account of life at Walden served to remind readers that the refuge they were seeking was in truth within themselves.

2

"TO BUILD, AS TREES GROW, SEASON BY SEASON"
Henry Ward Beecher's Domestic Organicism

As Thoreau was critiquing contemporary trends in home building and housekeeping from a Transcendentalist perspective in Concord, the popular preacher Henry Ward Beecher had begun to contemplate similar developments from the vantage point of his rapidly expanding church in suburban Brooklyn. Influenced by the work of his sisters Catharine and Harriet and inspired by his own enjoyment of gardening and interest in domestic pursuits, in his writings for periodicals during the 1850s and early 1860s he directed readers' attention to the architecture of the home as central to any man's consideration of what it means to live the good life. Although *Seven Lectures to Young Men,* Beecher's foray into the conduct-book genre, had garnered praise and laid the groundwork for what would become a career-long investment in the fate of manhood in the industrial era, by midcentury he found himself, as life guide to the clerks and merchants who filled his congregation, less interested in warning adherents away from dangerous environments and behavior than in helping them to cultivate inner passions and establish roots in a new society. Like Beecher himself, these men had become increasingly anxious about the potentially soul-killing effects of the urbanization that in many ways governed their daily rhythms and routines, even as they also valued the innovations and efficiencies of the very technologies that made them feel vulnerable.

While the interest in articulating a philosophy of home that appealed particularly to men's lifestyle concerns links him to Henry David Thoreau, the example of Beecher represents a counter-strain in midcentury domestic ideologies that invited men to embrace the central conundrum of their lives by envisioning suburban retreats as unexpected canvases for latent creativity, happy by-products of a rapidly industrializing nation. Even as Beecher recognized that for the average man a house represented "compromise between his heart and his pocket," as well as "a memorial of his ingenuity in procuring the utmost possible convenience and room from the least possible means," he urged his readers to demand and expect more.[1] Seeking to identify the "point of transition at which a material thing touches the immaterial" in order to harness the power of one's surroundings to affect mental states and communicate spirit, he encouraged American men to embrace a domestic mentality as a tonic for stresses associated with their urban work lives (*SP,* 100).

Combining Romantic philosophy with a new form of liberal evangelism, Beecher applied a governing metaphor of organic growth to a new form of life advice that sought to integrate pleasure and obligation, desire and necessity. In addition to its potential applications in spiritual matters, he suggested that the natural world offered an unparalleled model for the gradual gratification of domestic visions and wishes. In Beecher's formulation, a home must be designed, appointed, and maintained with an eye toward "serv[ing] our bodily wants, our social domestic wants, and our social public wants" (*SP,* 287). Certain rooms would satisfy specific urges and needs. Ideally, a house should grow alongside its inhabitants in a similar way to branches on a plant, with new plans and improvements flowering forth from sturdy foundations in their appointed time. Beecher represented the "fully blossomed" home as the incarnation of a life story.

At the same time, by imbuing individual rooms with a regenerative function, he characterized the house as a sort of "second self," an offspring that would bestow a nourishing, affirmative influence on its cultivators and society at large. "All decisions will have been aimed at some real want, and, meeting it, will take their subtle air and character from it." he advised. "Thus, one by one, the rooms will be born into the house as children are into the family. And, as our affections have undoubtedly a certain relation to form, color, and space, so our rooms will in their forms, dimensions, and hues, indicate the faculties which most wrought in their production" (*SP,* 289). In a circular process of inspiration and embodiment, a man's house might, as "a result of his own growth," communicate (to himself and others) the expression of his soul, the fruit of his core beliefs and labors. It would "secure the mazy diversity" (291) of an erstwhile unassuming businessman. In essence, his approach to home life promised to transform bourgeois masculinity by uniting seemingly incompatible categories of self and other, leisure and labor, society and spirituality, in a loosely defined program of privatized domestic benevolence.

SUBURBANIZING THE IMAGINATION IN AN ERA OF PROTESTANT REVIVALISM

Beecher's celebrity at midcentury was unparalleled in American culture. In the 1850s his Sunday services at Plymouth Church in Brooklyn attracted three thousand people at a time. The weekend ferries that shuttled between Manhattan and the growing suburb were affectionately called "Beecher Boats" in reference to the object of many sightseeing missions. The press's fondness for referring to the church itself as "Beecher's Theater" speaks to the minister's novel approach to his congregation's religious life. In an era of competing amusements, Beecher made church a destination. A skilled rhetorician with an affable, welcoming personality, he deftly combined entertainment and self-reflection in sermons intended to awaken people to the manifold opportunities for embrace that surrounded them. As shocking as this approach was to many onlookers, Beecher maintained that pleasure need not be avoided universally. Indeed, at various points in his life he argued that it was precisely the routine denial of pleasure and concomitant lack of acceptable outlets for the gratification of desires he associated with the soul's inmost needs that led so many Americans, but particularly men, into dangerous moral territory. By validating his adherents' aesthetic and experiential longings and by locating a place for amusement and entertainment within a religious framework, Beecher sought to suburbanize pleasure for his audiences by linking it to usefulness and framing it as a potentially character-building enterprise.

Much of Beecher's success can be attributed to his masterly ability to identify broad-based ideological shifts and capitalize on them in his professional life. Familial background had provided a strong grounding in Calvinist doctrine: his father, Lyman Beecher, was one of the last great evangelists of the Puritan line, a man known for his Congregationalist emphasis on man's depravity and unrelenting faith in the efficacy of religious revivalism. From an early age, though, Henry struggled with Lyman's orthodoxy, even as he recognized that the elder Beecher's spiritual demands were motivated by parental love and concern. Although many of his frustrations with a particularly dogmatic approach to religion were exacerbated, no doubt, by his atypical upbringing, he was one of many young Americans in the early decades of the nineteenth century who were looking for new perspectives on how to integrate spirituality into their daily lives in an era of rapid urbanization, industrialization, and specialization.

Fresh from a hotbed of religiously motivated self-improvement at Amherst, Beecher came into his own in a nation awash in awakenings that sought to ignite youthful longings untapped by the previous generation of enthusiasts. During the first half of the nineteenth century, a series of revivals that came to be known collectively as the Second Great Awakening swept the nation. Spurred by the fervor of itinerant preachers and infused by European Romantics' and American Transcendentalists' emphasis on a spirituality grounded in nature, the movement privileged love and acceptance over repentance and denial. In the midst of this renewed fervor, Beecher, like his contemporaries Ralph Waldo Emerson and Horace Bushnell, felt inspired to forge his own path in a post-Calvinist world.

From today's perspective, it is tempting to read Beecher's "innovations" as *only* theatrics: performances that carefully utilized rhetoric to align private and public good through a process of sneaky substitutions and uneasy elisions. Whether we designate it "Christian nurture," "secularized Protestantism," "romantic Christianity," or simply Protestantism, there is certainly evidence that Beecher and others of his generation perfected a linguistic (and bodily) balancing act that allowed their adherents to have their cake, materially speaking, and eat it too, religiously. It would be a mistake to dismiss their motivations too quickly, however. Like William Stowe, I resist the urge to flatten the work of these reformers by relegating them to the category of dilettantism and, instead, take seriously Beecher's interest in nature as something that involved more than "help[ing] justify the privileges of a comfortable, white, native-born, urban middle class by providing midcentury Americans with a liberalized, relatively undemanding form of Protestantism that reconciled their pleasures and material possessions with the religious beliefs they inherited from their forebears."[2] Just as his sister Harriet Beecher Stowe would capitalize on a newfound interest in sympathy in order to change the way people thought about slavery, Henry Ward Beecher offered audiences a form of Christianity that transformed doctrine into an ongoing process of self-actualization by way of a carefully groomed middle path of aesthetic gratification. If we can approach sentimentalism in a light that recognizes complexity in its motives, manifestations, and effects, we likewise should be capable of reading this religious moment in ways that open, rather than shut down, opportunities for interpretative engagement.

By the time he established himself as a minister in Indianapolis, Beecher had found a way to unite secular and spiritual strivings in what at first glance would seem to be a contradiction: a celebration of spontaneity in a package-able moral program. Beginning with his 1843–44 Indianapolis lecture series that would be repackaged in book form and become a best-seller under the title *Seven Lectures to Young Men,* Beecher identified a need for a new sort of guidance oriented to men like himself who felt overwhelmed and alone in the city, even as their lifestyles, geographic destinations, and career choices simultaneously registered dissatisfaction with the opportunities available in their rural hometowns. Knowing they were consumed with the complex process of learning how to navigate a new environment of alien patterns and signals at the same time that they were managing the more mundane activities of establishing and maintaining jobs, domiciles, and social net-works, he offered to walk with young men through the urban landscape as a friend familiar with their unspoken, most cherished desires. Despite taking a "stand against all demoralizing pleasure," the popular preacher acknowl-edged "the *necessity* of amusement" in their lives.[3] In doing so, he embarked on a multi-decade effort to instill in the bourgeois mind a new, spiritually inflected appreciation for the more circumscribed gratifications of a domes-ticated manhood in nature.

Recognizing the reality of the displacements his readers experienced on a daily basis, whether it be the gulf between their work and home lives or the less visible but nonetheless ubiquitous compartmentalization of the inner life of the individual (at work or at home) as something separate from the more display-oriented social self, he encouraged them to transform poten-tial liabilities into opportunities. Warning that "the mind has no kitchen to do its dirty work in, while the parlor remains clean. . . . [D]ishonesty is an atmosphere; if it comes into one apartment it penetrates into every one" (*SL,* 43), Beecher claimed that the distinctions governing their daily routines were surface level only; behavior in one sphere necessarily bled into another.

The problem for young men in urban environments was that they had left their familial roots but didn't know how to establish and nourish new ones. As a result, "we are such a migratory, restless people, that our home is usually every where but at home" (174). The solution was to help men fashion a home space that would act as a nourishing "platform" (8) for all other activities, a wellspring of inspiration and growth that would attend to the material, aesthetic, and spiritual inclinations of its inhabitants.

Employing architectural metaphors to describe the state of men's inner lives, Beecher compared the "shattered houses, abandoned by reputable persons" that stood "upon the outskirts of towns" to "idle men's imaginations—full of unlawful company" (21). His goal was to evict the vagrants and undesirables from their tenements to make room for repair and renovation of what had the potential to become valuable property on the fringe. By suburbanizing the imagination, he hoped to help men learn how to channel their dreams, to transform desire so that it did work for them rather than becoming something that needed to be suppressed or kept in check. Directly addressing merchants, clerks, and mechanics in a moment of economic depression, Beecher bemoaned a nationwide epidemic of debilitated manhood perpetuated by migration born of "restlessness" and a lack of self-nourishing, buoying "hearty industry," even in moments of leisure (8, 174). He urged them, in what would become the mission of his career, to recover and develop a "real, native mirthfulness," an "elastic cheerfulness and hearty enjoyment," and "a manly joy of usefulness" in the space of the home (82, 8, 9).

Beecher would spend the rest of his career constructing and furnishing that space for his followers in words. In order to capture men's attention and differentiate his approach from those of his sisters, he defined his domesticity in relation to the satisfaction rather than the denial of sensory "appetites" (171). Above all, domestic routines should bring happiness; if designed correctly, following natural growth patterns, their architectures would be predisposed to do so. Material consumption would contribute to aesthetic refinement, relaxation would rejuvenate, entertainment would improve the mind and body. Every impulse would contribute to the development of character, every activity serve a purpose. As a site of productive leisure, the domestic environment would meet men on their own terms and enrich them with a sense of accomplishment and pride. There would be no need to discipline "the habit of reverie and mental romancing"; given access to a "higher flavor of stimulus" that conferred "moderate but long-continued excitement" over the "intense but short-lived" variety (113), many of the dangers of modern life would fall away on their own.

"THE BUSINESS OF LIFE"
A Revisionist's Account of Accommodation

If it is true, as Andrew Lawson argues, that in 1844 Beecher's notion of what constituted manhood was "something known negatively, by what it is not, rather than by what it might be," something "intangible and precious, a quality that must be preserved, saved from the wreckage wrought by financial panics,"[4] by the 1850s he had found language suitable to evoke that essence. Recognizing that his target audience, both in the pulpit and on the page, consisted of a class of Americans who would reshape culture as the century continued, Beecher carefully aligned professional and material dreams with more abstract longings that traditionally had been associated with religious worldviews. In uniting pleasure and usefulness in the realm of the domestic, Beecher presented readers with a solution to their moral quandaries from multiple angles and simultaneously cast an investment in "homely" matters as manly (*SL,* 17). First, he suggested that men need not look beyond the home for the gratification of pleasure. Second, he mitigated fears about contributions to society or personal legacy by insisting that the home was *the* place to be useful, a spot where "sound judgment" and "close application" in the "ordinary business of life" would *pay* in visible ways (17). In the domestic sphere, "intellectual Industry and patient enterprise," which would both give men something to do with their time and gratify them with its results, could serve as "a substitute for Genius" (17, 16). Finally, and perhaps most important, he contributed to a widespread articulation in print culture of a rationale for the superior restorative power of nature, especially of a semi-tamed middle ground, for the man of business.

As well known as Beecher became in Indianapolis for his sermons, it was his potential to utilize the written word to communicate a message of self-love to a wider audience of young men in urban areas that attracted the attention of the New York merchant W. T. Cutter and facilitated Beecher's rise to national prominence. From an early age, Beecher had read popular literature with an ear for the relationship between rhetoric and reception, and before long he sought to bracket moral guidance with accessible tone and stirring sentiment in his own writing and speeches. In an October 1835 journal entry he had mused, "He is sure of popularity who can come down among the people and address truth to them in their own homely way and with broad humor—and at the same time has an upper current of taste and chaste expression and condensed vigor."[5] The success of *Seven Lectures* enabled him to see a path whereby text might accomplish that work on a scale never before imagined. While his original audience had been limited to the particular conditions of a young western metropolis, print productively broadened his distribution and generalized his message at the same time that it collapsed spatial, situational, and temporal gaps and united author and reader in the shared liminal space of the page. The content appealed to a wide range of individuals, and a heightened sense of intimacy enabled Beecher to insert himself into the family circle, or in many cases as a stand-in for a family that had been left behind in the country.

This was not simply a strategic ploy, however. Upon accepting the job at Plymouth Church in Brooklyn in 1846, Beecher had found himself in a position that was not so dissimilar to that of his parishioners. Debby Applegate notes: "Plymouth Church was packed with young men who had left rural villages to seek their fortune in the city—clerks, apprentices, students, those torn between ambition and homesickness. 'It was a common remark in those days that, whereas the average church congregation was made up in the proportion of five women to one man, in Plymouth Church the proportion ran the other way,' recalled one parishioner, with only slight exaggeration. Most had been raised in the stern Yankee tradition but came of age when the old truths and virtues no longer seemed so self-evident or desirable."[6] Like these men, Beecher had made a deliberate decision to relocate near an urban center. Despite his warnings about their dangers, he was cognizant of the draw of cities and would become increasingly unwilling to abandon or denigrate their opportunities, amenities, and amusements as the years wore on. At the same time, he retained a very real sense of what had been left behind: farm, family, prayer, and purpose. His geographic location in Brooklyn, he soon realized, mirrored his split mindset—and the same must be true of his constituents.

Connected to Manhattan across the East River by the Fulton Ferry, Brooklyn promised a safe, relatively quiet home base for men who worked in the city but valued (and could afford) an escape that reminded them of their rural roots. As Milton Rugoff describes it, in 1847 Brooklyn "was a highly respectable suburb of New York, a refuge for a middle class intent on escaping from Manhattan's increasing congestion, rising costs and waves of immigrants. . . . Substantial homes, pretty gardens and some forty churches framed its tree-lined streets, especially on Columbia Heights, overlooking the East River and New York Bay. And Manhattan—a metropolis crowding the southern half of a narrow island—was only a penny ferry-ride away."[7] Brooklyn—and eventually Brooklyn Heights, in a secondary wave of sub-urbanization that occurred in response to the unprecedented growth of the initial suburb into one of the largest cities in the Union—was a bustling community of daily commuters bound by similar backgrounds, values, and goals. They also shared anxieties about the fate of bodily health in the indus-trial age. Whether threatened by the encroachment of immigrants and the supposed disease and dirt they brought with them or the effects of constant noise and movement on already frazzled nerves, early suburbanites looked to an intermediate space between the city to which they had to return (for livelihood, for posterity) and the country from which they had come (in haste, in youth) to smooth and mediate the tensions that defined their lives.

Beecher capitalized on this embodied ideological state of in-betweenness in his midcentury periodical essays, many of which would be republished in book form as *Star Papers* (1855) and *Eyes and Ears* (1862). Whereas in *Seven Lectures to Young Men* he had assumed the role of a more knowledgeable men-tor, only a decade later he claimed to occupy the same position as his readers. Discussing his need for quiet and the effects of his occupation and the pace of urban life on his nerves in "Back Again" from *Eyes and Ears,* for instance, he confided that "there is no taxation comparable to an incessant various conver-sation with people for whom you must think, devise, and for whose help you feel yourself often utterly incompetent."[8] By exposing his own professional frustrations and feelings of inadequacy, he lent an aura of authenticity to what might otherwise come across as reformist dogma. He repeatedly associated the country with much-needed space for "retrospection, a mental state which is almost denied to public men in the life of a city," as he phrased it in "The First Breath in the Country" from *Star Papers* (143), and urged men to consider a suburban home an investment in their long-term health.

Linking nervous disorders to sensory overload in the city, he depicted its sounds and rhythms as artificial and man-made, products of "sound-making agencies" (*EE*, 128). To Beecher's mind, the city stirred up the imagination in the same heated, extreme way that dangerous hobbies did in *Seven Lectures*, while the natural rhythms of the suburban sphere promised to invigorate and reset the senses. Drawing from his personal experience of returning home to Brooklyn Heights after a day of ministry at Plymouth Church, he evoked Manhattan as a vast soundscape, one that was surprisingly open to manipulation by the commuter: "The grinding of wheels in paved streets, the clash and din of a half-million men, mingling, form a grand body of sound, which, however harsh and dissonant to those near by, becomes at a little distance softened, round, and almost musical. Thus, from Brooklyn heights, New York sounds its diapason, vast and almost endless. The direction of wind greatly influences the sound. When the air is moist, and the wind west, the city sends a roar across like the incessant break of surf upon the ocean shore. But with an eastern wind, the murmur is scarcely greater, and almost as soft, as winds moving gently in forests" (128). The city's impressive output could be overwhelming to any single individual within it. A small distance would do much to palliate the effect.

In addition to fostering an artistic appreciation for such a massive undertaking, periodic separation would provide a space where one's career need not define him. As ambient sound, it could be blocked out or invited in at will. Better yet, it could be transformed into something else through the imaginative process. In passages like the one just cited, Beecher's language performed the very elasticity that he advocated philosophically. By turning a tired description of a known environment into an opportunity for creative expression, he suggested that while certain characteristics of their lives and environments were fixed, urban businessmen need not passively accept the entire package; they had the power to bend and frame the view to suit the needs of their souls.

An essay from *Star Papers* titled "Towns and Trees" details the characteristics of the ideal domestic setting for the clerk, lawyer, or merchant who wanted to reassert control over his surroundings: "A place . . . that unites the refinements belonging to society in large towns with the freshness and quiet of a secluded village, imbosomed in trees, full of shaded yards and gardens, broad, park-like streets, soon opening out into romantic rural roads among pine woods along the rocky edges of dark streams—such a place, especially if its society is good, if its ministers, teachers, civilians, and principal citizens, are intelligent and refined, and its historical associations abundant and rich—must be regarded as of all others the most desirable for residence" (129–30). Whether this location was suburban in the manner of Brooklyn, Brooklyn Heights, or one of the literati outposts such as Lenox and Peekskill (Beecher's chosen vacation towns) was irrelevant; the key was that these sorts of communities combined a taste of the country with the amenities of the city. At the same time, they responded to the necessity of establishing a clear geographic separation between one's place of business and one's domicile. In the best scenario, "residences are so separated from the business part of the town" that one who "wanders about under [the suburb's] avenues of mighty elms, and among its simple old houses, or its modern mansions, would take it to be a place of elegant repose, without life or business" (131). It was an illusion, to be sure, but one to which everyone would willingly bow.

For Beecher, the magic of such places was that they interpreted the suburbanized imagination in material forms. When he told readers that in such a suburb they "can have the joys of the breezy wilderness at home" (*SP,* 132), he made no attempt to hide the fact that he was molding the view to his liking. Indeed, he intimated that this was the exact sort of revision in perception that needed to occur in order for them to embrace the lives they led in the present moment. "A man should put his heart into everything he does," he advised in "Honour Your Business" from *Eyes and Ears* (218). Even so, he shouldn't waste time meditating on annoyances, disappointments, or temporary setbacks. Instead, the spirit and energy that informed his original impulses should enable him to enliven and beautify an otherwise mediocre lifestyle. When Beecher exhorted readers in "Fence-Corners" that "it makes a great difference whether we look at things with an exact business eye, or with the eye of poetry and beauty" (*EE,* 321), he didn't mean that they should act one way at work and the other way at home but rather that they should be satisfied with their lives on all fronts and rely on natural intuition to guide them as to the appropriate approach or response in a particular moment.

This was where spirituality came in. "Let a man adopt his business, and identify it with his life, and cover it with pleasant associations," he urged, "for God has given us imagination, not alone to make some men poets, but to enable all men to beautify homely things. Heart-varnish will cover up innumerable evils and defects. Look at the good things. Accept your lot as a man does a piece of rugged ground, and begin to get out the rocks and roots, to deepen and mellow the soil, to enrich and plant it. There is something in the most forbidding avocation around which a man may twine pleasant fancies, out of which he may develop an honest pride" (*EE,* 218). In Beecher's formulation, the impulse to "cover" was not a weakness, and he certainly did not consider it an unnatural, forced manipulation. Rather, this was the intended outlet for the imaginative capacity, suburbanization in its most elevated form. Comparing a man's "lot" in the sense of fate to a plot of land that he owned flipped the situation completely. He might be stuck with a certain geography, but it was one that he had selected himself, and he should claim it by digging into the earth and improving the view. The openness of such an endeavor, the vulnerability inherent in any application of "heart-varnish," would ensure that the end result was a source of pride rather than an embarrassment, an "honest" performance of the parts one had been assigned.

Among the amenities of suburban oases, Beecher made clear, were other people. They just needed to be of the right sort. While his advice centered on the life of the individual male reader, he frequently connected practices of personal soul-searching in nature to the development of "social sympathy" (*EE,* 94) and "social largeness" (*SP,* 288). The man who made his living as Brooklyn's most famous religious figure certainly believed in the beneficial influence of community and recommended suburban domiciles over rural sites precisely because they offered more opportunities for fraternal bonds to form between like-minded men. The sympathy was not expected to extend, however, to individuals of different classes, occupations, or ethnicities. Much of the allure of the suburb for Beecher lay in its self-selecting, gated quality: men were less likely to be led astray in the terms he had depicted in *Seven Lectures* if the types of people and architectures typically associated with those behaviors did not exist in that particular locale. In a protected—one might say willingly staged—environment, the simple act of living among others of similar persuasion in a "good-natured" way was represented as an act of generosity and liberalism.

In a watered-down and self-realizable version of Jonathan Edwards's paeans to the "inward sweetness" of God's grace, Beecher's spiritual guidance posited the no less mysterious "possession of *good-nature*" (*EE,* 231), which he connected to "a sweet justice in common things, and a forbearance toward men in all the details of life, and a placable, patient, and cheerful mind" (233), as a persuasion that would revolutionize his adherents' lives. Practices of looking to nature for inspiration and guidance in domestic activities gave the impression (Beecher would deny it was an illusion) of outward orientation, acceptance, and invitation without the obligation or ugliness. Yard maintenance, ornamental tree planting, participation in recreational activities as a family, and even wholesome family dinners were elevated to demonstrations of virtue and patriotism. In this sense, Beecher's domesticity mirrored his sisters' articulations. The difference was that women's domestic programs typically channeled these activities through rhetorics of selflessness while men's philosophies were unapologetically and even protectively self-centered. Inwardly directed reflection and meditation, especially if it produced palpable, recognizable (to individuals in one's social sphere) results such as a well-manicured home or a happy, healthy family, constituted a form of privatized benevolence for its practitioners. This, in turn, was deemed an acceptable substitute for—even the intelligent man's solution to—civic engagement.

In line with so many of the era's conduct guides and self-improvement manuals, under Beecher's tutelage, the discipline of learning to watch one's own mind became *the* ultimate form of self-denial; there was no need to move outside the self in any other sense. It was only through this process, moreover, that self-realization could occur. Just as the suburb enabled one to view the metropolis in a new, holistic way—and, significantly, to possess it imaginatively and redeploy the revised vision to suit one's needs—an ability to discern one's own character as a result of careful observation would reward the effort involved. It was the same argument Thoreau had made in *Walden,* but Beecher insisted that a job pushing paper in the city and a trendy home in the suburbs offered no impediment to this new perception. In all likelihood such "baggage" would facilitate the process, because the businessman who embraced commodity culture and enjoyed society would be more likely to understand not only the difference between character and appearance but also the necessity of each.

In *Eyes and Ears,* Beecher defined character as formed from "a man's real inward habits and mental condition" (230). Appearance, Beecher continued, consisted of "the outward exhibition" of that character in everyday life, and as such was responsible for a man's reputation, or "the impression which he has made upon other men" (231). Neither could be entirely dispensed with by anyone who lived in any sort of proximity to other people, and both were valuable to the man of business. Rather than worrying about making their mark in a big way, though, he recommended that his readers concentrate on "the business of life," which "is made up of minute affairs, requiring only judgment and diligence" (293). In an oligarchic justification of a hierarchical society, he asserted that whatever they might have thought previously, genius was not a necessary character trait for the vast majority of men; there was no need to stand out from the crowd as an impressive thinker or innovative artist. The characteristics of keen perception, common sense, cheerful willingness to work, and patience on the relatively small but not unimportant scale of life's "homely duties" would do much to influence a man's appearance and thereby assure success in whatever sphere he found himself.

Without denigrating their careers as nothing more than a way to earn a living, Beecher urged his readers to embrace "pet notions" of their choosing in the domestic sphere in order to develop these manly characteristics: interests and hobbies that would bring them pleasure, challenge their bodies and minds, improve the state of their family, and foster a sense of pride in one fell swoop. "Almost all men, have some queer spot," he observed in "Pet Notions" (*EE*, 185). "We have known men quite addicted to sewing and knitting. They hemmed towels with an earnestness betokening a proper regard of this useful accomplishment of sewing" (187–88). Whether a man exhibited a fondness for flowers, a passion for cooking, an interest in horses, or an appreciation of the sewing machine, it was not something to hide or mock; such niche interests demonstrated that men, too, belonged in the space of the home and that their ideas and contributions should be taken into account. "These peculiarities are not simply amusing," Beecher admonished would-be detractors. "They are a testimony, often, of a yearning after things more fine than belongs to a trade, more beautiful than every-day business furnishes, and purer and truer than many of the experiences of every-day life. Sometimes they may be but vanities; but it is charitable rather to imagine that they are irregular exhibitions of a longing in everyone to be something more and better than he is" (188). If these outlets for the imagination succeeded in counteracting creeping feelings of "disenchantment" (358) with the mundanities of daily life, they were worth celebrating and nurturing.

AN "UNDISTURBED REIGN OF JOYOUS DISORDER"
The Domestic Liberty of "Unlopped Men"

Although he valued his close friendship with his sister Harriet, at a moment when she and their older sister Catharine were mapping a science of home economics for American housewives in domestic handbooks, novels, and periodical articles, Henry Ward Beecher took a different path in his domestic advice for suburban men. Railing against what he saw as women's misinformed and ill-fated frenzy for classification, neatness, and mastery, Beecher committed himself to the process of aligning American men with an organic state. In an article from *Eyes and Ears* he warned: "Women are in danger of excess in carefulness. They run into radical notions of order, and even flame forth into fanaticisms of neatness. Then neatness becomes most afflictive" (161). If his tone was humorous, the representation offered a pointed condemnation of female control of the domestic sphere:

> The housewife becomes a knight-errant. Ghosts and giants are nothing to her. Castles and encounters of freebooters she turns over to nursery credulity. She has her broom and brush in hand, her armature of cloth and wash, for that deceitful, stealthy, ubiquitous foe of all domestic peace, universal dirt. All nature is her enemy. All winds are averse which bring dust. All phenomena are regarded as good or bad from their dirt-producing tendencies. The economy of life is arranged with supreme reference to the virtues of order and neatness. Comfort is nothing, ease is nothing, happiness is nothing, good dispositions are nothing. Neatness is the one grace. That determines when you must get up, what you must wear, where you may sit down, what you may touch, what rooms are useable, what days of the week are home days, or endurable days. Life has not one moment's respite from unwinking vigilance! Not one moment is there that the great arch-enemy of connubial felicity does not threaten a speck or spot upon something. You live under a perpetual and sounding, "Take care." It is, "Take care! don't touch that silver, you will tarnish it." "Take care of that sofa, it is newly covered." "Take care! don't sit on that clean chintz; you ought to know better than to sit down on such a chair!" "Take care! let that hat alone, you will soil it." "Take care! pray don't go near that sideboard, you'll scratch it." "Take care! a stick! a knife too!! Whittling in the parlour!!! Go out—out with you; go out of the yard, go into the road; go behind the barn, where the wind won't blow your shavings back." "Take care! don't eat apples in the sitting-room—you always drop some seeds." "Take care, child, come away from that door. You are not going into that room; it is just put in order!" And thus, family discipline, domestic life, and the whole end of living seems to be, to avoid dirt and secure neatness. Is there anything so tormenting as

ecstatic neatness? Oh for a morsel of dirt, as a luxury! How good dust looks! A ploughed field with endless dirt—all hail! The great sentence itself, which consigns man finally to dust again, becomes a consolation! (162–63)

Presenting interactions between husband and wife as small skirmishes in an epic battle, Beecher criticized not only women's method but their goal as well. The wife is firmly in control in this sketch, ruler of a demesne that trembles at her every command. She regards her husband as just another child, infantilizing and denying his inclinations for fear that those whims, if allowed to mature, would threaten the holy mission. Relics of Enlightenment rationalism, women robbed homes of the comforts and restoration they should, by their very nature, be designed to bestow on inhabitants. Reversing gender roles by turning attributes formerly deemed the male prerogative into a critique of women's domesticity, the essay challenges men to do something better with their allotted portion.

What did Beecher propose instead? The closing essay in *Eyes and Ears* stakes men's claim to the domestic sphere as preferable to that of women. In "The Good of Disorder" he rejected the inherent privileging of order over disorder by questioning their definition: "What is order, as applied, I mean, to things? It is simply arrangement according to some notion, and disorder is simply arrangement according to some *other* notion. They might be called primary order and secondary order" (387–88). As evidence, he cited the artistic requirements of the picturesque, whereby "irregularity [was] valued," he noted, "even in polite circles" (388), as when furniture in a parlor was arranged in a way that communicated use, or a lawn was periodically punctuated by trees and shrubs that lent mystery and enchantment to the view. "What is the natural or picturesque style of landscape-gardening?" he asked, asserting that such a mode sought to evoke the patterns and order of the natural world: "It is a system based upon the rejection of any absolute rule. It aims to arrange things just as they would be if they never had been arranged at all" (388). Nature itself, he suggested, refuted women's insistence on the virtues of neatness and organization. According to Beecher, the beauty and variety of plants and flowers, trees and animals offered a better guide: "Everything in creation lies around loose, or is mixed up in the most inextricable disorder. Not in confusion. Disorder is never to be confounded with confusion" (389). Just as it took a man of a certain disposition (and class, and education) to distinguish leisure from laziness, it was a mark of culture to posit a rationale for deviating from conventional wisdom, especially if the alternative had the potential to become an acceptable outlet for an activity or belief previously thought to be dangerous or detrimental to the health of the populace.

Beecher characterized women's domestic arrangements as an offense to good taste in that they left nothing to the imagination. The endless meddling of women quashed any semblance of sentience in the world of objects, fating them rather than letting them breathe and discover their own destinies. He depicted himself wincing as he opened his dresser drawers, post-regularization by his wife: "There repose the snow-white shirts, the pile of handkerchiefs . . . like Egyptian dead in rows and shelf-like order. . . . And so it is with the next, and the next. So it is with the closet, with parlour, and entries. The same rectangular fate presides in parlour and diningroom. Nay, it stealthily creeps into the very study" (390), that inner sanctum of men's activity. He mourned the sacrilege committed there as the ultimate insult to a man's sensibilities:

> We left this room a Paradise, we find it a Purgatory. Our table was blossoming all over with a luxuriant and tangled abundance of letters, papers, scraps from newspapers, books, and books on books. It was a journal. Each day's deposit for weeks was there, almost with the regularity of geological strata. We could go back as in a register, and recall the topics of each several day, until memory failed, and the lower strata of papers, the very primitive formations, went back to dim and remote times inexplorable. Like an onion or tulip-bulb, the table was constructed in layers. Fatal absence! Misplaced confidence! We returned to find everything death-struck. All was order! Our articles sorted, our letters filed, our scraps classified, our pens collected and huddled like raw recruits in awkward squads, the scissors, the knife, the pins [sic], the ink, the mucilage, standing round like officers dressed for a parade-day. A month will not suffice to bring back again the admired disorder, the graceful melange. (390–91)

Contrary to the dominant narrative, the passage suggests, the ministrations of women were not motivated by innate sympathy; to them, relations were threatening unless adequately premeditated and responsibly chaperoned. Nothing living was deemed safe until it had been rendered inert—dismembered, scrubbed, and mounted by a woman's "remorseless" (391) hand.

By exposing what he saw as hollowness at the core of women's domestic busyness, he called out their claims to revolutionize the civic and moral state of the nation from that space as pretensions. Pre-skirmish, in contrast, Beecher's study stood as a living, material autobiography of a man in "benevolent sympathy" (391) with nature, one of those "unlopped men, whose side-branches, having had room to grow, give the full and noble proportions of manhood from top to bottom" (63). It had a life of its own, "blossoming" in unexpected places. In addition to housing an accessible, if idiosyncratic, history of his thoughts, interests, and actions, the room had a seemingly haphazard appearance with a rhythm and complexity that appealed to the eye and engaged the mind through its "unexpected contrasts": "Nothing was tame. Everything was fitted to excite surprise in a well-regulated housekeeper's mind. It was a stimulating sight. No art could have designedly arranged it. It was the workmanship of distributive and gradual chance. Like frostwork on the window, it defied invention and challenged imitation" (391).

Beecher ended the sketch by looking forward to that day in the summer when his wife and children were to depart for vacation, leaving him alone in their abode. It was then that he would return the house to its proper state without worry that his efforts would be thwarted by a well-meaning but mistaken-minded female enthusiast:

> We shall be sole monarch. Then, descending, we shall overturn the despotism of the parlours, and bring to the solitude of the house the joyful boon of disorder! We will forget to put anything in its place. The sofa shall sprout with strange things. Every corner be planted with new commodities. The book-case door shall never be shut. The chairs shall never have less than half-a-dozen books. Engravings shall lie in heaps. Right in the midst of manuscripts shall be seen bread and cheese and apples that had begun to be eaten; the ashes shall heap itself [*sic*] in gray disorder; kindling-wood and waste paper shall ruffle the hearth; and everything see everything doing what it was never expected to do. Brooms we hate as we do a tyrant's rod. We will expel them! Dust-brushes are an utter abomination. We will drive them forth! At present we think it meet to submit. But we snuff the balmy air that tells us that the vernal days are coming. To us they mean grass, leaves, lambs, birds, flowers, and odorous smell of soil and vegetation. But to us they mean also domestic liberty, the end of tyrannous order, the restoration of nature to the house, the undisturbed reign of joyous disorder. (392)

Whereas a woman spent all her time preparing and staging to the exclusion of enjoying and living, a man's only housekeeping job was to foster an environment for growth by resisting the impulse to meddle. Somewhat counterintuitively, it was only through a willingness to sit and watch something unfold that a bona fide domesticity could emerge.

In "The Life of Flowers," Beecher made a startling proposal. He asked his readers to consider how the "conce[ssion] now, by vegetable physiologists, that plants have a real *life*—not by a figure of speech, not a slight analogy of life, but a real vegetable life, which connects them with the long chain of more perfectly developed life above them" (*EE,* 353–54) would affect their interactions with these domestic ornamentals. Proclaiming the announcement "a great comfort" to him because it mapped paths of relation between the human and vegetable kingdoms, he vowed to "plant them with some sense of the dignity of seeds!" (354) from that point forward. The only appropriate response to such a discovery, he argued here and elsewhere, was enthusiastic reception, imaginative embrace of the reality of "soul-life" (356) in another form. In this simple affirmation of the creative potential of each of his readers—that is, their faith in the existence of the "invisible and intangible" (*SP,* 285) currents and spirits—Beecher traced the path by which the issue of those impulses, whether in the "detritus" of a disorderly room or the garden surrounding a cottage, might "return to us through some of the physical senses" (285) in the apprehension of nature. A domesticity that grafted its structures (ideologically and practically) onto those of the natural world was inherently generative. Reciprocally, the architectures, physical and procedural, of that "home-life" in all of its dimensions would speak "to several inward tastes" through eye and ear (285), thereby spiritualizing one's material existence.

Beecher was adamant that his domesticity required no special talent, no genius or background knowledge. The faith in organicism he advocated did not preclude discipline; anything worth doing took effort, but it was of a different sort from what women required. Rather than learning how to fold napkins, iron clothing, and organize dresser drawers, he announced, men should focus on training and elevating their relational capacities. As he stated in "Second Summer Letter": "Things must begin to be familiar before we feel their full meaning; not by putting at things, as a burglar would at the lock, punching and screwing, but by a natural and gradual opening of things to us, by a growing sensibility in us to them. For there is always to be an education. Man is for ever a disciple, and not a master, before nature" (*EE*, 36).

The method mattered, for the goal was not to tame the environment by forcing it to bend to human systems, but rather to allow the world to open of its own accord, gradually unfolding its own architectures, to the surprise and wonder of the witness. If coaxing was involved, it must be of the softest, most sympathetic and supplicating variety. This was the same method Beecher utilized in the pulpit and constituted what he saw as the great power of print culture. The most effective proselytizing announced itself as unadorned in the sense that it eschewed directives and obligations in favor of nurturing the growth of inner beauty in response to external stimuli. There was not even a need to reference Christianity explicitly; apprehension of the embodied mystery was so immediate that it existed on a plane beyond speech. As he phrased it in *Star Papers:* "Words belong to the body. But when we are 'in the spirit,' thoughts and feelings are expressed by the very act of existing, and syllable themselves by their own pulsations" (53).

Beecher's interest in the domestic sphere lay in its potential to soothe and recharge men who had become enervated by the frenetic pace of urban life. His governing metaphor of organic growth posited an essential, immutable relationship between man and earth which could be strengthened and developed through thoughtful devotion to a home in nature. The necessary activities involved in plotting a landscape to satisfy one's bodily, spiritual, aesthetic, familial, and social needs would help a young clerk familiarize himself with the most essential elements of his character. In that way, house and man would grow and change together in a mutual process of self-discovery. By limiting his engagement with the number of chores and obligations associated with home ownership (or, more accurately, by relegating them to the silent acquiescence of women, even as he chided them for attempting to turn their own burdens into productive enterprises), he transformed the domestic environment into a stage for safe experimentation, play, and leisure.

Many of his essays in *Star Papers* and *Eyes and Ears* center on possible productions on such a stage, all of which emphasize physical movement, fresh air, nature-based rhythms, and simple pleasures. Some of these include fishing and playing games with children, reading books in the open air, baking pies with rhubarb grown in the garden, bird-watching, walking, gathering eggs, arranging a library, testing new technologies such as sewing machines and lawn mowers, writing letters to friends, and propagating plants. By advertising these sorts of activities as small adventures and "pet notions," Beecher prevented them from becoming sources of anxiety or stress. Suburban hobbies balanced men's urban occupations by providing outlets for untapped energies and interests. Moreover, they could serve as sources of pride in two senses, each of which promised to relieve the burdens of the other. On the one hand, they were buttressed financially by one's career in the city. On the other hand, they gratified the body and mind independently of one's professional successes or failures. This symbiotic, forgiving relationship affirmed the suburbanized landscape as the ideal location for manhood to bloom in an industrialized nation.

BOOK-FARMING AND ITS DISCONTENTS

When Beecher published *Plain and Pleasant Talk about Fruits, Flowers and Farming* (1859), he was at the height of his career in Brooklyn. The essays contained within the volume, however, had been penned over a decade earlier for an agricultural journal he started in 1846 in Indianapolis, *The Western Farmer and Gardener.* Beecher recounted the early history of those original articles in the preface to the volume, explaining that in his early days as a preacher in the aforementioned western town, he would "drive the sermon out of our heads" through practices of "alterative reading."[9] In an effort to redirect his mental energies, he turned to books about horticulture, agriculture, and architecture. Soon he began renting a plot near his home where he could transmit book learning into practical innovation. His experiential learning, in turn, eventually credentialed him to author advice on the basis of his trials. He credited a passion for literacy, kindled in youth and continued for relaxation as much as for education, as responsible for the foundational transformative spark that led him to think and see differently. Here was an outlet for the imagination that combined self-improvement and entertainment. Asserting that "a seedsman's list, a nurseryman's catalogue, are more fascinating to us than any story" and claiming that his time spent with such volumes "paved the way for our editorial labors" (*PPT,* iv), he welcomed readers, first in western outposts and later in bustling suburban metropolises, to a genre that promised safe escape and embrace at once.

It is worth lingering on the appeal of *Plain and Pleasant Talk about Fruits,*

Flowers and Farming, especially given Beecher's target readership. What need would Brooklyn businessmen have for a volume about judging varieties of ornamental flowers, selecting and preserving seeds, planting an orchard, preparing pies or strawberries and cream, and completing monthly tasks for the owner and cultivator of multiple acres of land? After all, on the surface level, Beecher's essays would seem to have little resonance beyond their original readership, a motley cohort of wealthy gentlemen farmers interested in learning how to stake dahlias and keep plants alive indoors through the winter, and, perhaps more tentatively, a hardscrabble group of farmers and mechanics who worked their properties for a living. The agricultural paper itself was a relatively new genre in the early decades of the nineteenth century, and Beecher's articles reflect this fact. He expends a lot of energy instructing his readers on the value of this category of reading material, whatever their occupation. While extolling books and periodicals as the universal pathway to intelligence and success, he frequently employs the phrase used by the clerk quoted at the beginning of chapter 1, "book-farming," to characterize the reader's relationship to the genre.

Describing himself and other "agricultural writers" as "visionary" (48) and practical at once, he urges readers from a range of backgrounds to "select, modify, and act according to their own native judgment" in their consumption of the page. If approached with the reader's particular needs and interests in mind, this genre of writing could "answer a double purpose" (49). Most obviously, such works "convey a great amount of valuable practical information." More significantly, he maintained, "they then stir up the reader to habits of thought; they make him more inquisitive, more observing, more reasoning, and, therefore, more reasonable" (49–50). In essence, they helped suburbanize the imagination. Instead of lingering on any immediate benefit on the level of content, he rationalized the purchase of this "alterative reading" as a more comprehensive—and unavoidably more intangible—investment in the self. "Intelligent boys work better, plan better, earn and save better," he argued, "and reading a good paper makes them intelligent" (102). It was as simple as that.

Of course, such a rhetorical maneuver was not simple at all. "Those who are prejudiced against book-farming," he quipped, "are either good farmers, misinformed of the design of agricultural papers, or poor farmers who only treat this subject as they do all others, with blundering ignorance" (47).

Although Beecher took pains to represent his *Western Farmer and Gardener* essays as a democratizing force that would spread good habits and commendable behavior through print-based self-education, he also tacitly condoned a widespread population shift of newly minted urbanites to a middle landscape within commuting distance of the city which was displacing the very farmers with whom he also claimed affinity. Commenting on "a spirit for enterprise" that drew "the business men—merchants, lawyers, physicians, and clergymen of large cities" away from the rural landscapes of their youth, he praised the "system of *circulation*" (55) that led these same young men to reacquaint themselves with their youth—on new terms—in the many suburbs that were forming around major metropolitan centers. Even as he invited "professional" farmers to join hands with the self-proclaimed "hobby" farmers (of whom he was one) through shared literary interests, Beecher lauded the trend of what he saw as more open-minded, capable, industrious, thinking men looking to populate the geography just beyond the urban center.

It was only in *Plain and Pleasant Talk* that Beecher even gestured at speaking to lower-class rural people. By the time he penned the essays compiled in *Star Papers* and *Eyes and Ears,* colonization of the countryside was in full swing, and most farmers had been forced to relocate to a more remote fringe. These essays written in the 1840s remind us, then, of a population that has been silently excised from the author's midcentury vision. In a series of entries about manners, organization, and cleanliness from *Plain and Pleasant Talk,* he criticized specific habits of unpolished country people, apparently with an eye toward helping them improve their condition. He warned in a seemingly lighthearted way, for example, "It is a filthy trick to borrow of or lend for others' use, a tooth-brush, or a tooth-pick; to pick one's teeth at table with a fork, or a jack-knife; to put your hat upon the dinner table among the dishes; to spit generously into the fire, or at it, while the hearth is covered with food set to warm; for sometimes a man hits what he don't aim at" (36). From depictions of the decrepit rural shack tenanted by an Irish laborer to careful differentiations between idleness versus laziness and disorder versus dirtiness, though, Beecher was as interested in helping a *new* population identify and distinguish themselves from lower-class practices (and, he hoped, to initiate the process of neighborly "conversion" of their own accord) as he was in communicating hints for improvement to the farmers whose homes and choices he publicly critiqued.

The questions of audience and intent raised by these articles for *Western Farmer and Gardener* enable us to see clearly the extent of staging involved in Beecher's organic, benevolent suburban ethos of the 1850s and 1860s, a quality of masculine domesticity that would become more apparent in the writings of Donald Grant Mitchell and Nathaniel Hawthorne. For all his protestations against women's regimes in *Star Papers* and *Eyes and Ears,* Beecher, too, was motivated by desires for order and achieved his goals by eradicating any hint of social, political, or human dirt from the scene. Sadly, the erasure seems to have included his own immediate family as well. According to Debby Applegate, from his relocation to Indianapolis until his death in 1887, he was never able to balance the demands of career and family. Although he wrote voluminously on the subject of home life and argued for the necessity of men's active presence in the domestic sphere, he spent little time in his own home. His wife's letters to friends and to Beecher himself communicate a sense of abandonment, one that must have been especially difficult to deal with given the deaths of multiple children, frequent miscarriages, and one stillbirth. Applegate describes how Beecher, after a brief mention in his diary of the Indianapolis burial of their stillborn son, "changed the subject abruptly, writing in the next line, 'Began my garden. I wish to keep a little record of progress of things. Rose bushes, honeysuckle, willow trees have been in leaf for some days.'" He never mentioned his wife or children again in his diary; entries on gardening took over the space.[10]

These details put a darker spin on Beecher's proclamation in *Star Papers* that a "house is the shape which a man's thoughts take when he imagines how he likes to live" (285). He and other practitioners of masculine domesticity turned to nature for consolation and healing, but also for escape and a return to the innocent anticipation and enchantment of childhood. And yet, just as Catharine Beecher's unmarried state and Harriet Beecher Stowe's dislike of housework did not nullify the legacy of the home vision they espoused, Henry's domestic tragedies and shortcomings should not limit our engagement with his revisionary philosophy. Ultimately, his ability to pull off a seeming impossibility, the spontaneous performance, was his great gift as a rhetorician, whether in print or on stage. He could lend a sense of moral urgency to the renovation of self and other and do so in a generalized tone that radiated love and compassion. This was, after all, what made *Plain and Pleasant Talk* marketable to a completely different readership in the late 1850s and early 1860s. Every essay invited readers to apprehend its message in material and spiritual terms at once. The sheer volume of his articles on domestic horticulture and architecture makes it clear that these topics were not crafted as covers for more straightforwardly religious concerns. If anything, he insisted that his heart lay with the natural world; God became interesting to him—as, he hoped, he himself would to his followers—as a spirit influencing the various shapes and destinies of these more palpable loves.

While his content reflected the passion of a man devoted to his subject, though, he univocally asserted that his foremost interest lay in the ability of his hobby to alter his state by facilitating a new vantage point for viewing his surroundings and his own life. In the garden, whatever the garden happened to be for his readers, came renewal and balance. The closing essay of *Plain and Pleasant Talk* reminded even the most literal-minded readers that Beecher was always also talking about something else: "Have we, like the trees which we love and care for, made growth, of root and branch? Everything in nature has gradually assumed a preparation for winter. Those frosts and that ice which would have sent such mischief upon the leaves of summer, now lie, without harm, upon orchard and garden. Are we ripe and ready, too, for such a winter as adversity brings upon men?" (420). With the help of manly patience, natural perceptiveness, quiet industry, and hearty imagination, they could be.

Even an urban clerk could connect to these sorts of statements. Compromise was inevitable; business (whether in the sense of one's career or one's life) necessitated flexibility. Beecher promised to help men reenvision acts of accommodation and settlement in architectural terms—through suburbanization—as opportunities to furnish the mind afresh. Rather than picturing themselves as cogs in a wheel, mediocre handymen of a system that did not value their contributions, they could recast acts of adjustment formerly understood to be signs of weakness and vulnerability as virtues aligned with elasticity and radical relationality. He undoubtedly believed that access to green grass, a slight separation from the urban work world, and domestic loves would do much to help men establish the roots they would need to weather any future storms that happened their way.

3

"A MAN'S SENSE OF DOMESTICITY"
Donald Grant Mitchell's Home Relish

The writings of Thoreau and Beecher articulate a need for new direction and orientation in young men's lives in response to midcentury industrial expansion and its attendant developments. In their own ways, both authors identify a source of self-nourishment for businessmen in a semi-tame middle ground between country and city. The writers at the heart of this chapter and the next, Donald Mitchell and Nathaniel Hawthorne, explore the motivations and ramifications of such a movement in literature, self-consciously representing themselves as willing yet hesitant cultivators of the newly cleared plots they picture. Their semiautobiographical narrators find themselves drawn to positions of liminality both in person and on the page, even as they recognize their complicity in a trend as rooted in desires for evasion as in embrace. As urban-savvy men in search of domesticity on their own terms, they long for intimacy with others but also fear that commitment, whether of the professional or personal variety, will require them to sacrifice themselves in some essential way. In a protective response of distancing, they cast themselves as characters in their own lives and posit the suburbs as the ideal place to role-play.

In the course of mapping the geographic coordinates of a collective dream, though, Mitchell and Hawthorne suggest that men can't help but fall into the very plots they fear in their endless quest for alternate plots to self-actualization. Even though the resulting portrayals fall short of substantive critique or professional opportunism, they begin the process of theorizing suburbanization by thematizing the tactical maneuvers involved in turning life into a production. Indeed, it is these writers' own liminal position in their works, as insiders and outsiders at once, that makes them such fascinating markers of their suburban moment. Their writings demonstrate attachment to a vision they clearly have no plans to give up, even as they seem cognizant of, and at times somewhat embarrassed by, the rhetorical staging needed to realize and maintain their pose.

Drawing on metaphors from an emergent leisure culture that celebrated the benefits of recreation to mind and body, Donald Grant Mitchell attempted to flip the table on a domestic destiny that felt depressingly fated to many American men. Over the course of his literary career, he suggested the possibility of rewriting the marriage plot in suburban landscapes. On the surface, his prose invokes familiar sentimental literary dichotomies of bachelorhood and marriage that equate the former with idle reverie and the latter with its relinquishment. At the same time, he subtly invites readers to inhabit his writing on another plane, one that welcomes experiences of excitement, passion, and thrill-seeking into domestic routines. Whereas Henry Ward Beecher sought to suburbanize the imagination—by making it safe to indulge—in his writings about men's home lives, Mitchell hoped to set the suburbs on fire imaginatively, to prove that it was possible for men to live like bachelors even within the confines of that seemingly most tame of environments. In his careful deployment of a respected, established genre to voice illicit, unspoken desires, he shows how reverie might buffer a life governed by necessity and obligation. Conflating relational, geographic, and literary plots, he proposes that men approach their domestic lives as games, stories governed by fixed boundaries and rhetorics but also open to the influence of skill, strategy, and chance.

Throughout *Rural Studies, with Hints for Country Places,* a collection of essays compiled in 1867 as a meditative guide for men who sought to relocate beyond America's urban centers, Mitchell personifies the domestic landscape by characterizing it as a desirable woman whose attentions and trust must be won by way of artistic intuition, an appreciation for mystery, and attentive persistence. "A country home," he asserts, "will not yield its largest enjoyments to any who adopt it in virtue of a mere whim; there must be love; and with love, patience; and with patience, trust. The mistress who wears the golden daffodils in her hair, and the sweet violets at her girdle, and heaps her lap every autumn time with fruit, must be conciliated, and humored, and rewarded, and flattered, and caressed. She resents capricious and fitful attentions—like a woman; receiving them smilingly, and sulking when they are done."[1] Later, he suggests that a house should "court" its visitors, appearing to be mysterious and witty as it reveals its charms by degree. The approaching drive, the placement of the house on the lot, and the positions of trees and shrubs, according to Mitchell, contribute to a sense of excitement and allure for resident and visitor alike. Referring to the "partial concealment of the beauties that confront the eye" in the design of home and landscape as "art management," he asks readers to consider possibilities for desire, suspension, and ultimate gratification in the experience of domestic life, arguing that such qualities "quicken the zest with which the natural beauties, as successively unfolded, are enjoyed," effectively "wed[ding] the home to the view . . . drap[ing] the bride, and teach[ing] us the piquant value of a 'coy, reluctant, amorous delay'" (*RS*, 178–79).

In an effort to theorize what he called "a man's sense of domesticity" (273), Mitchell aestheticized the domestic sphere and classified home design and even the act of living as a form of art. Criticizing housewives for a brand of utilitarianism that left no room for "true home relish" in their unceasing commitment to pragmatics, he designated "livab[ility]" as the ultimate goal of men's domestic efforts, associating it with attitudes and decorative elements "that suggest easy comfort, ample room, odd loitering nooks, indefinite play of fire-light and lamp-light, wide and unpretentious hospitality" (273). In his country books from the 1860s, Mitchell returns to his earlier literary portrayals of bachelorhood to craft an alluringly reflexive, even onanistic domestic system whereby the occupant-designer of the home stages a scene of seduction for himself by choosing to role-play his own life. Like Thoreau and Beecher, Mitchell formulated and refined these ideas over the course of his literary career within the context of larger trends in community formation, both geographically and in print. Replacing fears of subjugation and stasis with the pleasures of an elaborate game, Mitchell locates in suburbanization a solution to the frustrations with feminine domesticity that he had voiced early on.

DREAMS OF A DIFFERENT DOMESTIC LIFE
Immobilizing Visions in Reveries of a Bachelor

The few critics who discuss Donald Grant Mitchell in the context of nineteenth-century print culture have focused on the popular success of *Reveries of a Bachelor, or, A Book of the Heart,* which sold fourteen thousand copies in its first year of print and was reprinted almost one hundred times between its appearance in book form in 1850 and Mitchell's death in 1907.[2] Organized as a four-part first-person contemplation of bachelorhood, marriage, family, and home narrated by Paul, a single man in his mid-twenties, it is also a meditation on life and death. Relaxing in a comfortable chair in his Connecticut cottage with a dog at his side, Paul stares into the fire and dreams about past, present, and future. Readers are invited to follow his flights of fancy and to sympathize with him as he voices various hopes and fears through imaginative rehearsals of domestic married life, weighing the possible pros and cons of settling down with wife and children versus remaining a bachelor indefinitely.

Mitchell was already a relatively successful periodical writer when *Reveries* was published, contributing frequently to the *American Review,* the *Morning Courier* and *New York Enquirer, The Knickerbocker,* and *Graham's Magazine.* He had authored two collections of essays, *Fresh Gleanings* (1847) and *The Battle Summer* (1850), in addition to a popular series of pamphlets criticizing New York society, originally published anonymously, called *The Lorgnette* (1849–50). When *Reveries* hit bookstores under the pen name Ik Marvel, however, Mitchell became a literary celebrity almost overnight. *Harper's New Monthly Magazine* called it "one of the most remarkable and delightful books of the present season," praising especially its "truthfulness and freshness of feeling." Claiming that "the author stamps his heart on these living pages," the *Harper's* review asserted that Mitchell "risked more than authors can usually afford, by dealing with the most exquisite elements of feeling, but he always forces you to acknowledge his empire, and yield your sympathies to his bidding."[3] Although the *New York Tribune* did not neglect to mention a calculated quality to the pathos elicited from readers, its reviewer similarly argued that the book's achievement lay in its ability to propel and channel emotion without sacrificing sincerity.

The Mitchell scholar Lisa Spiro demonstrates that *Reveries* fit into an established tradition of bachelor fiction that had been written in America since the early 1820s. Magazines like *Godey's Lady's Book, The Knickerbocker,* and the *Southern Literary Messenger* regularly published short stories and essays about bachelor life, and numerous books treated the same subject. Titles such as *Adventures of a Bachelor; or, Stolen Vigils* (1837), "The Bachelor Beset; or, The Rival Candidates" (1839), "The Bachelor Reclaimed:

A Sketch from Real Life" (1841), *Castle Dismal: or The Bachelor's Christ-mas* (1844), and *The Bachelor's Escape from the Snare of the Fowler* (1845) positioned bachelorhood within a sentimental framework for American readers during the first half of the nineteenth century by characterizing the single male as a troubled, confused individual but with a good heart, some-one who feared marital commitment even as he harbored secret hopes of eventually finding his soul mate.

Popular interest in bachelorhood in the first half of the nineteenth century reflected desires to control and channel proclivities that were per-ceived as dangerous to the health of society.[4] As the century unfolded, single young men came not only to represent the liberty, wit, and entre-preneurial spirit associated with Revolutionary America, but also to em-body fears about private meditations, unchecked passions, and headstrong youth. Sentimentalized representations of bachelorhood sought to defuse fears of masturbation associated with single men alone in rooms in front of fires by insisting they were dreaming about future wives and children—and nothing else. By letting readers into the mind of the bachelor through fiction, writers effectively removed the barrier between self and other that was the source of so much anxiety. As long as the bachelor's musings and actions reflected a desire to marry and join the majority of responsible adults, their mysterious tendencies and passion for cigars, fireplaces, dogs, alcohol, leisure hours, and sporting culture were indulged as youthful foi-bles and harmless quirks.

True to the popular representation of bachelorhood in these texts, Paul of *Reveries* dreams about women—a lot. He exhibits a hesitancy to com-mit to marriage and maintains a strong allegiance to his male friends. He includes an extended meditation on the pleasures of fireplaces and cigar smoking, and he reflects almost unceasingly on the passage of time as he tries to envision his ideal wife and family. In important ways, however, *Reveries of a Bachelor* moves beyond the plot and theme of earlier bachelor fictions. As Vincent Bertolini argues, Mitchell employs the language of sen-timent to protest traditional domesticity rather than to reassert its power. The narrator's reveries mark him as an earnest young man who professes commitment to a future marriage and domestic life while at the same time they enable him to escape the necessity of actually settling down with a wife.

Even so, Paul does not enact a thorough rejection of the domestic in this text. Instead, he projects a sense of unease toward the prospect of female control of the home space, which he seeks to mitigate through imaginative play. He relishes his cottage in the Connecticut countryside, commenting in the opening pages, "I take a vast deal of comfort in treating it just as I choose."[5] Whether he decides to spend the day dreaming or planning home improvement projects for the next year, he oversees his domestic environment. As he relaxes in the chair near the fire, he wonders how many of his fellow men have the "good fortune" to enjoy such evenings of "sober and thoughtful quietude" (*RB,* 17). The publication success of *Reveries* did not constitute a case of masterly literary trickery in which Mitchell conned readers and reviewers into believing that a bachelor narrator wanted something that in reality he did not. Rather, it reflected an attempt to grapple with men's anxieties about their current and future home lives while also documenting their investment in the domestic sphere in a way that would resonate with the real concerns of many readers, both male and female, over power negotiations and responsibilities after marriage.

Reveries does not successfully resolve the tensions it identifies, but it does voice specific frustrations that men might experience with what they perceive as female-centered theories of domesticity. Even as Paul vows that he will not remain a bachelor forever, he obviously enjoys being single, describing his solo existence as carefree, respectable, idle, and comfortable at various points throughout the narrative. He fears that marriage, by contrast, will be "absorbing, unchanging, [and] relentless" (19), that he will lose his dignity and freedom in a house where his wife will make all the decisions. He worries about becoming a "captive" (22) to the woman he marries or that his home life will be so unbearable that he will make excuses to stay late at work in an effort to escape its imprisoning clutches. In his dreams, he returns again and again to anxieties about losing respect and control.

Paul's reveries beg for alternatives to the sort of advice promulgated in the housekeeping handbooks that had become so popular during the first half of the nineteenth century, such as Catharine Beecher's *Treatise on Domestic Economy* (1841), which identified women as keepers of the home and sought to awaken them to their wide sphere of influence. According to Beecher, "The only legitimate object of amusements, is, to prepare mind and body for the proper discharge of duty."[6] In her taxonomy of potential applications for the housekeeper's time, she places "*novel reading* and *castle building*" under "the head of excessive mental action" on account of their "indulgence of the imagination." For Beecher, the dreamy propensities exhibited in *Reveries* operate as a "perverted" "stimulus" that "undermines the vigor of the nervous system" in addition to "wast[ing] time and energies."[7] In place of recreation and free time, books like Lydia Maria Child's *Frugal Housewife* (1829) and Eliza Leslie's *House Book* (1840) valued women's commitment to service, economy, health, and child rearing. Domestic fiction written by women celebrated many of the same ideals, from Catharine Maria Sedgwick's *Home* (1835), which detailed the positive effects of feminine virtues of temperance, cleanliness, kindness, and hospitality on the family as a whole, to Susan Warner's *Wide, Wide World* (1851) and Harriet Beecher Stowe's *Uncle Tom's Cabin* (1852), both of which appeared shortly after *Reveries of a Bachelor* and posited the quiet power of women to correct men's misjudgments and model Christian behavior through their extraordinary capacity for sympathy. Paul's hesitation to commit to life with a wife in *Reveries* stems from just these sorts of characterizations of women's rule over the home space; he fears that he will be constrained within a regime that leaves no time for self-definition, no space for artistic play.

Mitchell outlined Paul's nightmarish visions of married life most dramatically in the "First Reverie," which appeared as "A Bachelor's Reverie, In Three Parts" for the *Southern Literary Journal* in September 1849 and again in the inaugural issue of *Harper's New Monthly Magazine* for January 1850. Retitled "Smoke, Flame, and Ashes" for the expanded book edition, the section introduces readers to the narrator, whom they find seated in front of his fireplace in a cottage located on a country estate inherited from his mother after her death. Staring into the fire and listening to his tenants putting their children to bed in the next room, he ponders his own domestic future, bravely resolving to "pursue the thought wherever it leads" (*RB*, 18). As it soon becomes clear, though, the seemingly comic resolve is warranted: Paul's imagination conjures vivid incarnations of domestic possibilities that would complicate his ability to conceive of his home as a welcome refuge from business in the city.

He envisions life with a wife whose family is rich, and the ways in which a seeming boon could become a major annoyance if she controlled the purse strings and preached economy to him, or if she were to manifest an interest in stocks and begin to question his investment decisions. He also considers problems that might occur when "plaguey wife's-relations" (22) drop by unexpectedly, as aunts and uncles contribute unwanted advice and nephews make noise and eat all the good food. He next dreams of a bookish wife who relegates her domestic duties to hired help in order to free up time for her own pursuits, resulting in a nightly routine that is anything but relaxing: "The nurse is getting dinner; you are holding the baby; Peggy is reading Bruyère" (28). If a wife were to grow ugly or lax in her appearance in the midst of taking care of other duties, that could become problematic as well. What if he were no longer attracted to her, or worse, if she were attracted to someone else? Or perhaps she would be a terrible cook who was unsympathetic to protestations or suggestions for improvement: "I think I see myself—ruminated I—sitting meekly at the table, scarce daring to lift up my eyes, utterly fagged out with some quarrel of yesterday, choking down detestably sour muffins, that my wife thinks are 'delicious'—slipping in dried mouthfuls of burnt ham off the side of my fork tines,—slipping off my chair side-ways at the end, and slipping out with my hat between my knees, to business, and never feeling myself a competent, sound-minded man, till the oak door is between me and Peggy!" (25–26). Indeed, what if circumstances were so bad that he could not stand to be in the house with her? The more negative the scenarios Paul generates in *Reveries,* the more entrenched he becomes in front of the fire, preserving his hearth from the fated plot—whatever its specific manifestation—that is marriage.

After all, even if he were to choose a good wife, one who was attractive and sympathetic, who took care of all the necessary domestic offices without either overzealousness or dissatisfaction, his life would become much more complicated, especially in terms of emotional attachment. In marriage, according to Paul, "there is a heart-bond that absorbs all others; there is a community that monopolizes your feeling" (44) and decimates any hope for a carefree existence. It also would mark an end to male friendships, as the "hundred connections" he had forged with other men would "now seem colder than ice" (44). There were potential benefits to consider, however. Paul imagines that the right woman would cause him to be guileless and benevolent, in addition to returning him to a state of boyish enthusiasm and vivacity. Certainly he would be less lonely; he would have someone with whom to share sorrows as well as joys. He muses that he would enjoy playing with children and witnessing a mother's care for them. Paul welcomes the idea that someone could act as nurse to him if he became sick or cry inconsolably if he died unexpectedly. He theorizes that the presence of family would enliven the domestic environment, that love, like a flame, would "brighten up a man's habitation" (29). If his wife or children were to die, however, the pain would have a permanent impact. He also realizes that success in business would become increasingly important; if he were to lose his job or not earn enough money, the whole family would become poor. Responsibility for their welfare would be his province, and he could not stand to watch them beg or waste away from lack of food.

Despite unsettling reveries of married life, Paul's depictions of his home demonstrate commitment to a satisfying domestic existence outside the city. In fact, he claims that ruminations about the possibility of making the ancestral property a permanent home, considerations of whether "the little ricketty house would not be after all a snug enough box, to live and to die in" (17), were what gave rise to *Reveries* in the first place. Perhaps out of a sense of nostalgia for childhood, his country cottage acts as a central focal point in the narrative, with happy memories of the land and architecture serving as the standard against which he judges any visions of the future. Paul does not prefer metropolitan life; he readily admits that his rented "garret of the city" (58) offers little besides proximity to work. As he sits in an "office chair" in front of a "snug grate" (59), his thoughts reside in the country—with the little home's wide chimney, rattling windowpanes, cozy nooks, and opportunities for quiet, expansive contemplation. Whether we read Paul as a thinly veiled author figure or an urban clerk, it is clear that he associates home with a more natural landscape that is separate, mentally and physically, from his professional life.

Depictions of Paul's "quiet farmhouse in the country, . . . the only house in the world," he says, "of which I am *bona-fide* owner," offer a glimpse into a lifestyle that he believes to be threatened by marriage. He has fashioned a domestic environment that is self-consciously masculine, from the "saucy colored, lithographic print of some fancy 'Bessy'" that hangs at the foot of his bed to the "brown table with carved lions' feet," "heavy oak floor," "cosy looking fire-place," and small sleeping cabinet just the size for a feather-filled "broad bachelor bedstead" (15–16). Though he spends the weekdays in his city apartment because of its proximity to work, he is master of his domain in the country cottage on weekends. Having voluntarily whittled his responsibilities and necessities down to a bare minimum there, he can spend his days however he wants.

Every piece of furniture and knick-knack exists for him alone. His quest for comfort is not stifled by propriety, and there are no rules that cannot be broken. He brashly proclaims: "I manage to break some article of furniture, almost every time I pay it a visit; and if I cannot open the window readily of a morning, to breathe the fresh air, I knock out a pane or two of glass with my boot. I lean against the walls in a very old arm-chair there is on the premises, and scarce ever fail to worry such a hole in the plastering, as would set me down for a round charge for damages in town, or make a prim housewife fret herself into a raging fever. I laugh out loud with myself, in my big arm-chair, when I think that I am neither afraid of one, nor the other" (16). His cottage provides him with the very freedoms that are under attack in his dreamscapes. Even as he longs on some level for companionship, his material surroundings remind him that certain elements of his current existence are worth preserving.

From Paul's perspective, there is no need to orient home life around seemingly loftier, societally sanctioned goals: a domestic sphere that invites reverie at the end of the workweek would have its own restorative effects on the spirit. Title-page illustrations from the 1850 edition reinforce this assertion (fig. 5). The bachelor's pose is relaxed and comfortable; the hat and coat in the background and the house jacket he wears suggest an intimate relationship with his surroundings. In the right-hand image his dog has been replaced by a housekeeper, but both serve as trusty companions, confidants, and sounding boards. The open cabinet, roaring fire, scattered books and periodicals, and cigar have the quality of props designed to look careless (model representations of Henry Ward Beecher's domestic disorder) and help define this space as one whose sole purpose is to facilitate imaginative flow.

With that notion at the forefront of his mind, he does not worry about being immoderate as he heats his house, but basks in its warmth. He emphasizes his lack of obligation by bragging that he never takes a watch with him into the country, preferring to judge time by the progress of his fire. Even sleep is described in terms of pleasure rather than necessity, as

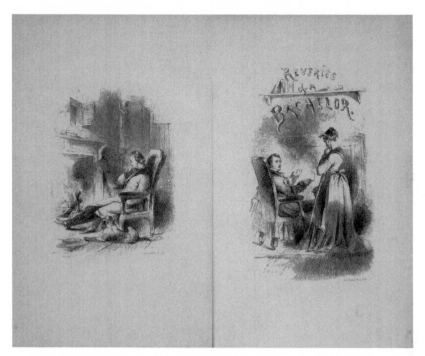

Figure 5. Title-page spread from *Reveries of a Bachelor* (1850). Courtesy American
Antiquarian Society.

"slip[ping] by the light of the embers into my bed, where I luxuriate in such
sound, and healthful slumber, as only such rattling window frames, and
country air, can supply" (17). Catharine Beecher and Lydia Maria Child
had it wrong: the home, in Paul's eyes, is ideally suited for cultivation that
leads inward rather than outward. Time and work are relative. If imagination, desire, and pleasure became integrated into the domestic ethos, work
there would not seem like work at all. Aided by a cigar, he enjoys letting
his mind wander along "all the ordinary rural topics of thought" (17) as he
considers various home improvement projects and changes that should be
made to the landscape.

Interspersed with the narrator's meditations on home renovation, interior design, and landscaping plans are dreams about women, as when he
beckons readers to conjure the body of a young woman alongside him in
part two of the "First Reverie":

> If now in that chair yonder . . . beside you—closer yet—were seated a
> sweet-faced girl, with a pretty little foot lying out upon the hearth—a bit

of lace running round the swelling throat—the hair parted to a charm over a forehead fair as any of your dreams;—and if you could reach an arm around that chair back, without fear of giving offence, and suffer your fingers to play idly with those curls that escape down the neck; and if you could clasp with your other hand those little white, taper fingers of hers, which lie so temptingly within reach,—and so, talk softly and low in the presence of the blaze, while the hours slip without knowledge, and the winter winds whistle uncared for;—if, in short, you were no bachelor, but the husband of some such sweet image—(dream, call it rather,) would it not be far pleasanter than this cold single night-sitting—counting the sticks—reckoning the length of the blaze, and the height of the falling snow? (30)

Mitchell makes no attempt to disguise the autoeroticism of the language here as it traces a sensory path along a completely passive body. The scene is staged from start to finish, from the little foot peeking out from the hem and hint of lace at the throat to escaped curls of hair and fingers resting listlessly on a gown. In this case, though, a premeditated self-seduction need not be anathema if performed in good faith. Mitchell's employment of sentimental language in this passage and others, rather than domesticating the bachelor figure, suggests that morally sanctioned sympathetic identification and unseemly demonstrations of erotic longing share more characteristics than most people were willing to admit. An embrace of their proximity, through the intentional use of sentimentalism to align bodily desires with those of the aesthetic, social, and spiritual variety, opens an underutilized but viable path to satisfying self and society at once.

Again and again in *Reveries,* Mitchell insinuates that for men at least, home works best as a backdrop, a stage for the performance and observation of successive life dramas. Refusal to demarcate a line between real and imagined life, in this respect, is central to the domestic ideology he espouses in 1850. When Paul asks, "Can any wife be prettier than an after dinner fancy, idle and yet vivid, can paint for you? Can any children make less noise, than the little rosy-cheeked ones, who have no existence, except in the *omnium gatherum* of your own brain? Can any housewife be more unexceptionable, than she who goes sweeping daintily the cobwebs that gather in your dreams? Can any domestic larder be better stocked, than the private larder of your head dozing on a cushioned chair-back at Delmonico's? Can any family purse be better filled than the exceeding plump one, you dream of, after reading such pleasant books as Munchausen, or Typee?" (21), we should not assume he is doing so rhetorically. Mitchell's narrator is feeling around for an escape from a story that has already been rehearsed, repeatedly, in all of its incarnations. That does not mean, as Bertolini suggests, that Paul wants to escape the domestic while *appearing* to embrace it. The representation of a bachelor's domesticity is solipsistic in *Reveries,* certainly, but so is Thoreau's: both are turning to imaginative life in the name of pushing against "the dull standard of the actual" (*RB,* 20).

In his impulse to search for an overlooked space between, to "determine limit" (43) for himself rather than accepting the reports of others, Paul asks readers to suspend disbelief just for a moment to consider what constitutes domestic communion and transformation. He defensively counters would-be detractors, critics who would place him outside the home: "What matters it pray, if literally, there was no wife, and no dead child, and no coffin in the house? Is not feeling, feeling; and heart, heart? Are not these fancies thronging on my brain, bringing tears to my eyes, bringing joy to my soul, as living, as anything human can be living? What if they have no material type—no objective form? All that is crude,—a mere reduction of the ideality to sense,—a transformation of the spiritual to the earthly,—a levelling of soul to matter" (53). By asserting that his imaginative rehearsals of the married state, and even the death of wife, children, and eventually himself, are real experiences—superior, in fact, to those with material corollaries—he follows sentimentalism to its logical conclusion. As a careful reader with his heart in the right place, he can imagine the lives of others with fidelity and sympathy. That orientation of openness, a willingness to be moved, paradoxically enables the self to transcend its boundaries by diffusing one's normal perspective through momentary and self-willed access to the life of another.

Such an assertion, after all, aligns with the central premise of *Reveries,* and the source of its popularity. Mitchell's narrative purports to provide readers authentic access to bachelorhood—an experience of otherness and relationality—across the space of the page. It follows, then, that Paul can claim to know the experience of marriage without ever removing from the hearth; he has tried it on (in the mind and on the page) in a way that is no less transformative than a permanent physical union. It is this category of quasi-disembodied play, in which the self, as part spectator and part participant, can shed its shackles and become medium, which the book advocates as the unique province of the man at home.[8] As an inwardly oriented stage, Mitchell's fictional domestic environment stands ready to support the seamless integration of material and imaginative life; in a word, it supplies the "feel" of home for inhabitants and visitors as they sentimentally role-play in an attempt to discover what it is they really want from their lives.

When Paul admits to selling the property in the book's final section, then, it comes as unexpectedly to readers as it does to the narrator himself. Following the path to his cottage one last time, he muses on its influence on his personal identity. Although he never explains his decision, the admission marks a limitation in his domestic vision. Through the loss of the country cottage in *Reveries,* Mitchell signals a narrative inability to carry out the claims that the text has espoused. Paul clearly wants to bring elements of a new urbanized manhood to the country landscape he loves, but he will be unwilling to relinquish permanently his rented city garret (or marry, for that matter) until he believes that he can live affordably and conveniently outside the city in a domestic landscape designed to serve as a conduit rather than an end, a realm where play is valued and even expected, where material incarnations of castles in the air successfully resist "a mere reduction of the ideality to sense."

SUBURBAN STAGING
Masculine Domesticity Revisited

Mitchell himself was a bachelor when *Reveries* was published, a fact that was not lost on readers who followed the movements of "Ik Marvel" as closely as the rambling dreams of his narrator. Their impulse was warranted: Mitchell's personal history bore more than a passing resemblance to that of the fictional character he had created. According to his primary biographer, Waldo Dunn, whose account (drafted in the deceased author's library with the permission of the Mitchell family) appeared fourteen years after Mitchell's death, there were many correspondences. Dunn claimed, in fact, that *Reveries of a Bachelor* constituted "the very best kind of autobiography" of the author's life prior to 1850.[9] After his mother's death in 1839, while he was still in college at Yale, Mitchell inherited a farmhouse and four hundred acres of adjoining land in New London County, Connecticut, where he settled after graduation, traveling twelve miles to Norwich for its market and paying for books and magazines to be delivered. His dog, like Paul's, was named Carlo, and various scenes and buildings from his biography correspond almost directly to those in Paul's boyhood reminiscences.[10] In letters written to his cousin Mary Goddard in 1848, he sounded much like the bachelor narrator of his book, admitting that he harbored hopes of regaining the land he had sold before going to Europe, that he "sometimes dream[ed] of having a great fortune, and going back there [to Connecticut], and reinstating everything in the old way, and so dream on again a life of happy idleness."[11]

At first, Mitchell welcomed the publicity generated by *Reveries of a Bachelor.* He attempted to capitalize on its success by issuing a sequel in 1851 titled *Dream Life: A Fable of the Seasons,* which continued in a similar vein by celebrating the power of the imagination and reflecting on the past. Soon afterward, he began to experiment with different styles of writing, mainly nonfiction for periodicals. His newfound celebrity-author status helped him in that regard: in 1851 *Harper's* invited him to write a monthly essay on topics of his choosing, which he titled "The Editor's Easy Chair."[12] He also agreed to write a regular column for *The Knickerbocker* in 1852, and fan mail poured in as both authorized and unauthorized editions of *Reveries* continued to be published each year. Around this time, he began a public lecture tour as well, and although listeners doubtless attended to see and hear the author of *Reveries of a Bachelor,* he chose to speak on topics related to artistic sensibilities, travel, and the domestic environment.

Eventually, however, his romantic relationship with Mary Pringle of Charleston provided the impetus for a shift in priorities. Their courtship was followed closely by the press, which hailed their marriage in 1853 as the unwritten conclusion to *Reveries.* Although Mitchell increasingly sought to distance himself from the best-selling text in public, appearing somewhat embarrassed and referring to it as a youthful book intended for young audiences, he occasionally channeled his fictional alter ego in his private life. He presented an inscribed 1852 edition of the book to Mary early in their relationship, and his letters to her during their engagement could easily have been penned by Paul. In a letter dated March 1–2, 1853, for instance, he mentioned a desire to escape his bachelor's den in New York

City: "I *do* look longingly forward to the day when in place of this solitary bachelor-room in a dim and dreary hotel, you will lighten my hearth and home with that cheery face, and give me such joys as have truly lived only in 'reverie.' "[13] A few weeks later he complained that his publisher, who was constantly pressuring him with writing deadlines, "would like me to take a room in his store 12 ft. x 8, one desk, one chair, one stone pitcher, six pens, and two reams of paper . . . [and] would advise me to keep there the rest of the summer, running up in the country to see you once a week; and in the winter, once a month."[14] Judging from the tone of these letters, the promise of "a country cottage home" with Mary had come to represent a refuge from publicity and a reprieve from a demanding writing schedule.[15]

As perhaps the most celebrated proponent of early suburbanization, the architect A. J. Downing helped popularize the notion that the environment in which the practice of domesticity occurred was just as important as the tasks and ideals themselves. Arguing that one's house should be a reflection of the self, Downing claimed that suburban spaces, with their unique combination of nature and civilization, offered unparalleled canvases for middle-class Americans who sought to transmit their personalities to their surroundings. It was his hope that "smiling lawns and tasteful cottages" would soon dot the countryside as testimony to American culture and democracy.[16] When Downing first published *Cottage Residences* in 1842, though, his plans were not viable for the vast majority of Americans. The description that accompanied the initial design, a "Suburban Cottage for a Small Family" (fig. 6), assumed it was possible for "a family of small means" to live "a comparatively retired life" in a modest-sized cottage, but his cost assessments contained inaccuracies, and transportation networks could not yet support individuals who needed to commute to work on a daily basis.[17]

Noting the discrepancy in an 1843 review of *Cottage Residences* that he wrote for the *New Englander*, Mitchell had chastised the reformer for misreading the needs of the American public. Perhaps chafing under the heavy responsibility of managing a four hundred–acre farm, he argued that few could afford to put the handbook's suggestions into practice and expressed regret that the sort of appreciation for aesthetic experience in the domestic sphere championed by Downing could not yet coexist with a simultaneous need for economy and convenience.[18] By 1847, though, recognizing the

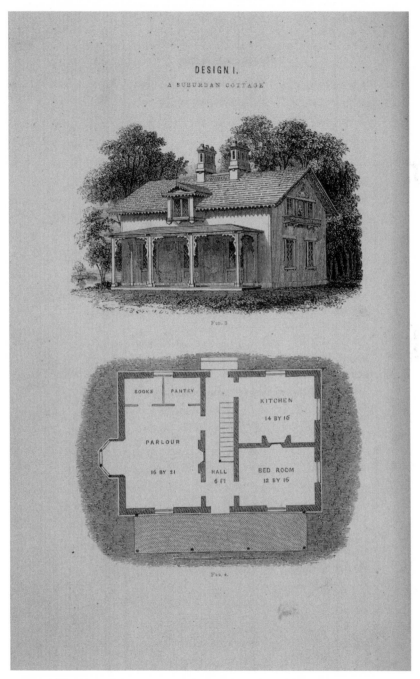

FIGURE 6. Plate from *Cottage Residences* (1842). Courtesy American Antiquarian Society.

potential in nascent trends toward suburbanization, he muted his earlier complaints for his review of a revised edition of Downing's *Treatise*. Even as he considered how to sell his farmland after the loss of his tenant caretaker, Mitchell praised Downing's efforts to readers of the *American Review,* arguing that the reformer was a man ahead of his time whose recommendations were only just beginning to be appreciated.[19] With the publication of *The Architecture of Country Houses* in 1850, Downing attempted to allay criticisms such as those voiced by Mitchell by explaining that his cottages were designed not with either the farmer or the aristocrat in mind, men who had "very different wants," but rather for "an industrious man, who earns his bread by daily exertions, and lives in a snug and economical little home in the suburbs of town."[20] By the time of Downing's death in 1852, his hopes had begun to be realized in towns throughout the Northeast, and a new generation of architects was eager to assume his mantle. Although Paul of *Reveries,* like Mitchell, had to sell his property in the country, during the 1850s and 1860s it became considerably easier to gratify an impulse to live in nature and commute to work each morning.

Mitchell himself purchased a suburban residence just outside the city of New Haven in 1855.[21] He would later recall in *Pictures of Edgewood,* a small gift book he printed privately for friends and relatives in 1869 which included lithographs of the homestead, "A friend called upon me shortly after my arrival, and learning the errand upon which I had been scouring no inconsiderable tract of country, proposed to me to linger a day more, and take a drive about the suburbs." As they toured the area outside New Haven—New York City, he reminded his wife, was only four hours away—he found himself on a farm at the edge of a wood, looking down on "all the spires of the city we had left, two miles away as a bird flies."[22] Accordingly, he named the property Edgewood and spent the next five years landscaping and renovating it. During that time, he disappeared from the public eye.

When Mitchell finally reappeared on the publishing scene in the early 1860s, he must have seemed like an altogether different writer to many of his readers. The pose of the sentimental bachelor anxious about marriage and career had been replaced by that of a family man consumed by home improvement projects. After he settled at Edgewood, almost everything he wrote for the rest of his career centered on life there: the experience of shaping a landscape, designing and building a home, establishing a garden, and enjoying the pleasures of domestic life in the suburban countryside. *My Farm of Edgewood: A Country Book* (1863) grew out of a piece called "Agriculture as a Profession; or, Hints about Farming," which appeared in the *New Englander* in November 1860. His next book, *Wet Days at Edgewood* (1865), was a compilation of essays about rural writers that he had contributed to the *Atlantic Monthly* between April 1863 and September 1864 under the title "Wet Weather Work." In 1867 he gathered together articles written for *Hours at Home* and *The Horticulturalist* in a book titled *Rural Studies*.[23]

All of this later work shares two important characteristics: a concern for domestic life outside American cities and a focus on the integration of gamelike play into everyday lived experience. While it would be easy to dismiss Mitchell's books from the 1860s as the fruit of a middle-aged man's complacency, which on one level they certainly were, these writings are more than material records of the quiet extinguishment of a celebrated bachelorhood. In the course of outlining what he referred to as "a man's sense of domesticity," Mitchell demonstrated that the thrill of the chase and a passion for cigar-induced reverie need not exclude a desire for companionship and visions of home. Just beyond the urban periphery, a man could begin the process of turning a physical space into an embodiment of selfhood, a stage where self-actualization could unfold and enshrine itself.

In theorizing as well as detailing the practicalities of domestic staging for male readers, Mitchell drew from a new interest in the beneficial properties of play in an expanding American leisure culture.[24] During the first half of the nineteenth century, popular amusements such as opera, theater, public balls, museums, parades, amusement parks, dance halls, and gambling emerged to service a burgeoning youth culture of new urbanites in search of entertainment outlets to fill their free time and social needs. Bars like Pfaff's and restaurants such as Delmonico's quickly became bastions of white-collar culture, and proprietors began to pay new attention to the potential of interior design to transform rectangular boxes into oases of conviviality and stimulation. Toys, games, musical instruments, books, and other recreational commodities also proliferated in this period, along with increased discussion in popular periodicals of specialized hobbies as offering necessary "relief," in the words of Donna Braden, "from the monotony of repetitive work" and "adherence to the clock" associated with the industrialized era.[25] Proponents of play advocated the adoption of favorite home amusements, for adults and children alike, as both necessary breaks for overtaxed minds and opportunities to maintain and develop skills and perceptions typically neglected by the work world.

In turn, the games themselves reflected the values of a changing society. Developed by Milton Bradley in 1860 as a secularized version of the Mansion of Happiness (1843), the Checkered Game of Life, for example, turned what Jennifer Jensen describes as a "typical virtue-versus-vice race game," in which the goal was to reach heaven through accumulations of virtuous behavior, into a pleasure-tour celebration of life milestones, in which success was defined in material, social, and medical terms.[26] At a moment when men like Mitchell's Paul were voicing feelings of entrapment, domestic playfulness—whether through the embrace of board games and sports, conversation, or even the layout of the home and surrounding landscape—promised to restore a sense of fluidity to a relatively fixed plot of obligation (to career, marriage, children, and religion). By lending a sense of mystery and intrigue to what had come to look like a tired and banal yet nonetheless essential environment for careworn businessmen, play reintroduced the feelings of pleasure, camaraderie, exploration, and freedom from direction that young professionals remembered from childhood but saw nowhere in the regimes of women or in their work lives.

The hope was that such an approach would be restorative on multiple levels. The slight self-distancing integral to the experience, whereby all players temporarily agree to abide by a set of rules that place everyone on an equal playing field, effectively made the familiar (including selfhood) foreign. This self-conscious staging worked to protract the enjoyment of a known environment by openly manufacturing enchantment. Additionally, the dreamlike quality of games allowed, in the words of Kenneth T. Jackson, "some combination of luck, strategy, and knowledge to give their players the kind of clear victories and successes that are so rare in real life."[27] As William A. Gleason argues, new theories of play in the nineteenth century sought "to substitute for the fading American ideals of—or more precisely, the vanishing American opportunities for—individual autonomy, creativity, and agency."[28] For Mitchell and other proponents of masculine domesticity, a play-based approach to home life promised to reconstitute a manhood that had been lost along the march to productivity and innovation, and more important, to keep it inviolate to future incursions.

Mitchell's late-life writings can be classified as country books, a now forgotten genre, discussed in detail in chapter 6, which flourished in the 1860s in response to changing patterns in population and land use. Henry Ward Beecher loosely fashioned *Star Papers* and *Eyes and Ears* after country books of the day, and other famous practitioners included Frederic Cozzens, Robert Barry Coffin, Nathaniel Parker Willis, and Lewis William Mansfield. Part autobiographical essay, part architectural pattern book, and part domestic treatise, the genre celebrated the new availability of what Willis would refer to as "country life within city reach" and modeled an urbanite's relocation experience for an audience that might be considering a similar transition. In country books, however, there was always a gap between the class positions occupied by author and reader. Even as writers preached economy and simplicity, arguing that it was possible for middle-class Americans to move to the suburbs and enjoy lives similar to their own, the images and descriptions of their homes made it clear that celebrity afforded them unique privileges and opportunities. The popularity of country books depended in large part on the fame of the writer, as they offered opportunities for voyeurism alongside information about the suburban experience.

In line with other books of this genre, Mitchell's stated purpose was to provide guidance to individuals who wanted to move to the suburbs, even though he also dwelt extensively on the particular details of acquiring and maintaining Edgewood. Despite acknowledging that the impulse to dream about the perfect home was natural to both sexes, Mitchell suggested that suburban life was particularly well suited to men's needs. Addressing himself to men from urban areas who harbored a "very determined wish to reap what pleasures they can out of a country life, by such moderate degree of attention and of labor as shall not overtax their time, or plunge them into the anxieties of a new and engrossing pursuit" (*RS,* 26), he hoped his accounts of finding and renovating his property would help the reader determine what to plant and how "to establish a cozy home, where his children can romp to their hearts' content, and he—take a serene pleasure in plucking his own fruit, pulling his own vegetables, smelling at his own rose-tree and smoking under his own vine" (31). He invited readers to use his writings as inspiration in the design and care of their own suburban homes, promising that they, too, would find solace and happiness in the suburbs.

In addition to detailed discussions of fences, ornamentation, and vegetation outside the house, Mitchell's country books included recommendations for furniture, fireplaces, paint colors, and wall décor. He paid particular attention to distributing "the aesthetic element" (*MFE,* 167) throughout the interior, explaining how architectural and decorative details could impact mood and communicate a life philosophy. In this he drew from Downing's applications of the picturesque to American architecture and landscape design. Speaking of the "notion of associationalism" at the core of Downing's romantic philosophy, Steven Fink reviews the architect's emphasis on balancing use and beauty, as well as his further division of the category of beauty into the two subcategories of "absolute" and "relative" beauty.[29] While "absolute" beauty appealed to principles of symmetry and proportion, variety and unity, which were supposedly universal (to civilized men), "relative" beauty originated in the "personal or historical *associations*" of the inhabitant and communicated particular unique beliefs and ideas to visitors and onlookers.[30] Returning to the faith in dream and reverie from his *Reveries* days, in his country books Mitchell translated Downing's associationalism into a domestic philosophy that privileged staging over doing.

His rationale was that attention to the design and appointment of the space itself, as a conduit to engaging, invigorating, and satisfying role play, would amply repay the homeowner. The smallest details, from paint color and chair placement to types of trees and maintenance of paths, precipitated subtle mood shifts and triggered latent memories in ways that could be utilized both to influence and to extend the experience of enchantment. Mitchell oriented his instruction, therefore, toward helping potential homeowners identify their most cherished memories and ardent longings in order to tap them, associationally, via an aesthetic sensibility. What his readers did in those spaces once the stage was set (or reset with renovations or updates, as the case may be) was their own business: the domestic performances that couldn't help but unfold from a thoughtfully prepared and maintained home would be self-initiated and self-directed, and happily for author and reader, also unregulated.

This domesticity did not have precise rules; in an effort to distinguish his approach from those espoused by popular proponents of feminine domesticities, Mitchell claimed that even his methodology was intended to approximate a man's way of thinking. Rather than closing down opportunity and eliminating pleasure through detailed step-by-step instruction, he presented his guidance with words like "suggestion" and "stimulation," as if hoping to inaugurate a new understanding of what sorts of experience the home could encompass when men took the initiative to participate actively in shaping the domestic environment. The lack of explicit instruction was meant to foster a sense of possibility rather than restriction, to suggest that the home was a canvas for personal artistic expression rather than a prefabricated kit. The home, he insisted, should reflect the individual needs and personalities of its occupants. He urged readers to cultivate "homeliness," insisting: "I like hugely that good old English word—homeliness. It ought to have again its first meaning. Pretty-faced women have corrupted it. It describes all that is best about a country house" (*RS,* 274). For Mitchell as for Henry Ward Beecher, a slight disarray was desirable; it signaled the presence of mental and physical activity and encouraged inhabitants and visitors to value stimulating inquiry and open exploration over concerns about manners or morality.

Even as Mitchell ultimately equated the sentimental rhetorical apparatus of *Reveries* with juvenilia, he honed an "adult" version of that style in his writings about suburban home ownership. In *Reveries,* Mitchell had suggested that courtship, an activity that might appear to be a harmless game, a sport for young bachelors, could turn out to be something much more serious. A seemingly straightforward hunt for a wife could go horribly wrong if a young man entered the situation naïvely. Paul complains:

> I have trouted, when the brook was so low, and the sky so hot, that I might as well have thrown my fly upon the turnpike; and I have hunted hare at noon, and wood-cock in snow-time,—never despairing, scarce doubting; but for a poor hunter of his kind, without traps or snares, or any aid of police or constabulary, to traverse the world, where are swarming, on a moderate computation, some three hundred and odd millions of unmarried women, for a single capture—irremediable, unchangeable—and yet a capture which by strange metonymy, not laid down in the books, is very apt to turn captor into captive, and make a game of hunter—all this, surely, surely may make a man shrug with doubt! (22)

In the suburbs, however, the fear of entrapment in married domestic life evaporates; the game extends indefinitely, as Mitchell's country books urge readers to approach their homes as an unfinished picture, not dissimilar to a reverie that materializes, bit by bit, over the years.

As the dreamer is now master of the game, so too have concerns about capture been replaced by anticipations of seduction. "No troutfisher who is worthy the name, wants his creel loaded in the beginning," Mitchell asserts in *Rural Studies*. "He wants the pursuit—the alternations of hope and fear; the coy rest of his fly upon this pool—the whisk of its brown hackle down yonder rapid—its play upon the eddies where possibly some swift strike may be made—the sway of his rod, and the whiz of his reel under the dash of some struggling victim." As fisherman, the man is now a seasoned veteran. This time, though, the trout he seeks is not a desirable marriageable woman but rather a home that suits him: "It is a mistake, therefore, I think, to aim at the completion of a country home in a season, or in two, or some half a dozen. Its attractiveness lies, or should lie, in its prospective growth of charms" (114). Secure in the knowledge that he will gain his intended object, he has chosen to go fishing for pleasure, and he longs for an exciting outing. The elements are not completely in his control—and he wouldn't want it any other way. Working with the fixed facets of one's environment, or under unexpected or unavoidable constraints, the self-assured man can artfully enhance the view to his advantage.

Just as romance, in the appreciative view of an intelligent man, should unfold through artful delay, the home should not give away all its secrets upon first glance. Mitchell urges readers to factor in elements of unexpected pleasure in the architecture and landscaping of houses. Taking Downing's associationalism in a new direction, Mitchell emphasizes that the layout of one's entire property should incite curiosity and reward exploration. Downing had asked property owners to take their cue from nature; Mitchell hints that men might do well to think about the qualities that make a woman desirable as they decide where to place shrubs and trees and how to appoint their entryways and piazzas. As he coyly remarks in *Rural Studies,* "Nature is a mistress that must be wooed with a will; and there is no mistress worth the having, that must not be wooed in the same way" (27).

Catharine Beecher had set "a relish and desire for high excitement" in opposition to "the more steady and quiet pursuits and enjoyment of home" in her *Treatise,* even as she simultaneously issued a call for American men to prioritize familial over social obligations.[31] Mitchell, in contrast, unabashedly enjoins men to cultivate "a true home relish" as a means to happiness. Whether we interpret his choice of the word "relish" architecturally (as a joint providing extra support to a structure), sensorily (as a condiment or embellishment that adds flavor or complexity), aesthetically (as an individual taste or proclivity), spiritually (without construction), sexually (implying enjoyable anticipation of bodily pleasure), or as a gesture at a quality or characteristic that eludes categorization (as a trace or tinge of something), it asserts the presence of an essential essence in men, inwardly generated and directed, which expresses itself most palpably in the domestic realm. In the nineteenth century, relishes were thought to aid digestion, and Mitchell's domesticity was designed to perform a similar office for the circumscribed trajectory of men's lives.

Even though Mitchell makes it a point to detail the practicalities involved in any move to the country, warning that it is a mistake "to make an easy thing of it" (*RS,* 26) and recommending that newcomers from the city hire help to assist with various domestic tasks, he conspicuously avoids mentioning standard activities such as food preparation, child rearing, and housekeeping in his country books. His wife and children rarely appear in accounts of life at Edgewood; although he occasionally mentions their presence by the fireside or at play in the yard, for the most part they remain silent appendages to the landscape, almost like decorative elements. Whereas in *Reveries* he voiced fears about the capacity of family to intrude on private moments and claim valuable time and space, Mitchell's country books suggest that the suburbs would enable husbands, wives, and children to pursue their separate interests alongside one another.

Ultimately, after all, suburban life was designed to meet the needs of men. As they left every morning and returned in the evening, the change in surroundings would cue different mental states and modes of behavior. To Mitchell and his readers, there was no reason to believe that "the man who plants a garden, and builds a cottage" could not entertain a realistic hope "of shaking off the dust of the city under green trees upon his own sward-land, where some—nameless party—in white lawn, with blue ribbon of a sash (as in Mr. Irving's pretty picture of a wife), stands ready to greet him, after an hour of torture at the hands of our humane railroad directors" (62–63), so long as he knew that he would play a large part in maintaining the suburban vision himself. In any case, Mitchell's guidance insinuates that a suburban house could come to embody the most alluring characteristics of women from a man's perspective, taking on the role of the "nameless party" if need be. It would not matter if a woman became consumed in her children or in housekeeping activities after marriage; men could continue to experience sensations of flirtation and enchantment at home. Always offering up new challenges and rewards, the domestic environment could function as a stand-in that was simultaneously more cunning and more attentive than a wife.

Asking his male readers to rethink their notions of what a home could be, Mitchell describes his domestic program as "the fruit from a graft of the fanciful, set upon the practical" (*MFE*, 221). So was suburban America. In an era of dizzying change, this liminal space provided a necessary distance to process that change or enjoy a temporary reprieve. It had the benefit of being both nostalgic and forward-looking, allowing individuals to feel connected to a simpler, less hurried or less complicated past at the same time that it took full advantage of the newest developments in transportation and the most popular trends in home design. At his home on a hill overlooking New Haven, Donald Grant Mitchell discovered that the fears of his youth, which he fictionalized in *Reveries,* were unwarranted. Although it had seemed impossible that his bachelor reveries could coexist peacefully with the realities of married home life, he eventually discovered that they need not be mutually exclusive in the suburbs. In his books about Edgewood, he sought to share that discovery: while women might have their own ideas about how to run a household, husbands had opinions, too. If readers followed his advice, their homes would grow with them, as living incarnations of their beliefs, motivations, desires, and joys. Even the reveries of a bachelor could positively impact the shape and feel of the American home. "This is a style of grafting," he assured his readers, "which is of more general adoption in the world than we are apt to imagine" (*RS*, 221).

4

ADVANCEMENT AND ASSOCIATION, NOSTALGIA AND EXCLUSION
Hawthorne and the Suburban Romance

B etween March 1842 and September 1843, Horace Greeley, publisher of the *New York Tribune,* allocated a daily front-page column to the Fourierist social reformer Albert Brisbane. The *Tribune* was the most widely read American newspaper of its day, and Brisbane used the medium to outline the benefits of Associationism, a communitarian reform plan that was based on the writings of the French theorist Charles Fourier. In the paper's series "Association; or, Principles of a True Organization of Society," Brisbane expanded on the ideas he had espoused in *Social Destiny of Man* (1840) by suggesting that America's problems, which included class struggles, labor disputes, gender inequalities, and slavery, could not be remedied politically; rather, they required social action. Opposing Transcendentalists like Emerson and other reformers who promoted individual regeneracy in thought and action as the indispensable seed for large-scale change, Brisbane argued that reorganization of society must come first.

Specifically, he suggested that men should collectively purchase land outside but within reach of major cities in order to live according to a community system, sharing in the mental and physical labor required to reform the world and bring happiness to all classes and individuals. Collective investment, thought, and action, he claimed, would reward members in ways that individual effort could never match, facilitating increased production that would lead to cheaper and better living. He promised readers that Association would "dignify Industry," which he identified as all branches of "Agriculture, Manufactures, and Mechanics," and "render it *Attractive,*" which would be "the first practical step to be taken to emancipate and elevate the Laboring Classes."[1]

Brisbane used his columns to educate the *Tribune's* readership about

Fourier's philosophy and to lay out a practical plan for a community based on Associationist principles. He hoped that the medium would correct misconceptions about Associationists, clarifying their stance on private property and voicing their appreciation for individual skills and talents. In his March 21, 1842, column, for example, he assured readers that "the privacy of domestic life will be fully maintained, while the advantage and pleasure of wide-spread and friendly social relations will be open to all."[2] At the same time, he enumerated the concrete benefits of communal living, such as universal education and health care. Soon he began advertising his books and providing notice of Fourierist and Associationist meetings that were open to the public.

Most significantly, however, in late March 1842 he began to outline "Means of Making a Practical Trial" of Fourier's theory in the United States. By October of the same year, he had announced the need for money to fund an experimental Associationist community in the United States. Within five months of his first column, Brisbane was able to accomplish in the United States what Fourier could not in France: the establishment of a model community on Associationist principles. By June 1843 the North American Phalanx, in Red Bank, New Jersey, was in the process of organization. It would become one of the largest and longest-lasting utopian reform communities of the nineteenth century, but it was only one of many Associationist communes, unions, and periodicals whose formation was greatly influenced by Brisbane's writings.

The success of Brisbane's vision was attributable in large part to his medium: his *Tribune* column enabled him to connect with readers from a wide range of classes, professions, and backgrounds, from urban businessmen to rural farmers. The weekly edition of the *Tribune* circulated nationally, and in an age of reprinting, the columns were republished in many other papers. Above all, Brisbane understood the power of the newspaper, and knowing that it would be the key to effecting change on a mass scale, he placed his reform scheme in Greeley's hands in an effort to reach the largest possible number of people. Brisbane utilized the popular press to galvanize the hopes of his readers for a better life, encouraging them to imaginatively inhabit suburban reform communities through his descriptions and promises.

Emerson remarked in an 1840 letter to Thomas Carlyle: "We are all a little wild here with numberless projects of social reform. Not a reading man but has a draft of a new community in his waistcoat pocket."[3] Albert Brisbane was one of many popular literary figures who were instrumental in the creation of an imaginary realm of model communities and visions in the mid-nineteenth century—a list that also includes Angelina and Sarah Grimke, George Ripley, Fredrika Bremer, George Foster, and George Lippard. Hawthorne's *Blithedale Romance* has long been held up as a model literary representation of this midcentury reform craze. At a time when many writers were using print culture to suggest shapes for suburban growth, Hawthorne plays with the notion of physical landscape as imagined community in *Blithedale*. He uses the character of Miles Coverdale to link a new physical space in America—that of the suburb—to the literary genre of the romance. As an outpost slightly removed from the ordinary course of travel, in which people and objects can play with predetermined identities and roles, the suburban environment is a space that invites forgetfulness and encourages arcadian idealism. At the same time that it presages hope and embodies newness, though, the suburb, like the romance, is inherently a lament for a moment that has already passed, a requiem on the part of its planners and inhabitants for a way of living, interacting, and perceiving the world that they deem no longer a possibility.

In the decade following his own sojourn at Brook Farm, Hawthorne came to understand early suburbanization in the United States as a transformative process whereby radical reformist impulses are ideologically contained and mitigated, packaged for middle-class consumption. Its ultimate manifestation becomes compensatory in the sense that it stands as a defensive reaction to change, the "dummy American['s]" exchange of what D. H. Lawrence refers to in his essay on Benjamin Franklin as the vision of the "soul of man [as] a vast forest" for "a neat back garden."[4] In *The Blithedale Romance,* though, Hawthorne insists upon suburbanites' acute awareness of the loss inherent in such a trade. Trapped in a cultivated limbo of their own making, afraid to commit in either direction, they enact the very forms of alienation that their planning and scheming were intended to correct. Their dreams hover around the edges of daily life just as Coverdale circulates in his own narrative, as sad, solipsistic evasions that reject commitment and nurse regret. Hawthorne's view of suburbanization in the 1840s and early 1850s, in other words, mirrors that of Lewis Mumford in the late 1930s: "So much for the weakness of this movement. One must realize nonetheless that like so many other impulses of romanticism it was a healthy reaction, to be condemned, not for what it did, but for what it omitted to do."[5]

SUBURBAN AMERICA AND MIDCENTURY ASSOCIATIONIST REFORM

In search of privacy to experiment with new forms of community organization, Brisbane was especially drawn to possibilities for communal organization and activity in the suburbs. In their desire to correct labor exploitation and individual corruption, Fourierists sought to reshape the landscape between urban and rural America in a more formal way than traditional land prospectors and commuting businessmen did. According to the historian Carl J. Guarneri, American Associationists frequently followed Fourier's recommendation to establish communities called phalanxes in agricultural areas that were in close proximity to large cities (ideally no more than fifty miles away): "The Fourierists' suburban 'new industrial world' was meant to reconcile the machine and the garden (to use Leo Marx's terms). Like good utopians—and many other nineteenth-century Americans—Associationists felt they could blend old ideals and new techniques."[6] In that sense, they did not seek to escape industrialization altogether; rather, they hoped to improve upon the status quo by outlining a way of living that would address and mitigate the challenges inaugurated by new technologies and population shifts. Brisbane and his followers envisioned the suburban landscape as a space where classes could intermingle and the necessary work required to run a community could be shared among its members. The hope was that by attracting a broad range of people with different talents and backgrounds, they could fashion a self-sufficient association that combined, in the words of the historian of suburbia Dolores Hayden, "industry and agriculture, offering the advantages of both city and country."[7] Through their model suburban communities, they sought to provide Americans with alternate ways to organize their work and home lives.

As the son of a successful land speculator from Batavia, New York, a small town between Buffalo and Rochester, Brisbane had witnessed firsthand the process by which transportation developments could transform sleepy villages into bustling urban satellites. He first met Fourier in 1832 while studying abroad in France and immediately was drawn to the philosopher's theory of improving people's experiences with labor by restructuring society into settlements of 1,620 people in the pastoral countryside (two each of the 810 basic personality types identified in Fourier's theory of the passions). Brisbane also appreciated his mentor's business sense. While working as a traveling salesman, Fourier had experienced both the numbing ennui of white-collar labor and the power of marketing to cultivate an aesthetic and sell a product. His theories of attractive labor and passional attraction promised to reform society by integrating a shared sense of beauty and responsibility from an earlier era into revitalized constellations of commerce and industry. When Brisbane returned to the United States in 1834, he vowed to popularize Fourier's ideas among American readers. Marital problems and economic setbacks delayed his plans, though, as the Panic of 1837 demolished the savings he had hoped to invest in real estate for a model Fourieristic community.

Fourier died in 1837, but it was not until 1839 that Brisbane was able to regroup from financial losses and earnestly contemplate the practical adaptation of the philosopher's theories to American audiences. In *Social Destiny of Man,* he outlined the tenets of a new Fourieristic reform movement, which he designated "Associationism." Half of this 480-page tract consisted of a translation of Fourier's writings, while the other half showcased Brisbane's own theories and reflections. Central to his message, as he explained in the March 16, 1842, issue of the *Tribune,* was the belief that "the interest of the Individual would be the interest of the Mass, and the interest of the Mass that of the Individual."[8] Associationist principles maintained that if an individual's desires for health, beauty, and financial stability were met, he or she would become a more efficient worker, and society as a whole would benefit. At the same time, by taking a communal approach to the organization of domestic life, individuals could pool their resources when it came to housekeeping, child care, and meal preparation, leaving more time and energy for leisure activities.

It was a delicate balancing act: even as he claimed that society operated best when individuals worked together toward a common goal, he insisted that personal needs and interests would not be sacrificed to the larger system or group. As he elaborated in his 1843 pamphlet *Association,* each member would own shares of the community's stock (comprising "the lands, edifices, flocks, implements, machinery and other property of an Association—that is, its personal and real Estate"), as with "the capital of a bank or railroad."[9] All individuals would operate as "joint proprietors," and as such would feel more invested in the community's fate than they would in a society composed of isolated households (31). Therefore, although an individual member could sell or buy shares, the property itself could not be divided or sold without the agreement of the entire community. He frequently claimed that Associationist ideology would enable even individuals from the poorer classes to enjoy satisfying food and shelter as they contributed to the well-being of themselves and others.

In all of his writings, Brisbane suggested that new developments in suburban architecture such as those being popularized by A. J. Downing and A. J. Davis could be used to facilitate Associationist goals. Indeed, he intimated that recent innovations in home, industrial, and commercial design could attain an unparalleled pinnacle of achievement in reformist communities. Through an "architecture of combination and unity," which he designated "the architecture of the future," the material landscape would speak to "all the sentiments and wants" of man's nature by "combin[ing] in the highest degree the useful and the beautiful" (*SDM*, 362). A central building, the phalanstery, would function as the hub of domestic and social activities. Private rooms and apartments would be separated by partition walls with doors opening onto a large gallery, which would serve as an indoor main street for the community, thus combining "the charm of domestic privacy and the pleasures of social life" (*A*, 23–24).[10]

Brisbane thus likened the design of the phalanx to "a town under one roof" with "an avenue or public way, corresponding to a street, which will form a means of communication with all quarters of the building" (*A*, 20). The central hall would be approximately twenty-four feet wide in a large Association; "by means of it, the inhabitants could, in the depths of winter, visit each other, go to parties, public assemblies, concerts, lectures, etc. without knowing whether it snowed or rained, or whether it was cold or blustering" (20). He characterized such accommodations as a great improvement both for the urban poor, who were confined to unhealthful tenements, cellars, and garrets, and for families who felt isolated in the countryside. Residents would benefit from shared spaces such as libraries, reading rooms, galleries, and indoor gardens. To that end, varieties of plants and trees would be chosen for their beauty as much as for their production. Since a plum tree was less attractive than a pear tree, for example, fewer plum trees would be planted on the grounds than pear trees (*SDM,* 352).

Before any construction began, however, an advantageous site needed to be located, which he identified in *Social Destiny of Man* as "adjoining a forest, and situated in the vicinity of a large city, which would afford a convenient market for its products" (350).[11] While the suburbs offered privacy, space, and accessibility, Brisbane also insisted that such locales were key to the reformation of society on a much larger scale. Calling attention to the ways in which recent economic depressions, population shifts, and housing trends had perpetuated already disconcerting class tensions and lifestyle discrepancies, he identified the gap between rural and urban America as indicative of the detrimental effects of a society that valued individual prosperity above all else. He criticized the "rural scenes" that were celebrated by many of his contemporaries by pointing out that such fields were "cultivated . . . by poor laborers, whose condition excited pity" (390). The pleasures afforded by the natural environment in its current state, according to Brisbane, stood in "constant contradiction of civilization, in which the *beautiful* exists only at the expense of the *useful*" (390). When aesthetic gratification aligned itself with leisure and stood in opposition to labor and productivity, everyone suffered.

Associationism promised to reunite use and beauty, and it would undertake their reunion in the suburban landscape. In addition to the proximity to markets and necessary facilities that suburbs afforded, their transitional status in the middle decades of the nineteenth century made them uniquely malleable. By establishing their communities near major cities, reformists would gain adherents more quickly while maintaining the necessary privacy to experiment with nontraditional organizations of domestic life. As Brisbane phrased it, the association should be near a large city so as "to be at once more generally known, and lead to a more rapid imitation" (*A,* 16), for "[if] we can substitute peaceably and gradually Associations . . . in the place of present falsely and defectively organized townships, we can effect quietly and easily . . . a social transformation and a mighty reform" (73–74).

Gaining exposure through articles, books, and lectures, Brisbane's vision began to be tested in earnest in the 1840s. According to Dolores Hayden, "those most receptive to the communitarian call tended to be without education or substantial funds, small business owners and urban working people like Fourier himself, who chafed at the inequities of daily life enough to commit themselves to drastic changes."[12] Although the North American Phalanx, located forty miles outside New York City near Red Bank, New Jersey, was the largest and most successful result of Brisbane's plans, many other reformers established communities in suburban landscapes following his recommendations.[13] Between 1842 and 1852, almost thirty phalanxes formed in the United States.[14] By 1846, the American Union of Associationists had set up headquarters in New York City. Horace Greeley became a sponsoring member of the "Industrial Home Association Number I," a community formed in Mount Vernon, New York, which was fifteen miles from the center of Manhattan and boasted three hundred families in residence by 1852. Headed by John Stevens, a tailor, the association occupied 370 acres, divided into quarter-acre lots, with no member allowed to have more than one share. The plan included four half-acre school lots and another half acre set aside for a railroad station that would serve the New York, New Haven, and Harlem lines.[15] Similarly, the Raritan Bay Union phalanx of Eagleswood, New Jersey, farther south along the coast from the North American Phalanx, was formed in 1853 by Marcus Spring, a wealthy merchant from New York, who converted to Brisbane's philosophy and invited A. J. Davis to design the central collective dwelling. While almost all Associationist colonies were relatively short-lived, their success did seem to correlate with relative size and proximity to major metropolitan areas. Although it was founded by New York City mechanics, for instance, the Sylvania Association selected 2,300 acres of land in the mountains of eastern Pennsylvania, one hundred miles from New York and forty miles from the nearest railroad. The group's rapid dissolution illustrated the prudence of starting with a small property as close as possible to a large city.

The most famous "practical trial" of Brisbane's Associationist plans took place at Brook Farm. Eight miles west of the center of Boston in West Roxbury, Massachusetts, the 170-acre former farm was bounded on one side by the Charles River and on the other by Baker Street, a thoroughfare that connected the nearby towns of Roxbury and Dedham to Newton. An early advertisement for the community marketed its location as an amenity, describing it as a "place of great natural beauty, combining a convenient nearness to the city with a degree of retirement and freedom from unfavorable influences unusual even in the country."[16] Although the reformers did not formally adopt Fourier's theories until the winter of 1843–44, Brisbane's ideas were certainly on the mind of founder George Ripley when he first discussed his idea for Brook Farm with the Transcendental Club a few weeks after reviewing *Social Destiny of Man* for the *Dial* magazine.[17] Writing to his friend Ralph Waldo Emerson about his plans to join with others in purchasing the farm where he and his wife had boarded in the summer of 1840, Ripley explained that he wanted to "combine the thinker and the worker, as far as possible, in the same individual; to guarantee the highest mental freedom, by providing all with labor, adapted to their tastes and talents, and securing them the fruits of their industry; to do away with the necessity of menial services, by opening the benefits of education and the profits of labor to all."[18]

From the beginning, as Carl J. Guarneri notes, individuals were drawn to Brook Farm after becoming dissatisfied with certain elements of their work and home lives: "Unsuccessful in business or unable to live with the pressures and compromises of the outside world, fledgling ministers, lawyers, clerks, and artisans found congenial places in Fourier's New Industrial World as teachers, farmers, and administrators."[19] Single young men, especially, turned to Brook Farm and other Associationist communities for direction and definition at home and at work. Struggling to remain afloat in urban areas, they looked outside the city for new opportunities and approaches to everyday living. Ripley's initial vision attracted a large number of artists and intellectuals, but as he drifted toward Fourierism and decided to place a greater emphasis on communal living and industrial labor, lower-class blue- and white-collar workers began to join the group. Although the recently formed Brook Farm Phalanx never recovered from the fire of March 1846 that demolished its central building, the Phalanstery (it was under construction at the time, and members could not recoup the financial loss), Ripley achieved his greatest success in the effort to counteract lifestyle discrepancies based on education and class after the conversion to Fourierism in 1844. For a relatively short period in midcentury America, he and other reformers envisioned the suburbs surrounding major cities as ideal places to experiment with new theories for social reformation and economic and cultural rejuvenation. Although the Brook Farm property was eventually sold at public auction for $19,000 in 1849, the plans and layouts of it and many other failed Associationist groups influenced the shape of suburban community formation in the late nineteenth century and into the twentieth.

THE SUBURB AS ROMANCE

In the preface to *The Blithedale Romance,* Hawthorne says that he wants to write a type of fiction that "is allowed a license with regard to every-day Probability, in view of the improved effects which he is bound to produce thereby."[20] It was a notion he had toyed with in various earlier writings, from *Mosses from an Old Manse* (1846) to *The House of the Seven Gables* (1851). In this 1852 book about a group of reformers who locate themselves a little beyond the city and attempt to fashion a community that promises to reform the world, his statements about the romance take on peculiar intimations. Referring to himself in the third person, he speaks of his desire to fashion a "theatre, a little removed from the highway of ordinary travel, where the creatures of his brain may play their phantasmagorical antics, without exposing them to too close a comparison with the actual events of real lives" (*BR,* 1).

His comments attempt to frustrate anyone who might be inclined to read the story as a thinly veiled account of his experiences as one of the sixteen original members who arrived at Brook Farm in April 1841; he warns readers not to look for exact one-to-one correspondences in events, persons, or places. At the same time, his claim that "among ourselves . . . there is as yet no Faery Land, so like the real world, that, in a suitable remoteness, one cannot well tell the difference, but with an atmosphere of strange enchantment, beheld through which the inhabitants have a propriety of their own" (2) appears somewhat hollow—especially as he simultaneously characterizes his "old, and affectionately remembered home, at Brook Farm, as being, certainly, the most romantic episode of his own life—essentially a day-dream, and yet a fact—and thus offering an available foothold between fiction and reality" (2). Even as he denies doing so, Hawthorne equates Brook Farm with his notion of a "Faery Land" in the sense that it occupies a space that is physically and ideologically distinct from both the urban and rural ways of life, a landscape that attempts to erase all historical traces of previous occupants and their labor in an effort to start fresh in the creation of a new and better order.

Over the course of his narrative, Hawthorne exposes the inherently romantic nature of the suburban vision by exploring gaps between artistic outlines and material incarnations. In depicting Blithedale as a "Modern Arcadia" and its inhabitants as "A Knot of Dreamers" (the titles of chapters 8 and 3, respectively), he certainly criticizes the reformers' vision as one mediated by class anxieties. While he might agree with his character Zenobia when she protests the efficacy of any project that insists on the ability to "remove ourselves, at pleasure, into an imaginary sphere" (107), he makes it clear that he also recognizes a beauty in bourgeois philosophies and plans, despite what he sees as the inevitability of their failure. Early on, Hawthorne admits that the story that follows will end with a disintegration of ideals; nevertheless, he asserts that something valuable comes into existence (even if only momentarily) in the space between dreams and reality: "Yet, after all, let us acknowledge it wiser, if not more sagacious, to follow out one's day-dream to its natural consummation, although, if the vision have been worth the having, it is certain never to be consummated otherwise than by a failure. And what of that! Its airiest fragments, impalpable as they may be, will possess a value that lurks not in the most ponderous realities of any practicable scheme" (10–11). Hawthorne's choice of genre coincides with a refusal to cast Blithedale in a completely negative light.

Reiterating these sentiments, he takes the opposite position from that of Thoreau in *Walden*: "Therefore, if we built splendid castles (phalansteries, perhaps, they might be more fitly called,) and pictured beautiful scenes, among the fervid coals of the hearth around which we were clustering—and if all went to rack with the crumbling embers, and have never since arisen out of the ashes—let us take to ourselves no shame. In my own behalf, I rejoice that I could once think better of the world's improvability than it deserved. It is a mistake into which men seldom fall twice, in a lifetime; or, if so, the rarer and higher is the nature that can thus magnanimously persist in error" (*BR,* 20). Aware of the effects of his own class lens on his ways of perceiving himself and his environment, he makes it clear that both he (in the preface) and his characters recognize their oscillations between embrace and evasion as endemic to the bourgeois approach to reform. Their (and his) selection of the suburban landscape as the ideal location for their experiments, then, becomes emblematic of their ideological limitations in the sense that it physically reproduces the mediated viewpoint of its inhabitants. As Lewis Mumford suggests, despite the best-laid plans to correct inequalities and plot democracy, "the very popularity of this move to escape partly robbed it of its success. Land values went up on the outskirts of every town, sometimes in sound agricultural territory, in expectation of suburban developments. . . . Except for a small detail of tradesmen and handymen, the suburb was a one-class community: it boasted, in fact, of its 'exclusiveness.'"[21] In its middle-class refusal of the less desirable elements of either city or country life and its simultaneous demand for the amenities of both, the suburb poetically incarnates a liberal refusal to commit to the causes to which it pays lip service.

Through the figure of Coverdale specifically, Hawthorne considers the complex aesthetics that shape suburban life and intimates that suburbanites are not always able to remain blissfully forgetful of the irony of their situation. As the Blithedale population expands, Coverdale muses on the extent to which members are playing at labor and leisure, and at reform more generally. Before Hollingsworth gives his sermon at Eliot's Pulpit one Sunday, he remarks that the "modern cottage[s]" dotting the property appear "so like . . . plaything[s] that [they] seemed as if real joy or sorrow could have no scope within" (*BR*, 117–18). Zenobia's flower, the masquerade, the legend of the Veiled Lady, and the woodland festival corroborate Coverdale's assessments. When he visits the lyceum, he notes the young men in the audience "all looking rather suburban than rural" and insists that "in these days, there is absolutely no rusticity, except when the actual labor of the soil leaves its earth-mould on the person" (197). Like George Ripley, the founder of Brook Farm, who prepped himself for his experiment by borrowing books on farming from the Boston Athenaeum, Coverdale insinuates that members of the Blithedale community are born consumers rather than producers, and that no amount of idiosyncratic theatricality (in words or action) could overcome, in Mumford's phrase, "an impulse that had, from the beginning, a constant air of unreality."[22]

Despite Coverdale's claims to distrust Blithedale's "spick-and-span novelty" (*BR*, 129–30), though, his narration also claims sympathy with the suburban utopian vision. Reflecting on the snow as he transitions from city to country, he remarks that even it cannot help but look "inexpressibly dreary" and almost "dingy" as it falls "through an atmosphere of city-smoke, and alighting on the sidewalk, only to be moulded into the impress of somebody's patched boot or over-shoe" (11). When the caravan abandons pavement for country road, he happily exclaims to himself that "there was better air to breathe. Air, that had not been breathed, once and again! Air, that had not been spoken into words of falsehood, formality, and error, like all the air of the city!" (11). Like N. P. Willis, who in 1853 would extol the sense of ownership conferred on him by the suburban environment (referring to a "delicious consciousness of being the first to be waited on, the one it was all made and meant for" over an April day in the city that seems "potted and pickled, and retailed to other customers as well"),[23] Coverdale associates the extraurban environment with a much-coveted and increasingly rare sense of newness and possibility, one that affords a healthy, original relationship of self to world.

Upon his arrival at Blithedale, he marvels at the change in outlook produced by his new surroundings, a difference that is manifest even in the superior satisfaction of a country fire over the coal grate's wan glow: "I felt, so much the more, that we had transported ourselves a world-wide distance from the system of society that shackled us at breakfast-time" (*BR*, 13). A simple removal from the everyday urban environment promised to reshape perception and reinvigorate human interaction. Self-reflexive to the very end, Coverdale manifests the same painful prescience that lies at the heart of any true literary romance: a belief that imaginative play is the only available response to the realization that the truth or reality or intimacy that we seek is always and unavoidably mediated in one way or another.

The Blithedale Romance was the first book Hawthorne wrote in the first person, and his correspondence supports apparent parallels between fictional characters and individuals involved in the Brook Farm project and Transcendentalist philosophy. In an 1851 letter to William B. Pike, he mentioned that his next romance would revolve around notions of community and include reminiscences from his time at Brook Farm.[24] Certainly, Coverdale's coded references to Fourierist ideas reflect Hawthorne's engagement with questions of an individual's relationship to the community of which he is a part; Hawthorne had borrowed a few volumes of the philosopher's works from an old Brook Farm associate while writing *The Blithedale Romance*. When Coverdale debates the merits of Fourier's plan with Hollingsworth after being struck by "the analogy which I could not but recognize between his system and our own" (*BR*, 52–53), despite the fact that the commune's structure is not organized according to Fourieristic principles, Hawthorne invites readers to consider the fictionalized society he presents within the context of midcentury reform movements. Moreover, the fact that Coverdale admits to having read the volumes in their original French suggests that he was contemplating the unexpurgated version of Fourier's writings, which includes a system of short-term sexual matching based on personality type. Through the narrator's stated wish to introduce the "beautiful peculiarities" (53) of the project into life at Blithedale, Hawthorne begins to call his characters' motivations into question.

Not coincidentally, Hawthorne's own motives in joining Brook Farm had more to do with personal domestic desires than with the promise of communitarian reform: while secretly engaged to Sophia Peabody, he had traveled to Roxbury with no property or income in hopes of obtaining an economical cottage suitable for a young couple. As Brenda Wineapple remarks in her biography, "in need of a home, an income, and a place to write, Hawthorne gladly gambled on Ripley's arcadia" by purchasing two shares in the community and paying an additional $500 for a detached home.[25] The letters he wrote to Sophia soon after his arrival focus almost exclusively on Brook Farm's potential to satisfy their plan for a picturesque, comfortable, affordable, and convenient home life. On April 28, 1841, mentioning a longing "for thee to stray with me, in reality, among the hills, and dales, and woods, of our home," he marveled at the sense of "seclusion" he had discovered "so short a distance from a great city," assuring Sophia, "If we were to travel a thousand miles, we could not escape the world more completely than we can here."[26] The original layouts of both Brook Farm (which was at that time a private cooperative organized as a joint-stock company) and Blithedale reflect Brisbane's Associationist notions that in a reformed world, private and public need not be in conflict. Coverdale describes the relationship in the following way: "The bond of our Community was such, that the members had the privilege of building cottages for their own residence, within our precincts, thus laying a hearthstone and fencing in a home, private and peculiar, to all desirable extent; while yet the inhabitants should continue to share the advantages of an associated life" (BR, 80). Ideally, individuals could join the movement in the hope of establishing a better life for themselves and their families while simultaneously advancing a new organizational model for American society.

Ultimately, Hawthorne remained at Brook Farm only through October 1841. Despite his initial enthusiasm, he began to tire of physical labor (members supported themselves by means of the school and the farm they ran) as the months wore on and complained to Sophia that he did not have the energy to write after spending hours working in the fields. As early as May he had begun to reflect on the gap between a dreamscape and one's day-to-day material existence, or as he lamented in a letter written on May Day, "Alas, what a difference between the ideal and the real!"[27] In the same note he contemplated the process by which language enacted a similar discrepancy: "Every day of my life makes me feel more and more how seldom a fact is accurately stated; how, almost invariably, when a story has passed through the mind of a third person, it becomes, so far as regards the impression that it makes in further repetitions, little better than a falsehood, and thus, too, though the narrator be the most truth-seeking person in existence. How marvelous the tendency is! . . . Is truth a fantasy which we are to pursue forever and never grasp?"[28] It was not that the vision itself was flawed, nor that the act of living and breathing compromised the integrity of the unsullied dream. Somewhere in the translation, though, a loss occurred. The location of that loss, whether on a page, in conversation, in mind, or in action, had geographic coordinates; it traced a path, left records, and invoked its own unfulfilled resolutions at each step of the way.

The notion that such a gap could operate as both an asset and a liability was something that Hawthorne carried beyond his experiences at Brook Farm into his writing career. After leaving the community and starting a family with Sophia, he turned to the genre of the romance in order to explore the liminal space that he had identified in the early 1840s. By choosing to mediate his representation of Blithedale through the perspective and voice of Coverdale, Hawthorne problematizes the reformist project at the same time that he recognizes his own complicity in it. As readers assess the narrator's interest in and engagement with the reformist community, they must grapple with any individual's relationship to the society of which he or she is a part.

Upon his arrival at Blithedale, Coverdale seeks communion with others in a natural environment, secure in the belief that he is more likely to find it, and thus to live consciously and happily, outside the city than within the urban environment. Although he manifests interest in Hollingsworth's ideas, he craves "the long-sought intimacy of a mysterious heart" (*BR,* 90) more than anything else. In highlighting the tension between communal vision and individual prerogative, Hawthorne insinuates that suburban space is defined by a shared sense of lack. Despite its best efforts, the suburb evoked phantom hopes of intimacy, even in the mid-nineteenth century. United in a homogeneous desire to locate selfhood in nature without having to sacrifice the convenience and amenities of industrialized America, neighbors lead parallel lives that cannot help but be literary, grounded in imaginative visions. As Benedict Anderson describes the phenomenon in *Imagined Communities,* "it is *imagined* because the members of even the smallest nation will never know most of their fellow-members, meet them, or even hear of them, yet in the minds of each lives the image of their communion."[29]

Coverdale struggles to reconcile his need for solitude with a bitter awareness of his own loneliness throughout his time at Blithedale. In the book's opening chapter, reluctantly facing the fact that he is "really getting to be a frosty bachelor, with another white hair, every week or so, in my mustache" (9), he heroically takes one last puff from his cigar and, he says, "quitted my cosey pair of bachelor-rooms—with a good fire burning in the grate, and a closet right at hand, where there was still a bottle or two in the champagne-basket, and a residuum of claret in a box, and somewhat of proof in the concavity of a big demijohn—quitted, I say, these comfortable quarters, and plunged into the heart of the pitiless snow-storm, in quest of a better life" (10). The legitimacy of an exodus into the suburbs in the quest for "a better life" on the part of upper-middle- and middle-class Americans, of course, remains in question throughout *The Blithedale Romance,* not only for Coverdale but for the author and the reader as well.

Although he is immediately struck by the ways in which the change in scenery signals an improved mental and physical state, Coverdale manifests an awareness of his position in a liminal landscape almost immediately. Even as he navigates a new type of space at Blithedale, he constantly refers to his old way of life. As if in response to the stress of adjusting to a new locale, he becomes sick soon after his arrival, which compromises his ability to work. In the chapter titled "Coverdale's Sick-Chamber," he reminisces about his urban existence and second-guesses the rationale that led him to his current spot, asking: "What, in the name of common-sense, had I to do with any better society than I had always lived in! It had satisfied me well enough" (40). From his "pleasant bachelor-parlor, sunny and shadowy, curtained and carpeted, with the bed-chamber adjoining; [his] centre-table, strewn with books and periodicals, [his] writing-desk" to his leisurely walks to libraries and galleries amidst "the suggestive succession of human faces, and the brisk throb of human life, in which [he] shared" (40) and evening dinners out, followed by concerts, clubs, theaters, and parties, he wonders what sort of paradise he had envisioned outside the city. Convincing himself that his illness is a sign that his body is not ready for the new environment he has found himself in, he mocks the experiment and his fellow travelers as deluded dreamers. Even as he claims not to regret, he says, "that I once had faith and force enough to form generous hopes of the world's destiny—yes!—and to do what in me lay for their accomplishment" (11), he is forced to grapple in unanticipated ways with his own self-delusions and fantasies over the course of his sojourn at Blithedale.

Much of his disillusionment stems from interactions with other individuals in the community. As someone who prides himself on his ability to read other characters without revealing his own stake in the activity of observation, Coverdale takes pains to conceal himself from Hollingsworth, Zenobia, Priscilla, and Moody at the same time that he seeks their friendship. Frozen into inaction by opportunities for communion, he worries about losing his individuality in a society that expects much from him in return for the benefits it provides. While he claims a need for periodic seclusion in order to regroup and rejuvenate, his desire for space also operates as a need for critical distance. Whenever he has the opportunity, he retires to the top of a white pine tree, which he designates as his hermitage. He prizes this "hollow chamber, of rare seclusion" surrounded by leaves and grapevines, and catalogues his minor domestic improvements to the space "to enlarge the interior, and open loop-holes through the verdant walls" (98). He maintains that it serves as an artist's retreat—a good place to write poems and essays, and to smoke cigars—and as such, he says, it exists as "my one exclusive possession, while I counted myself a brother of the socialists" (99). As a self-described symbol of his individuality, it is a place he seeks to keep "inviolate." From his hidden perspective, though, he spends most of his time watching over the group through "several of its small windows"

(99). The ability to escape at will enables Coverdale to remain both in and outside the social reform project at Blithedale. His elevation and distance diminish the scale and significance of Hollingsworth's visions and Zenobia's theatricality; privately he can mock the plan and its adherents even as he continues to enjoy group privileges and casts himself as a friendly listener upon his return.

Although he readily acknowledges that his status as spectator is what prompted him to leave his city apartment for open fields in the first place, he ultimately likens his role both at Blithedale and in the literary account that he constructs to that of the chorus in a play, as a commentator who is linked in sympathy with while nonetheless remaining isolated from the others. In response to new demands and exposures, he admits to "being, in truth, not so very confident as at some former periods, that this final step, which would mix me up irrevocably with the Blithedale affair, was the wisest that could possibly be taken" (8). Ultimately he finds himself unable to reconcile his own vision with the needs of others, and he describes himself as standing "on other terms than before, not only with Hollingsworth, but with Zenobia and Priscilla" (138). When his hope for the realization of personal intimacy disappears, he feels a strange sort of loss:

> It was the dreamlike and miserable sort of change that denies you the privilege to complain, because you can assert no positive injury, nor lay your finger on anything tangible. It is a matter which you do not see, but feel, and which, when you try to analyze it, seems to lose its very existence, and resolve itself into a sickly humor of your own. Your understanding, possibly, may put faith in this denial. But your heart will not so easily rest satisfied. It incessantly remonstrates, though, most of the time, in a bass-note, which you do not separately distinguish; but, now-and-then, with a sharp cry, importunate to be heard, and resolute to claim belief. 'Things are not as they were!'—it keeps saying. (138–39)

In a passage that evokes Hawthorne's description of the romance in his preface, Coverdale attempts to articulate the change that has taken place, describing his environment as "suddenly faded," noting that it had been "some principal circumstance" that "gave the bright color and vivid reality to the whole affair" (138). Indeed, it is the unshakeable awareness of a gap, or mediation, as the central defining characteristic of both his location and his life that situates Coverdale as a true suburbanite. Aware of his own culpability in constructing the fence behind which he has found himself, he nonetheless feels powerless to open the gate and walk out. Whether unmediated access or commitment to a "principal circumstance" was ever possible in the first place is unclear; what is certain is that he is no longer able even to play as though it were.

After this realization, Coverdale becomes more cynical in his views and takes refuge in the language of his narrative. As holes and exaggerations in his narration call his pronouncements and insights into question, he criticizes the project more openly and attempts to retreat further into himself. Voyeurism becomes his only means of experiencing a sense of closeness to other individuals. Eventually, he decides to remove himself temporarily from Blithedale in order to "take an exterior view of what we had all been about" (140). In the chapter titled "Leave-Takings," he returns to Boston and stays at a hotel for a few days. Sitting in his rented room, this time he welcomes the reprieve provided by the city and suggests that the reformist project is shaped by unrealistic expectations: "As matters now were, I felt myself (and having a decided tendency towards the actual, I never liked to feel it) getting quite out of my reckoning, with regard to the existing state of the world. I was beginning to lose the sense of what kind of a world it was, among innumerable schemes of what it might or ought to be. . . . No sagacious man will long retain his sagacity, if he live exclusively among reformers and progressive people, without periodically returning into the settled system of things, to correct himself by a new observation from that old stand-point" (140–41). Post-crisis, it is not so much that Coverdale objects to the type of reform that Blithedale seeks to popularize (although he certainly objects to Hollingsworth's single-minded pursuit of his cause above all else), but rather that he worries about the capacity of such schemes to warp one's understanding of the relationship between self and environment, private and public, on a more general level. He convinces himself that it is safest to maintain boundaries and baselines, lest they disappear altogether and threaten his sense of inviolateness in the process.

As if in validation of his fears, try as he might, he cannot shake Blithedale's influence on his perception of himself and his surroundings. Sitting in the hotel, he reflects on the odd predicament he has found himself in. Recent thoughts, conversations, and experiences have fundamentally shifted his

worldview, so much so that at the hotel he remarks, "The very circumstances now surrounding me—my coal-fire, and the dingy room in the
bustling hotel—appeared far off and intangible" (146). At the same time, he
feels removed from the life that has so recently consumed him: "Blithedale
looked vague, as if it were at a distance both in time and space, and so
shadowy, that a question might be raised whether the whole affair had been
anything more than the thoughts of a speculative man. I had never before
experienced a mood that so robbed the actual world of its solidity" (146). He
attempts to brush off the experiment's importance to his sense of identity
by insisting that he had "staked no valuable amount of hope or fear" (195)
on the enterprise and had never taken it seriously ("it had enabled me to
pass the summer in a novel and agreeable way, had afforded me some grotesque specimens of artificial simplicity, and could not, therefore, so far as
I was concerned, be reckoned a failure"), but it is clear that his interactions
with others at Blithedale have profoundly affected him. So although he
seemingly returns to his previous state at the end of his narrative, a bachelor who, even thirteen years later, cannot find a cause worth dying for, he
acknowledges, "More and more, I feel that we had stuck upon what ought
to be a truth" (245–46), regardless of the fact that "the experiment, so far as
its original projectors were concerned, proved long ago a failure, first lapsing
into Fourierism, and dying, as it well deserved, for this infidelity to its own
higher spirit" (246).

Comparing the allure of suburban America for midcentury reformers to
the possibilities of the romance genre for a writer like himself, Hawthorne
grappled with the notion of physical landscape as imagined community, of
a space, whether material or textual, where, as Brisbane insisted, the interest
of the individual would be the interest of the mass and vice versa. Even in his
preface he invoked the words of George Ripley, who had hoped that Brook
Farm would offer "a model of life which shall combine the enchantment of
poetry with the facts of daily experience."[30] Hawthorne was ever enchanted
with the notion that the visible world is not as legible as it appears, and so the
popularization of a physical embodiment of ideological liminality offered
him the perfect setting for a meditation on bourgeois evasiveness. For a
man whose house troubles followed him throughout his adult existence,
who struggled to provide for his family and demarcate lines between his

work and home life, *The Blithedale Romance* stands as an honest, if regretful, meditation on the limitations of a class lens which he, too, struggled to put aside. Similarly to Coverdale, Hawthorne sought domestic comforts while at the same time he chafed at familial obligations, futilely attempting to compartmentalize elements of his life and defensively erecting boundaries around himself. He even constructed a tower at The Wayside, his home in Concord, where he could write, as Wineapple phrases it, "high above the fray, entering his sanctum through a trapdoor, he told Longfellow, on which he'd plant his chair."[31] His efforts always seemed to fall short, however; late in life he voiced sensations of perpetual unsettlement and feared that he had "lost the capacity of living contentedly in any one place."[32] In *Blithedale* he identified an opportunity to channel personal dreams and demons into larger explorations of what, exactly, is at stake in reformist projects as well as the process by which retreat so often replaces initial embrace in situations that require true commitment to a person or a cause.

Toward the end of *The Blithedale Romance,* a defeated Zenobia confesses to Coverdale that she is "weary of this place, and sick to death of playing at philanthropy and progress" (227). Referring to existence at Blithedale as "mock-life," she reflects a loss of faith in person and plan that foreshadows her suicide soon afterward. To readers today, the utopian craze that swept America in the 1840s looks a lot like escapism. By the mid-1850s, all but one of the almost thirty phalanxes founded in the previous decade had failed, and their properties were relinquished to outsiders. Nonetheless, they left their imprint on the landscape, as well as in public structures, activist movements, and domestic routines. In their identification of the suburban environment as a location for reform and in their efforts to remedy social, political, and economic problems by mitigating the tension between public and private, self and other, individual and community through appeals to a shared aesthetic, they set the stage for later suburban development. Even in the twentieth century we can see traces of utopian idealism, attempts at associationist reclamation, in gated subdivisions and community bylaws. If it is "mock-life," which on some level it certainly is, the suburb encourages a form of play that has been enormously seductive and long-lived.

Ultimately, both Coverdale and Hawthorne conclude that narrative alone can assess what transpired at Blithedale and Brook Farm, since it, like them, would seem to be trapped in its own box. Even as they recognize that language is, by its very nature, inadequate to the task at hand, though, they simultaneously affirm the written word's power to do justice to the gap between dreams and realities, idealistic visions and daily routines. While writing cannot help but embody the distance (however slight) that it endlessly seeks to overcome, that doubleness testifies to loss and gain at once, to the inevitable failure of reformist schemes and to the recognition of truth seen and sought. The hope for a better life, author and character insist, is not misplaced; the desire to reshape and start over is not "a foolish dream" (227), however much Zenobia and the other characters at Blithedale would insist it is in moments of disillusioned frustration. If, in the clearing of space and constructing of "castles," a new host of transactions, associations, exclusions, and erasures ensure the impossibility of ever achieving desired goals, the failure lies with the approach rather than in the impulse itself. In what serves as both an apology for inaction and a playful offering with its own virtues and rewards, author and character turn to the page and trace the loss, mapping the "calamity" that Coverdale says nature "adopts . . . at once into her system" (244). "Human nature" would probably be more accurate, Hawthorne hints with his depiction of Coverdale in the final chapter, and the true poet reveals rather than conceals what is at stake in the suburbanization of the soul.

5

A NETWORKED WILDERNESS OF PRINT
Textual Suburbanization in Willis's Home Journal

In 1855 the popular writer, editor, and socialite Nathaniel Parker Willis published *Out-doors at Idlewild; or, The Shaping of a Home on the Banks of the Hudson,* a collection of essays written about his home, Idlewild, that had originally appeared in his *Home Journal* magazine between 1853 and 1855. Although the essays covered a wide range of topics related to life in the suburbs of New York City along the Hudson River, they shared a focus on the role of aesthetics in domestic life. Recalling his design for a gate to mark the entrance to Idlewild, for example, Willis mentioned taking "pencil and paper to bed" and spending "hours in the combination of lines and curves to express what I wanted the entrance of my cottage to say." Ultimately, he realized that his goal was essentially "an autobiography that would latch and swing upon a hinge."[1] Here and elsewhere in *Out-doors at Idlewild,* Willis communicated a desire to transmit his personality to even the smallest details of his home and the surrounding landscape. He asserted the notion that the right combination of "lines and curves" could embody something more than themselves; with the help of aesthetics, the domestic environment could voice selfhood. Through his writings about suburbanization in the Hudson River Valley in the early 1850s, Willis invited *Home Journal* readers to join him in a reconceptualization of the home as a reflection of personality and a mark of distinction.

Willis sometimes invoked nostalgia for an eighteenth-century European past, a time when aristocratic gentlemen signaled wealth and status through their agrarian estates, but he manipulated that impulse in his writings to suggest that Americans could display class markers (regardless of their actual earnings or pedigree) through tasteful home design, landscaping, and decoration. Influenced by the Jacksonian era's emphasis on principles of meritocracy and social mobility, Willis wanted to democratize taste by replacing inheritance (in the sense of both wealth and blood) as a mode of class distinction with one based on mastery of the art of living well.[2] His stated goal was to use the pages of the *Home Journal* to cultivate a republican "aristocracy of the mind" in the United States.[3] He wrote extensively about domestic architecture, landscape, objects, and décor in the magazine, arguing that attention to details in these categories would transfer a spirit of well-being and happiness to one's person and property. Taste, a sense that could be acquired by individuals of all economic backgrounds, would allow his readers to connect with the physical spaces and landscapes they inhabited in ways that previously had been available only to the elite.

Although Mitchell and Hawthorne registered dissatisfaction with the status quo regarding men's work and home lives and contemplated the potential of suburbanization to reconcile grievances and establish new lifestyle patterns, the authors discussed in this chapter and the next took their critique to the next level. Identifying a connection between concerns about the fate of manhood in the industrial era and the cultural fetishization of a utopian middle space between country and city, they honed literary modes that both theorized and manipulated the developments they witnessed. Willis's experience with his gate, and his decision to write about it in *Outdoors at Idlewild,* speaks to a complex sensibility that developed alongside midcentury suburbanization. Technological advances in publishing and wider distribution along new transportation routes facilitated the spread of information about suburban community formation, as I discuss in more detail in chapter 6. Over the course of writing about his relocation from New York City to the Hudson River Valley, Willis identified an opportunity to capitalize on these developments, linking the *Home Journal*'s readership with the geographic and imaginative space of the suburbs.

From his weekly letters about Idlewild to editorials by architects on suburban home building and advertisements for domestic appliances and furniture, Willis sought to fashion a print community that embodied a lifestyle associated with country life but within reach of the city. Even as he assured readers that his magazine offered a path to class mobility, though, he simultaneously hinted that the suburban ethos detailed in its pages was not open to everyone and that it was desirable *precisely because* it was exclusive. Inherent in his message, in other words, was the recognition that aesthetics could be applied for purposes of dissociation as well as association, especially in the suburbs, where home owners could leave behind the cares and obligations of the work world as they embraced a private sphere of cultivated leisure.

"Country Life within City Reach" at *Idlewild*

The first image readers saw when they opened *Out-doors at Idlewild*, even before the title page, was a drawing of the gated drive leading to Willis's estate (fig. 7). This frontispiece served as an orientation to the text. Though the title invited readers to follow the path to his home (barely visible above the trees) in the pages that followed, the gate in the engraving evoked a sense of exclusion, marking what lay beyond as a place of sanctuary where privacy was valued. Extending an invitation to partake in his private thoughts and simultaneously suggesting that his life could not be attained by others, the gated drive embodied the "close remotenesses" Willis mentioned inside the book.

Explaining that his "cottage at Idlewild . . . is a pretty type of the two lives which they live who are wise—the life in full view, which the world thinks all; and the life out of sight, of which the world knows nothing," he asserted control over his readers' curiosity even as he offered glimpses into his private domain.[4] He was able to add intrigue to his own domestic existence by intimating that neither he nor his house was an open book. *Out-doors at Idlewild* and the editorial letters in the *Home Journal* that had preceded it included small peeps into Willis's domestic space, transforming a relatively routine home life into an extended tease of self-revelation. In this way he modeled the techniques by which an individual, in the words of the critic Sandra Tomc, could learn to marshal the home space as "a site for the mobilization of energies of self-making" in a new society.[5] Taste and aesthetics were powerful in the domestic sphere because they *withheld* even as they invited appreciation, retaining the promise of future pleasures and signaling the presence of something too valuable to be put on display for all to see. The fact that Willis felt the need to construct a gate in the first place, after all, reflected an urge to mark the entrance of his property, suggesting that something out of the ordinary lay beyond.

So what *did* the gate enclose? In material and historical terms, it marked the boundary of Idlewild, a fifty-acre property located in a planned

FIGURE 7. Frontispiece to *Out-doors at Idlewild* (1855). Courtesy American Antiquarian Society.

development at Cornwall along the Hudson River. In 1836 Freeman Hunt, the future founder and editor of *Hunt's Merchants' Magazine and Commercial Review,* had called the Hudson "the greatest thoroughfare of the Union" and mused that the Hudson Highlands area in particular would soon be in demand: "Its scenery throughout is magnificent, and in this particular region sublime. Health and happiness dwell among its hills, and every luxury that the earth can yield is wafted by its waters. It is within a few hours' journey to New York, and the facilities of access are unexampled in convenience, economy, and opportunity. The day is not distant, when the entire banks of the Hudson will be dotted with villas of the refined and elegant."[6] Willis himself had commented on suburbanization along the Hudson as early as the 1840s, noting in an article for the *New Mirror* that "there is a suburban look and character about all the villages on the Hudson which seems out of place among such scenery. They are suburbs; in fact, steam has destroyed the distance between them and the city."[7]

In 1849, when the Swedish author and intellectual Fredrika Bremer was touring the United States with her hosts, Mr. and Mrs. A. J. Downing, she marveled at the interconnectedness of country and city along the Hudson:

> New York receives butter, and cheese, and cattle, and many other good things from the country; and the country, with its towns and rural abodes, receives coffee and tea, and wine, and wearing apparel, and many other things from New York, and, through New York, from Europe. The little town of Newburgh maintains alone, by its trade from the country and back, two or three steam-boats. When one sees the number and magnificence of steam-boats on the Hudson, one can scarcely believe the fact that it is not more than thirty years since Fulton made here his first experiment with steam power on the river, and that amid general distrust of the undertaking.[8]

The Hudson River Railroad would make its first trip from New York City to Poughkeepsie at the end of 1849, and it was running eight daily round-trips between Albany and the city only two years later. By midcentury the combination of efficient steamship travel (which became more cost-effective as a result of transportation competition) and frequent railroad access had transformed communities along the Hudson River into bustling New York suburbs, highly desirable to men of means who worked in the city a few days a week but preferred to live close to nature.[9]

Willis had a long-standing interest in writing about the benefits of living outside American cities; in 1839 he had published a popular book of sketches about life along the Susquehanna with his first wife, Mary Stace, called *A L'Abri; or, The Tent Pitch'd*, which became better known under its 1840 title, *Letters from Under a Bridge*. At Glenmary, the cottage in Owego, New York, that he had purchased in 1837, he found a welcome retreat from the bustle of New York City, as well as a private environment where he and his wife could start a family. As the letters to his doctor and friend that constitute the volume make clear, the domestic retreat influenced his feelings about the relationship between mind and matter. Detailing the ways in which a country existence had improved his outlook on life and overall state of health, he proclaimed, "I like my mind to be a green lane, private to the dwellers in my own demesne."[10] Although financial difficulties would force him to sell Glenmary and return to New York City in 1842, his experience there established a predilection for a home surrounded by nature, separated physically and mentally from the world of business.

After the death of his wife during childbirth in 1845, another escape from the city seemed especially necessary. A trip to Europe (accompanied by his young daughter, Imogen, and her nurse, the future author and abolitionist Harriet Jacobs) did little to quell his grief, though; for much of the visit he suffered from what his doctors diagnosed as "brain fever."[11] Upon his return in the spring of 1846, he threw himself into his work with a frenzy that belied his literary posturing as a man-about-town without a care in the world. Although his personal style and antics had made him one of the best-known magazine writers of his generation, there were certain aspects of his life that he sought to keep private.[12] Willis hoped that a combination of prolific writing, social engagements, and a new wife would help him recover from personal devastation and plaguing health problems.

Unfortunately, even a second chance at married life with a wealthy young woman named Cornelia Grinnell failed to assuage feelings of discomfort in either arena. Diagnosed with "rheumatic pleurisy" in 1848, Willis struggled with ailments that included vertigo, occasional blindness, and a persistent bloody cough. (Doctors would finally link his symptoms with epilepsy in the 1850s.) To make matters worse, he became embroiled in the most famous divorce trial of the century. Upon being identified by a servant as a onetime paramour of Mrs. Edwin Forrest, wife of the famous tragedian associated with the Astor Place Riot of 1849, Willis was tracked down and beaten by the actor in Washington Square in June 1850.[13] News of that spectacle and proceedings from the divorce trial kept Willis on the defensive between 1850 and 1852, in both print and society. Many in the press portrayed him as a weak (albeit humorously unfortunate) victim who had merely sought to protect an innocent woman. Although he was eventually exonerated, the ordeal exhausted him physically and took a toll on his nerves.

Given the circumstances, it is understandable that Willis sought a permanent removal from the city in the early 1850s. His time at Glenmary had made him keenly aware of the advantages of an unscrutinized existence, and his new wife's dowry provided more than enough money to purchase land and build a home in the Hudson River Valley. The Willis family took a particularly well-timed summer vacation in 1850 to a boardinghouse in the Hudson Highlands. That fall they purchased property in a new residential community called the Hudson Terrace. Willis engaged Calvert Vaux—the famous architectural associate of A. J. Downing who soon would partner with Frederick Law Olmsted to design Central Park—to fashion a house for him, and construction began in the autumn of 1852. His plan eventually graced the frontispiece of Vaux's 1857 home pattern book, *Villas and Cottages,* as an example of a model suburban domicile.[14] A home outside New York City promised to separate Willis's public from his private life, allowing him more control over who had access to him and when. Undoubtedly influenced by trends in home design and community formation that had initially been popularized by Downing, Willis would attempt to remake his image by endowing his new home with the tone and characteristics of his more ideal self.

Ensconced within the protective shell of his domestic surroundings, he could cultivate the aura of a retired, respected American author and tastemaker in the pages of his magazine and in selected outlets such as Vaux's handbook while also controlling the extent to which readers were aware of his illness. As an 1858 article on Idlewild in *Harper's New Monthly Magazine* illustrates, Willis took pride in sharing the landscape that he felt embodied his priorities and talents so perfectly.[15] Though he often wrote about visits from popular literary figures such as Washington Irving, J. P. Kennedy, Charles Dana, James T. Fields, and Bayard Taylor, he also opened his gates to tourists at designated hours and happily estimated that "five thousand people, at least, pass daily under my library window" along the Hudson.[16] Because his location allowed him to control access in a way that was not possible in the city, he could afford to welcome visitors, whether in person or in print, into his home space; after all, as he reminded readers at the closing of *Out-doors at Idlewild,* he decided when "the gate of Idlewild is here shut upon the pen that is their servant."[17] Especially with regard to his health, Willis valued his privacy. Even though he wrote fairly extensively about his respiratory troubles, dedicating *Out-doors at Idlewild* and his 1859 collection *The Convalescent* to "his fellow sufferers" and addressing many of his editorials as open letters to one of his personal physicians, T. O. Porter, he sought to keep his epileptic attacks a secret from anyone other than his wife and doctor. Largely as a result of selling his home in the city and taking up primary residence at Idlewild, he succeeded in doing so until his death in 1867.[18]

The Willis family sold their New York house in the spring of 1853 and moved to Idlewild on July 26.[19] Willis chronicled the relocation process in weekly letters to the *Home Journal* between April 2, 1853, and August 5, 1854. Through these essays he celebrated a new development in American domestic life which he referred to in the column's running title: "Out-doors at Idlewild; or, Country-Life within City Reach." Rather than focusing exclusively on his individual experience, Willis sought to communicate the joys of suburban living for readers who might be contemplating similar transitions, as the prefatory remarks from his co-editor, George Pope Morris, to the first column illustrate: "[Mr. Willis] proposes to give a series of sketches descriptive of Country-life within City-reach. . . . For the last year or two he has been taking advantage of the new facilities given by improvements in railroads and steamboats—uniting the repose and beauty of rural life with the comforts and advantages of easy access to the city. He finds much in this which is new. It forms a combination of the desirable qualities of the true mode of life, which he thinks well worth describing and making familiar to the world."[20]

Recognizing that "many" of his readers were "on the point of yielding to the new movement—business in the city, home in the country," Willis positioned himself as an expert on the establishment of suburban "comfort and loveliness."[21] Even though he failed to provide detailed advice in his columns on *how* readers should achieve the goal of a residence beyond the city, he offered an argument for their presence there, in addition to positioning Idlewild as a model of success to which they could aspire. Praising development along the Hudson in his first letter, he proclaimed that the river would soon be "but a fifty-mile extension of Broadway" and invited his readers to imagine its banks as a "suburban avenue—a long street of villas, whose busiest resident will be content that the City Hall is within an hour of his door."[22] There was no reason to remain in the city after work, according to Willis, when transportation could easily shuttle the man of business from the urban center to the beauties of nature. Outside but within reach of American cities, readers could participate in new domestic trends as they learned how to infuse their surroundings with a sense of self on an unprecedented scale.

In these *Home Journal* letters Willis presented facts about his life at Idlewild as local examples of what readers could expect from the suburban experience more generally. As he detailed his successes and failures in planting various trees, shrubs, and vegetables, or his desire to clear new paths and construct landmarks such as gates, benches, and bridges, he modeled the decisions involved in shaping a landscape outside but within reach of American cities, even as he recognized that the Hudson River Valley was suburban only in the loosest sense. Unlike many of his readers who would have been better served by establishing themselves in Brooklyn because of cost considerations and the necessity of commuting on a daily basis, Willis could afford to live in a community that was more "rural city" than suburb. Nevertheless, while surveying the Hudson on daily walks and horseback rides, he contemplated the restorative effects of nature on the spirit for Americans who were concerned about poor air quality that was due to the overcrowding of metropolitan areas. Descriptions of interactions with his neighbors and accounts of daily trips to Newburgh for groceries were meant to dispel fears of isolation for prospective middle-class home buyers from the city. Reflecting on his morning writing sessions in the study, family meals in the dining room, outdoor picnics with the children, and discussions with his wife at the hearth, Willis invited his readers not just to consider plans for their own houses but to imagine themselves moving through spaces that were similar in kind if not in degree and enjoying domestic activities in an environment that availed itself of the amenities of urban and rural areas while eliminating the drawbacks of each.

In an *Out-doors at Idlewild* essay from 1854, Willis reflected on the process whereby a personal aesthetic could evolve from an experience with a landscape. In a sense he was pinpointing a remarkable new method of branding that co-opted the domestic environment even as it defined itself in opposition to the goals and motivations of the business world: "Separate a rural spot from the rest of the world, either by poetry or property—only putting around it the fairy ring of thought-haunt, where your love and sadness are at home—and it is curious how you are made gradually conscious that there is a *genius loci,* a spirit, inhabiting just what you have fenced in with thoughts or rails."[23] As his articles about Idlewild gained a following, Willis sought to capitalize on the unique position that he occupied as editorial adviser to readers who were considering moving to suburban areas. He recognized that in the process of describing his surroundings in the Hudson River Valley each week, he was "indirectly advertis[ing]" a lifestyle that was defined by close remotenesses, both geographically and aesthetically.[24] His domestic environment was as much the creation of his mind as a physical landscape, and he invited readers to visit that space in his *Home Journal* columns. Once he realized that he was acting as gatekeeper both to his property at Idlewild and to more broadly based desires on the part of readers for information about how to transform their surroundings into reflections of their best selves, Willis attempted to extend his notion of a genius loci, or "thought-haunt," to his magazine as a whole.

A Spirit in Things
Periodical Culture as Textual Infrastructure

Beginning in the 1850s, Willis encouraged readers to think of the *Home Journal* as a suburban community in print. One of the major benefits of a home like Idlewild, or any domestic existence on the urban periphery, he insisted in his columns, was that it allowed its owners to feel that they could call a part of nature their own. In an essay in the May 14, 1853, issue he declared, "Each April morning, to drop the reins upon the neck of your horse, and look, charmed, around, seeing that Nature did *not* go to bed, used up and tired, the night before, as *you* did, but has been industriously busy upon the leaves and blossoms while you were asleep . . . is, somehow, a feeling that has in it the bliss of *ownership*." Indeed, "the morning seems made for you," he continued. "The fields and sky seem *your* roof and grounds. The air and sunshine, fresh colors and changing light—all new, and not a second-hand thing to be seen—nothing to be cupboarded and kept over for to-morrow, or for another guest—gives a delicious consciousness of being the first to be waited on, the one it was all made and meant for. A city April, in comparison, is a thing potted and pickled, and retailed to other customers as well."[25] Drawing from his own experiences in the Hudson River Valley, Willis envisioned a magazine that would provide readers with benefits similar to the ones he described. As publishing networks expanded and became increasingly difficult to navigate, Willis promised customized guidance in the *Home Journal.* Subscribers would no longer feel like anonymous statistics in a world that packaged material for mass consumption and maximum profits. Even if they did not own a home in the suburbs or failed to apply some of the recommendations contained within the *Home Journal* to their own lives, he urged readers to embrace the unique benefits of a lifestyle-based print network and to think of him as a friendly counselor who was devoted to their individual needs.

Willis had established the foundations for this innovative vision of readership over the course of two decades in the New York publishing world. As he had explained in an 1846 column for the *Evening Mirror,* "An apple given to you by a friend at table is not like an apple taken from the shelf of a huckster. . . . [T]he friend's choice alters the taste and value of the apple, as the individual editor's selections or approbation gives weight and value to the article."[26] Early on, Willis understood how to utilize the medium to his advantage, framing his editorial role as that of a helpful guide through a potentially overwhelming and disorienting forest of news and literature. He invited readers to get to know him through his "weekly visit" and made an effort to suffuse the magazines he edited with evidence of his personal style and interests.

It was his decision in February 1846, however, to found the *National Press: A Journal for the Home* with his longtime friend and collaborator George Pope Morris that laid the foundations for this new conception of a periodical as a textual neighborhood. Less than a year after the death of his first wife, Willis decided to ground his efforts in the domestic environment, a focus that he and Morris solidified in November, when they changed the title to the *Home Journal.* In keeping with their earlier ventures, the new magazine included forays into high-society gossip and information about cultural events in New York City, but for the most part it comprised articles, stories, and advertisements that appealed to readers' home interests and obligations. This in itself was not significant; after all, *Godey's Lady's Book* had been in continual publication since 1830 and was widely considered the most successful domestic magazine in America. What differentiated the *Home Journal,* however, was the editorial decision to name "the man of business" and "the Domestic Fireside and Family Circle" as its primary audiences, straddling a gap that previous periodicals had avoided by addressing either the businessman or the domestic sphere to the exclusion of the other.[27]

The first issue of the newly retitled *Home Journal* addressed itself "to the circle around the family table" and promised to "divert the mind" from business with "matter which is instructive, companionable, and amusing" at the same time that it "picks, arranges, condenses, and gives, in small compass, the 'cream and substance' of the week's wilderness of newspaper reading."[28] In emphasizing men's return home each evening to their families, the new magazine promised to bring the family together at the end of the day by reintegrating businessmen into the domestic sphere. Willis assured men particularly that time allocated to the *Home Journal* would be well spent: not only would they be kept abreast of important news, but also they would learn strategies for transporting a bit of the work world's efficiency and sense of purpose into the home environment.

A four-page weekly folio with seven columns per page and few illustrations, the periodical's structure reflected its goal of both providing pleasurable recreation for the family and fulfilling the need of readers to be informed members of society. Stories under headings such as "Romance and Reality" and "Gems of Prose" were typical page-one fare. The second page included Willis's weekly editorial letter, letters from correspondents, recaps of major news, and listings of cultural events around New York City. The third page was full of advertisements (for lamps, cakes, daguerreotype galleries, picture frames, *Godey's,* carpeting, folding bedsteads, wedding cards, "Batchelor's Hair Dye," and hemorrhoid cures), bank transactions, marriages and deaths, and a "Useful Information" column that addressed subjects such as how to grow trees and vegetables, home remedies, recipes, and price and quality comparisons of appliances such as refrigerators, coffeemakers, and ice cream freezers. The *Journal's* final page usually contained fiction reprinted from other newspapers, especially foreign ones, and included essays and poems as space permitted.

In each issue Willis argued for the importance of his role as an editor who carefully chose the most important news briefs and the most edifying stories. Invoking an early version of keeping up with the Joneses in the November 21, 1846, issue, he remarked: "In this enlightened age, people grow inferior to their neighbours, if they do not 'keep up with the times.' All who would be respectable must 'know the news.' Yet newspapers are numberless, and, in their very multitude, even those who have access to them become bewildered with the confusion of matter." Under his guidance, the *Home Journal* would cull material from other papers, enabling families to remain abreast of current events without having to sacrifice time set aside for entertainment.[29]

The magazine's growing popularity in the late 1840s and early 1850s testified to Willis's shrewd business sense. Even as Morris oversaw financial considerations and claimed to be the voice of practicality behind Willis's artistic genius, it was Willis's entrepreneurship that enabled the periodical to access middle-class fantasies of upward mobility. His editorial efforts in the 1830s had reflected a desire to appear more aristocratic than he was in reality, but by the mid-nineteenth century, he had found a way to portray his rough-edged outsider status as an asset rather than a handicap. Characterizing the *Home Journal* as a sourcebook for those who sought to integrate beauty into their daily routines, Willis figuratively annexed the home space as a location where individuals with a common bond congregated for conversation and inspiration. The periodical communicated a sense of thriftiness and accessibility even as column subjects and advertisements insisted that the opportunity to experience domestic refinement was a marker of American cultural advancement.

In his editorial capacity, Willis argued that attention to aesthetics would not only improve the quality of home life but also put individuals in control of their own class status. As he stated in a column titled "Society and Manners in New York," "to look well-bred has a value in this metropolis, at present, which gives more social rank than in any other capital in the world."[30] Luckily, taste could be learned, especially in the United States, where persistent effort, along with an earnest openness to new experiences, "puts Americans over time as electricity puts news over distance."[31] Just as the telegraph, which had begun to be used by newspapers in the 1840s, had created an invisible fence that brought individuals into a shared space regardless of their physical location, *"sympathetic association"* through a shared belief in the power of aesthetics in the domestic sphere would link readers of the *Home Journal* to one another.[32]

Willis's vision for the *Home Journal* mirrored his physical movement away from the city. In February 1851 he and Morris refined their primary goals in an attempt to fashion a literary space that would house the needs of a particular type of reader. A new tagline emerged, "For the Cultivation of the Memorable, the Progressive, and the Beautiful," which was followed by a quotation from Goethe: "We should do our utmost to encourage the beautiful, for the useful encourages itself." Advertising new features, the February 15, 1851, issue proclaimed, "This widely-circulated weekly is now acknowledged to be the most indispensable drawing-room gazette of the country." Flaunting the paper's popularity, the editors insisted that "a home is hardly complete, we think we may safely venture to say, without the HOME JOURNAL, which is the CHRONICLE OF ALL THAT INTERESTS ALL CLASSES OF SOCIETY, and of the intelligence which most enlivens an American Home."[33] Allocating more space and prominence to columns about life in the suburbs than periodicals such as *Godey's,* which marketed themselves exclusively to women, the *Home Journal* had found its niche.

Coverage of trends in home construction and community development suggested that country life within city reach constituted the ideal domestic arrangement for American men and their families. In the March 15 issue Willis incredulously asked why businessmen would not prefer to reside in nature, given recent transportation developments: "Cities will soon be places for business only—not for residence. Railroads will soon take you 'most anywhere' as quickly as an omnibus takes you up town, and then, who would make his home in the city?" He explained that the magazine's columns were written and selected "in anticipation of this spread of New-York over a rural city of fifty miles square." As a new geography for home life, the "rural city" and its suburban counterparts necessitated new orientation and advice, and Willis and his columnists professed "wisdom in the art of living,"[34] a masculinized approach to domesticity for spaces that had been designed with men's needs in mind. Form and function, as the author of a running *Home Journal* column, "Perfecting the Home," made clear, had more to do with each other than some might suppose, and the periodical's purpose was to help subscribers experiment with that relationship in their homes by providing "new or useful ideas on the means and manner of making life agreeable" for the family as a whole.[35]

Willis intimated that suburban home owners were more likely to devote themselves to the art of living well than were people who lived in urban or rural communities. Their decision to establish homes outside but within reach of American cities suggested that they had capital at their disposal but wanted to spend it intelligently, in ways that would improve their quality of life while remaining true to their democratic roots. Identifying *"comfort* and *fitness in a home"* as "a universal want," he offered to help readers navigate the more intangible but increasingly important qualities of "taste" and "style" in home design and decoration.[36] Channeling A. J. Downing as he articulated a desire for "counsel that is both cheaper and more practical" than the advice provided by architects and landscape gardeners to the wealthy, Willis understood that he was "mak[ing] a profession of *giving a start*" to his middle-class readers in the pages of the *Home Journal*.[37] He argued that just as editorial choices made his magazine a "welcome visitor" to his subscribers, so landscape, architecture, and interior decoration influenced the ways people experienced place. Using Idlewild as an example, he sought to demonstrate how objects and materials could become vessels for the spirit, manifestations of the owner's personality in the suburban environment in a way they could not in other locales. Customization was key in that regard: articles urged men especially to consider the type of family they wanted to have and what sorts of activities they wanted to pursue after work and on weekends, and to modify their layouts and appointments accordingly.

In the course of providing information about new railroad lines and planned developments, interior decoration and landscape architecture, Willis cast suburban home ownership as an "investment of a stock" in "secured health and renewed strength" for the entire family.[38] Commenting on the transformation of communities outside Boston, he even depicted commuting time as a boon to a harried businessman:

> The old residents, leaving the low and reclaimed land to foreign labourers, plant themselves in the suburbs. There they build tasteful houses, with flower-plats and gardens; availing of the frequent omnibuses, or of special

trains run almost hourly, and commuting for passage at $20 to $40 a year; they reach their stores and offices in the morning and at night sleep with their wives and children in the suburbs. No time is lost, for they read the morning and evening journals as they go and return. Some of the wards appropriate for stores thus rise in value, but diminish in population. The suburbs extend, and the commercial community grows in a widening semi-circle.[39]

Not only were the suburbs more cost-effective than urban environments, according to Willis, but also they enabled men to devote themselves completely to domestic cares each evening, with no loss of productivity during the commute. Country life within city reach promised to improve the quality of men's experience of leisure and amusement after work at the same time that it positively influenced the mental and physical state of their wives and children.

Throughout the 1850s Willis chose not to dwell on discrepancies between his own privilege and the aspirations of *Home Journal* readers, despite the fact that his property on the western side of the Hudson occupied some of the most desirable land outside the city. He did not ignore class altogether, however. Willis hoped that his magazine would support the creation of a new class of Americans whose distinction rested on the understanding and use of the domestic design principles that he and other experts promulgated through the medium of print. Willis spoke frequently of his desire to "strike a new level in American Home Life—(bringing some homes *up* to the mark, and some *down* to it)—which shall strengthen the right of our paper to its name, and secure to us the thanks of the home-loving and moderate-minded."[40] While he warned against the excesses of wealthy Americans, he also assumed that middle-class home owners knew that upward mobility was possible—they just needed to locate themselves in the right neighborhood.

For that reason he did not bemoan the fact that middle-class Americans were abandoning New York's urban center to the poorer immigrant classes, or that increased demand for residences in suburban communities was pushing farmers away from the city. In an early essay from *Out-doors at Idlewild,* he spoke of a neighbor who was moving his farm "twenty miles farther back, where a man could afford to farm, at the price of the land." According to Willis, the move was advantageous to both prospective home owners and the farmer himself: "His corn-fields on the banks of the Hud-son had risen in value, as probable sites for ornamental residences, and with the difference (between two hundred dollars the fancy acre, and sixty dollars the farming acre) in his pocket, he was transferring his labor and his associations to a new soil and a new neighborhood."[41] He continued, extolling the fact that "*a class who can afford to let the trees grow* is getting possession of the Hudson; and it is at least safe to rejoice in this, whatever one may preach as to the displacement of the laboring tiller of the soil by the luxurious idler."[42] Grouping himself with the class of "luxurious idlers" who were making life more difficult for farmers, he nonetheless insisted that individuals who appreciated the land for its inherent beauty deserved to own the most advantageous spots—in his case, along the Hudson River. The *Home Journal*'s goal was to teach that sort of appreciation.

In *The Industrial Book, 1840–1880,* John Nerone describes how a growing number of periodicals "invited readers into alternative and subaltern spaces segmented from the great public" in the mid-nineteenth century and, in doing so, "turn[ed] the transmission of information into a ritual of social continuity."[43] From the vantage point of his home on the Hudson, Willis became a powerful domestic reformer toward the end of his literary career. As the famed editor of the *Home Journal,* he turned personal necessity to his advantage by presenting his magazine as a textual suburb in an era of burgeoning print culture. In the process of inviting readers to visit him at Idlewild through his weekly columns in the early 1850s, he created a meeting place for Americans who had begun to demand more from their home lives. An 1858 article in the *Circular* praised his efforts: "No other popular writer has been so free to give his reader the incidents and experiences of his private home, taking them to his fireside and showing them the ways of family life at Idlewild." Acknowledging that people wanted life advice from the authors and editors they had come to view as friends, the writer commended Willis for welcoming readers "at the opened door" of Idlewild and showing them the benefits of separating themselves from the urban business world to fash-ion a domestic environment that embodied their personalities.[44]

By the time of Willis's death in 1867, Idlewild had become one of the most famous homes in nineteenth-century America. In what was, paradox-ically, the greatest measure of the success of his writings, the name Idlewild took on a life of its own as the century wore on, ultimately outliving the public's memory of the author. Willis claimed to have chosen it as a pro-spective home buyer when the seller declared the land to be of little value, *"only an idle wild* of which nothing could ever be made," a proclamation that "stuck captivatingly" in the author's memory.[45] It did not matter to him that the land was not workable as farmland; a place expressly identified as *un*suited for labor and production in a traditional sense was ideal for him. Through his appellation for and characterization of Idlewild in the pages of the *Home Journal* and eventually in *Out-doors at Idlewild,* Willis intimated that suburban domestic spaces were desirable precisely because they enabled home owners to dissociate their professional and private lives. By the mid-1850s, the word had entered the English lexicon as a general designation for homes whose architecture and layout celebrated nature for nature's sake, serving as retreats from the dust and grime of the city. Willis himself became fond of quoting periodicals that used the name Idlewild to describe houses other than his own. Over the course of the late nineteenth century and well into the twentieth, it was associated with numerous homes and parks, most significantly a town in rural Michigan, an amusement park in Pennsylvania, and what is now known as John F. Kennedy International Airport in New York. As for the *Home Journal,* it was renamed *Town and Country* in 1901, and is still published under that name today. It is the oldest continually published magazine in the history of the United States.

To his credit, Willis acknowledged that the road to upward mobility via aesthetics was not without its pitfalls. He occasionally wrote in the *Home Journal* about the drawbacks of certain suburban communities and proposed remedies for less than ideal domestic situations. For example, in the January 31, 1852, issue he called for either an underwater tunnel (like the Thames tunnel) or an "airy structure" (like the Menai Bridge in Wales) across the East River to decrease commuting time between Brooklyn and Manhattan. He proclaimed that "the large amount of dwelling-house property that lies, by airline, so close to the business heart of New-York, is object enough, and the 50,000 semiwives of Brooklyn who wish to be 'made whole' and dine, and tea with their husbands, are impulse enough" to remedy the unsatis-factory state of the "Long Island suburb."[46] Likewise, he sometimes printed letters from readers who regretted following his advice. In the "Correspon-dence" section from November 1853, for instance, a letter from one reader was titled "Country-Life beyond City Reach," emphasizing the difficulties involved in following Willis's advice. As a young man with a wife and baby, he'd decided to leave behind his business in the city (even though he was "in a fair way of becoming ultimately one of the 'merchant princes'" of New York) after reading "so much in your columns of Idlewild." He chose "a spot where my taste could be best displayed" but which was far from the railroads. Despite following advice from pattern books and periodicals, he and his wife had had trouble getting plants to grow, lacked society, and felt overwhelmed by home improvement projects. Wanting to persuade readers against the "rural mania, now so common," he argued, "Your Idlewilds are all very well for your wild, idle chaps who have plenty of money and nothing to do; but a man who can't afford to support two houses, one in the country for summer, and one in the city for winter, had better stay at home and attend to his business."[47] Although Willis and his contributors recommended that prospective suburban home owners who would need to commute to work each weekday choose land near regular and efficient transportation, it seemed that some readers could not afford that real estate. The column would ultimately be reprinted in other magazines, such as *The Spirit of the Times,* as a humorous warning about discrepancies between artistic visions and daily realities.

Even in Willis's own life, economic and practical considerations sometimes could not be helped, and the original vision of the gate might not be the one that materialized in front of one's house. As he recalled in *Out-doors at Idlewild,* he had originally attempted to design the gate himself, insisting that its form reflect his personality, but he relinquished his plan after "a laboring man by whose opinions I usually take the measure of my own" noted that it was not "pig-tight." As a result of its impracticality, he asked his architect, Calvert Vaux, to redesign it. Vaux's version admirably integrated form and function, but Willis complained in the essay, "It does not look at all as if it led to *me.*" Apologizing for an inconsistency between the gate's personality and his own, he nonetheless accepted the final design: "There it stands, however, leading to Idlewild. Friends will understand where it promises too much."[48]

One hundred years after its founding, *Town and Country* magazine recalled its first editor as a man who "led a generation of Americans through a gate where weeds gave way to horticulture."[49] Willis's reputation has not fared well in critical circles; only recently has his work begun to be considered something more than elitist, self-aggrandizing drivel. Despite, or perhaps because of, his contradictions and idiosyncrasies, though, it is worth returning to this writer who committed himself to improving the lives of his many readers even as his name became permanently linked with New York's "Upper Ten" in the mid-nineteenth century. Looking out his study window at the tourists on his lawn and the steamboats on the Hudson River, he sought to share his "aristocratic" experience with middle-class Americans. Recognizing himself as part of a larger economic and cultural phenomenon that would alter the shape of northeastern cities and towns, he embraced early suburbanization in the pages of his magazine, even going so far as to suggest that "country life within city reach" could actualize the "close remotenesses" that were commonly understood to be a novel facet of the reading experience. His enlistment of print culture in the project of preparing and welcoming a new class of individuals into a new type of space, as well as his radical effort to cast the suburb itself as text, set the stage for future lifestyle-based publications from *Esquire* and *GQ* to *Martha Stewart Living* and *Architectural Digest,* magazines that successfully banked on their ability to serve as aesthetic counselors to the masses. Willis's gate may have promised too much, but his was a promise that continues to build communities of readers, uniting them in the belief that the smallest material details, decisions, and practices contribute to ongoing personal narratives of economy and elegance, accomplishment and ascent.

6

SPECULATIVE MANHOOD
Living Fiction in the Country-Book Genre

In an episode from *Out of Town* (1866), the American humorist Robert Barry Coffin's midcentury account of suburban domestic life in Fordham, in what is now the Bronx, Barry Gray (Coffin's pseudonym and the book's narrator) persuades his wife to have a group of his "artist friends" over for dinner. The prospect throws his wife into a state of nervous excitement as she contemplates what she should serve to the group of "ten hungry men" arriving from New York City, knowing that they will not be satisfied with her traditional Saturday meal of "simple salt codfish and potatoes."[1] At the same moment that she proclaims her unwillingness to perform the task of hostess for such an occasion, an express wagon filled with twelve hampers of food and drink appears at their doorstep. The arrival of these provisions, ordered ahead of time by Mr. Gray, sets the stage for a banquet orchestrated by a man for his male companions. The delivery even attracts the attention of the local paper, and a journalist is sent to observe the party through a window. The published report (which Mr. Gray shares with his readers) focuses on the meal's extravagance and wildness, from the description of the "immense game-pie, composed of ducks, woodcocks, quails, and grouse" at the center of the table to the "jugged hare," "boned turkey," and "boiled ham, a round of beef, broiled spring chickens, ducks stuffed with olives, boned sardines, and other appetizing relishes" that surround it (*OT*, 59).

Both the article and Mr. Gray's account embrace a narrative of excess in their coverage of the event as they linger over the culinary delicacies and characterize the domestic particularities of the host as endearing quirks that elevate what would have been a simple dinner (if he had not taken the helm) to the status of an impromptu *occasion*. Attentive to the smallest details of his guests' comfort, Gray "pluck[s] a handful of mint" before their arrival, "bruis[ing] it against the gate-posts which command the entrance to [his] possessions" (53), in order to welcome them. As the first two men remark upon the pleasant aroma, Gray ushers them into his library, where "a dozen goblets gleaming with ice, golden with whiskey, softened with sugar, and fragrant with mint" (54) await them. Casting his domestic neuroses as charming ingenuity, the writer hosts a feast that caters to his friends' sensorial appetites while at the same time it showcases his home as an imaginative embodiment of a less tangible personal flair. Displacing his wife's moral economy, Gray directs a domestic theatrical production that broadcasts his epicurean proclivities in such a way as to protect himself from charges of dilettantism or dandyism. The scene just described is but one instance of many in which Coffin attempts to reconstitute American manhood, geographically and aesthetically, by introducing readers to suburban men linked by a shared desire to unite a feminine-coded romantic sensibility with a masculine hearty appetite.

A relatively short-lived but extremely popular narrative form that took as its subject male authors' relocation from urban to suburban environments, the country book, of which Coffin's *Out of Town* is an example, flourished throughout the 1850s and 1860s. Typically these were penned by periodical writers and published serially before being collected into book form. Standard examples of the genre such as Mitchell's *My Farm of Edgewood* and Willis's *Out-doors at Idlewild* celebrated the opportunities and amenities available for upper-middle-class Americans in the suburbs surrounding major northeastern cities.[2] Born of a flourishing celebrity culture that was itself a product of the confluence of rapid urbanization, a proliferation of popular amusements, and innovations in printing techniques, as we saw in chapter 5, the country book was a hybrid form. Framed as sanctioned exposés of the domestic lives of the popular writers who penned them, the incidents depicted were intended to be read as a sort of fictionalized memoir. Authors talked about their real homes and neighborhoods, and conversations with their spouses, children, and friends seemed to be taken from real-life events. At the same time, they admitted to shaping and pruning their accounts for the sake of interest and humor and frequently embellished characteristics of themselves and their acquaintances. The genre's depictions of suburban life drew from established literary precedents in the pastoral, sketch, and travel book but also borrowed new modes of product and property advertisement from commercial business culture.

As the form developed alongside the suburbs themselves, a group of country-book writers began to push the boundaries of representation by utilizing humorous theatricality to defamiliarize the home space for readers. Perhaps counterintuitively, in doing so they hoped to achieve a sort of realism in the depiction of men's domestic lives that they felt to be lacking in the more staid, whitewashed representatives of the genre. These more playful country books, *Out of Town* among them, portray communities of individuals who are actively (if unknowingly) contributing to their own shortcomings and failures through faulty rationalizations, especially in terms of their purchasing habits, housekeeping tendencies, and social behaviors. Eager to locate a place for themselves in a vision created and fostered by the print medium, newly minted suburbanites rush headlong into advertised home felicities without stopping to ask what constitutes true necessity and what might be a needless expense or even an occupational hazard. Their collective textual realization is especially powerful because country-book writers come to see themselves—as readers come to see them over the course of their narratives—as part of much larger machinations, willing, if unquestioning, participants in a domestic plot of epic proportions.

Fascinatingly, revisionist country-book practitioners identified opportunity in their rehearsals of co-optation. In their attempts to transpose a ubiquitous geographic netherworld onto the space of the page, the most successful examples of the genre paid homage to the contours of that genre while refusing to silence the feelings of liminality (related to gender identity, professional status, familial contributions, and creative potential) the authors felt in their own lives. In this final chapter I explore the cultural work of domestic eccentricity in country books by the popular humorists Frederic Cozzens and Robert Barry Coffin as revisionist inheritors of the textual suburbanization inaugurated by the writers treated earlier in this volume. In the "living fictions" they penned—meandering portrayals of the an author's alter ego living his life as a fictional fantasy—they found a way to thoughtfully finesse the anxiety typically endemic to the occupation of liminal states into experiments in autobiographical pastiche.

"A COUNTRY HOME FOR ME!"
Advertising a Dream

In 1850, the Swedish author Fredrika Bremer wrote to her sister of the astonishing difference between metropolitan New York and Henry Ward

Beecher's suburban Brooklyn: "Brooklyn is as quiet as New York is bewildering and noisy: it is built upon the heights of Long Island; has glorious views over the wide harbor, and quiet, broad streets. . . . It is said that the merchants of New York go over to Brooklyn, where they have their house and home, to sleep." She continued: "The friend with whom I am living, Marcus S[pring], has his place of business in New York, and his proper home here in Brooklyn, one of the very prettiest rural homes, by name 'Rose Cottage.' . . . From this place he drives every morning to New York, and hither he returns every evening, but not merely to sleep, but to rest, and enjoy himself with wife, children, and friends. Rose Cottage lies just on the out-skirts of town (you must not imagine it a little town but one which has one hundred thousand inhabitants)."[3] Bremer's description emphasizes both the scale of suburbanization at midcentury and the influence of men's business concerns on community formation. Designed with the needs of a commuter in mind, Brooklyn offered men who worked in the city a space for relaxation, hobbies, family time, and inner cultivation. By demarcating the line between work and home life, suburbs asserted that regardless of what happened in the weekday business world, the domestic sphere would remain inviolate, ready to welcome men back in the evening and on weekends.

The unstated reality, of course, was that the fate of the houses themselves as well as the families within them were inextricably tied to success or failure in business. Moreover, Brooklyn itself was a business, with speculators buying up acres of land, subdividing it into little parcels, and selling it for large profits. The first large-scale gated suburban community in the United States, Llewellyn Park, opened in 1853, twelve miles from the center of New York City by ferry and train. Llewellyn Haskell, a businessman who had made his fortune by selling wholesale pharmaceuticals, purchased a large tract of farmland in West Orange, New Jersey, and marketed his "Country Homes for City People" by delineating ideal residents and their value system in periodicals alongside train schedules into New York City from the development. He engaged A. J. Davis to design a community that combined privately owned tracts of land with common park areas that would be maintained through a homeowners' association. Residents ranged from wealthy businessmen and social reformers to religious enthusiasts, but everyone abided by a single covenant that dictated landscaping, decorating, and architectural guidelines. In addition to his professional career as a New York merchant, Marcus Spring, as mentioned in chapter 4, was a stockholder in the North American Phalanx in Red Bank, New Jersey, at the time he hosted Bremer in Brooklyn, and only a few years later he would form the Raritan Bay Union, another utopian community, in Perth Amboy, New Jersey. As this passage from Bremer demonstrates, even seemingly straightforward pattern books, advice manuals, and periodicals register business motivations and allegiances. Domestic trends buttressed the sales of commodities designed to support them, and print culture, in turn, offered the most influential venue for the diffusion of both.

Editors of rural magazines initially praised ailanthus trees, which Bremer mentioned in one of her missives, while in editorials and advertisements landscape designers and nurserymen recommended the variety as ideal for suburban yards. An article in an 1845 issue of *Dwight's American Magazine* extolled its virtues to readers looking for a trendy, adaptable, attractive, and low-maintenance shade producer for their gardens. Referring to the variety as "the most favorite tree in New York and other places where it is known," the author lauded recent widespread importation of the seeds. It also romanticized the tree's exotic origins, simultaneously tantalizing readers while obscuring its history and associative connotations: "The Ailanthus is a native of the East Indies, probably of Japan; and its name is said to mean in the language of that Island, the Tree of Heaven." Suggesting that the selection and arrangement of trees, shrubs, and plants in a yard communicated something essential (and special) about the homeowner, the article advocated colonialist curatorship as a form of self-expression. "It is important," its author insisted, "that those who appreciate the value of fine trees, and the embellishment of grounds, should be informed on this subject."[4]

Soon, however, people began to view the ailanthus as an invasive species. A front-page editorial in the August 1, 1852, edition of Downing's *Horticulturalist* exclaiming "Down with the Ailanthus!" reflects the regret of homeowners who felt tricked by print recommendations: " 'The vile tree comes up all over my garden,' say fifty owners of suburban lots who have foolishly been tempted into bordering the outsides of their 'yards' with it—having been told that it grows 'so surprising fast.' 'It has ruined my lawn for fifty feet all round each tree,' say the country gentlemen, who, seduced by the oriental beauty of its foliage, have also been busy for years dotting it in open places, here and there, in their pleasure grounds."[5] A spirited debate about the trees played out in many papers in the early 1850s, with many readers writing angrily about the armies of inchworms that the "Tree of Heaven" attracted to their yards. It was too late, though; the ailanthus had taken root throughout Brooklyn as a result of print trends, becoming an element that defined the landscape for residents and visitors alike (even into the twentieth century: the title of Betty Smith's 1943 novel *A Tree Grows in Brooklyn* refers to this species).

References to the tree's "true character" exposed the xenophobic fears that lay just under the surface of, and indeed fueled, consumer orientalism. Maligning the supposedly indigenous traits of populations that had been pictured more rosily (and distantly) in the original vision, Downing cast the plant as a wolf in sheep's clothing, a "usurper" with "the fair outside and the treacherous heart of the Asiatics," hell-bent on "mak[ing] foul the air, with its pestilent breath, and devour[ing] the soil, with its intermeddling roots." The ailanthus debacle, and Bremer's mention of the tree prior to its fall from favor, offer a telling glimpse of the fetishization and co-optation so central to the allure of suburban exodus for many Americans. While the defensiveness and anxiety motivating their removal to the suburbs may manifest themselves more openly in literature of the period, an aesthetic of domestic eclecticism enabled suburbanites to welcome into their homes the very diversity and wildness they supposedly sought to circumvent through relocation—but on their own terms, as accent pieces, in such choices as wallpaper and rug patterns, lamp and furniture shapes, and architectural and landscape styles.

By the early 1860s, most metropolitan papers had begun to publish news briefs from individual suburban towns, which typically included notices of new subdivisions and properties for sale in addition to scores from some of the first baseball games ever played, meeting locations for horticulture societies, and reports of public construction projects such as the erection of streetlights and sidewalks. Specialized papers had even begun to appear that addressed the suburban life exclusively, whether for an individual town, as in the case of the *Brooklyn Daily Eagle,* which debuted in 1855, or collectively, as illustrated by periodicals such as the *Suburban Reporter* and the *Suburban News,* which emerged in New York suburbs during the 1860s (fig. 8). Distributed at the office of the postmaster and at the railroad stations for

FIGURE 8. Masthead of the *Suburban Reporter* (1864). Courtesy American Antiquarian Society.

each suburb, these papers both reflected and cultivated a suburban aesthetic. Reports on the division of country seats into smaller lots, calendars that included strawberry festivals, and reviews of new hotels and railroad facilities spoke to a growing population of Americans who wanted to integrate leisure and recreation into their domestic lives, people who believed in the restorative effects of nature and hoped to erect monuments to themselves and their accomplishments in an environment that asserted mastery over the world of business.

At the same time, the papers themselves testify to a new marketing trend: newspaper *as* advertisement. This development represents a significant shift in thinking about business possibilities in the print medium. Although earlier papers had included advertisements on individual pages, periodical editors like N. P. Willis began to explore branding opportunities for the paper itself. As detailed in chapter 5, increased audience segmentation and appeals to niche interests of readers certainly evolved as a result of improvements in technologies for the manufacture and distribution of print, but we might also consider these explicitly "suburban" papers as a sort of pushback against what many readers had come to consider the hazy generalities and impractical schemes of pattern books from the 1850s. In place of romanticized views, this category of suburban propaganda traded in economy. As the periodical industry itself suburbanized, reaching beyond established audiences and routes toward new strategies for community building and customer engagement, representations of suburban life promoted by proprietors (whether editors, speculators, or merchants) became increasingly brief. Facts and figures predominated; distances to railway stations, lists of amenities, precise estimates of cost, and more explicit identification of potential buyers took center stage. Readers seem to have had a better sense of what they wanted (and sought to avoid); by this period, after all, bustling, growing suburban communities constellated at the edges of most large urban areas in the United States.

A closer look at typical advertisements of property for sale in these suburban papers provides a tangible sense of the shift from image to rationale. Language is direct and concise, with both content and style geared more explicitly to the requirements of its intended audience. These advertisements stick to the basics and are easy to absorb at a glance, ideal for commuters on trains who peruse and skim in a cursory rather than an intensive fashion. Even given the abbreviated descriptions, though, the ads manage to communicate a sense of excitement and energy (figs. 9 and 10). Brief references to clean water, railroad depots, suitable inhabitants, and sidewalks operate as surrogates that speak in a tangible way to larger concerns such as air quality, accessibility and convenience, like-minded neighbors, and modern technologies. These ads still reference a dream, but they do so in a very different way than the pattern books had. Significantly, they assume that it is a widespread vision, and one that, to varying degrees, all readers deserved to realize. Even as they admit that readers who harbored hopes for, in the words of figure 10, "A Country Home for Me!" are part of a much larger trend, they also reinforce the intelligence of such sentiments by invoking high city rents and the beauty and convenience of life in suburban areas. Whether they chose to rent or buy, readers were encouraged to conceive of a move beyond the confines of the city as the right decision—one that would improve the domestic life of families and make work in the city more palatable because of the ability to escape from it in the evenings and on weekends.

REVISING THE PARADIGM
Suburban Hijinks in Cozzens and Coffin

The advertisements I've detailed did more than attempt to sell specific products and real estate: they helped fashion a new architecture of domestic consumption. Publishing routes improved and expanded, broadening book distribution, with the result that phrases such as N. P. Willis's "country life within city reach" soon operated as shorthand for a whole host of

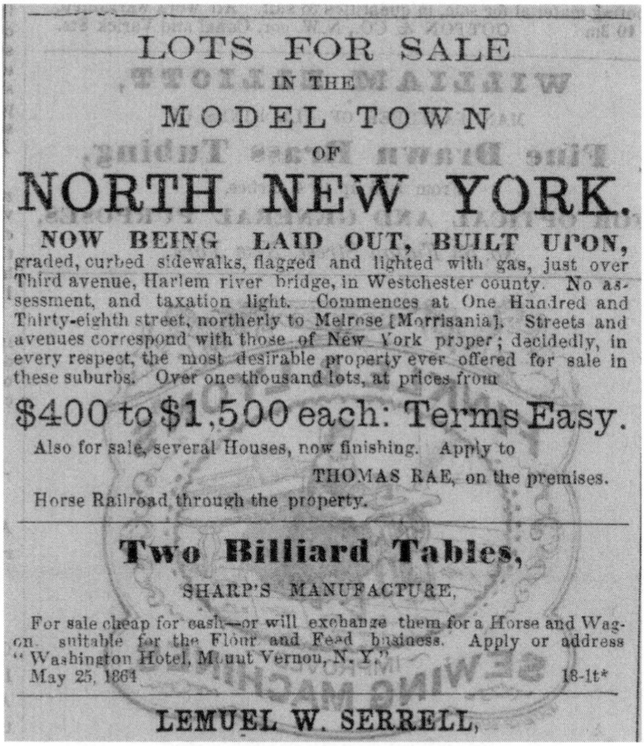
LOTS FOR SALE
IN THE
MODEL TOWN
OF
NORTH NEW YORK.
NOW BEING LAID OUT, BUILT UPON,
graded, curbed sidewalks, flagged and lighted with gas, just over Third avenue, Harlem river bridge, in Westchester county. No assessment, and taxation light. Commences at One Hundred and Thirty-eighth street, northerly to Melrose [Morrisania]. Streets and avenues correspond with those of New York proper; decidedly, in every respect, the most desirable property ever offered for sale in these suburbs. Over one thousand lots, at prices from

$400 to $1,500 each: Terms Easy.

Also for sale, several Houses, now finishing. Apply to
THOMAS RAE, on the premises.
Horse Railroad through the property.

Two Billiard Tables,
SHARP'S MANUFACTURE,
For sale cheap for cash—or will exchange them for a Horse and Wagon, suitable for the Flour and Feed business. Apply or address "Washington Hotel, Mount Vernon, N. Y."
May 25, 1864 18-1t*

LEMUEL W. SERRELL,

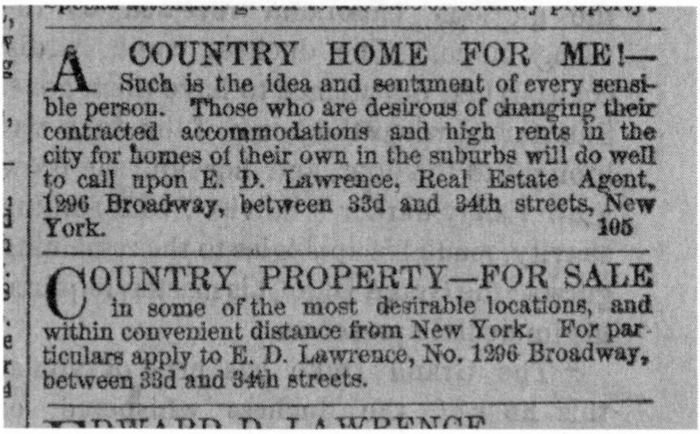
A COUNTRY HOME FOR ME!—Such is the idea and sentiment of every sensible person. Those who are desirous of changing their contracted accommodations and high rents in the city for homes of their own in the suburbs will do well to call upon E. D. Lawrence, Real Estate Agent, 1296 Broadway, between 33d and 34th streets, New York. 105

COUNTRY PROPERTY—FOR SALE in some of the most desirable locations, and within convenient distance from New York. For particulars apply to E. D. Lawrence, No. 1296 Broadway, between 33d and 34th streets.

FIGURES 9–10. Advertisements from (top) the *Suburban Reporter* (1864) and (bottom) the *Suburban News* (1867).

associations fixed in readers' minds by print culture. In a relatively short period of time, homeowners transitioned from a very localized sense of relationality between self and community to a more national understanding of market culture and one's identity as a consumer. New and more reliable transportation options gave Americans increased variety while standardizing expectations. Just as we can see evidence in periodical advertisements of this internalization and solidification of an ideal—what the middle-class home should look like, what purposes it should serve—so too can we trace the spread of a print-based, market-driven ethos in more explicitly literary forms.

Popular country-book authors really lived in the locations they described, so their accounts of the produce they grew, the ice cream they made, the meats they ordered, the spirits they brewed, and the meals they enjoyed constitute clues to the ways in which changes in food production and land use, combined with technological innovations such as the railroad, had begun to afford former city dwellers the amenities of the urban environment minus its hassles. Moreover, combining prescriptive advice with entertaining narrative and glimpses into the private lives of public individuals, these texts overtly promoted specific lifestyle decisions and poses. The agendas and perspectives of their authors, received from one another as much as self-fashioned, molded the reality the writers wished to evoke for readers hungry for details and desirous to replicate them. The concept of home, it turned out, was packageable, and there were textual pleasures (as well as financial incentives) to be had in both wrapping and unwrapping it.

Although books in this genre were not always designated as "country books" at the time when they were written, the subject, tone, and shape of the narrative were identifiable to midcentury readers, authors, and publishers. As examples of the form proliferated in the 1850s, though, representations of suburban domesticity contained within individual volumes started to feel stale. F. W. Shelton, for instance, penned an apologetic preface to *Up the River* (1853), in which he admitted that "many books have already been written of the like design."[6] As Shelton intuitively understood (and realized his readers did as well), the country book's popularity threatened the genre's primary raison d'être: its dedication to voicing the discovery of unique selfhood in a tailor-made environment. Attuning the scale of his narrative to the micro-details of daily experience, he insisted that "happily the subject of the country is still inexhaustible, and there is an infinite variety in the objects which it presents, and in the phases which afford themselves at every turn to the eye of the loving and faithful painter."[7]

Up the River offered small-scale ruminations on experiences of suburban life outside New York City as a textual crystallization of the long-sought intimacies of deep male friendship. In Shelton's estimation, the idiosyncratic jottings of an individual man should be received like a handwritten letter: as communicating a gift of the personal in an era defined by impersonal communication. "One is brought into good company in this book," he proposed, "wherein we have at least a gleam, a twinkle, and a recognition of beautiful thoughts which have been concealed in their setting."[8] Still, he remained painfully aware of the propensity of print to universalize even (and especially) the most original evocations, crafted "in the unwrought vein of epistolary richness." When it felt "true to Nature, the language came home 'familiar as Household Words' to the bosoms of those concerned," ready-made, as it were, to be "pasted in note-books, or folded up, duly endorsed with the date, and deposited in some pigeon-hole for future reference, as a document worthy of being preserved."[9]

In response, the best writers became visibly concerned with the question of how to avoid cliché and speak from the heart about this most loaded of subjects, the home. Some, like Shelton and his literary friend L. W. Mansfield, turned the conundrum to their advantage by intentionally relegating themselves and their readers to the edges of literary interest and accountability in the name of oft-overlooked and rarely voiced avocational domestic pleasures.[10] Others, like Frederic S. Cozzens and Robert Barry Coffin, utilized humor to critique established modes as inimical to the everyday lived experience of novice suburbanites and probe the trade-offs involved in such a massive shift from an earlier, more pastoral way of life to an inescapably networked—and overwhelmingly market-driven—domesticity. Through their exaggerated domestic portrayals, they made peace with the set phrases and pieces and heralded a new era of self-expression and aesthetic gratification through bricolage.

Frederic S. Cozzens was a wine merchant by trade. At an early age he opened a grocery and wine business in Manhattan—the first retail establishment in the state to sell native wines—which he managed through the late 1860s. In the posthumously published autobiographical sketch that opens *Sayings, Wise and Otherwise,* a collection of short essays, he attributed his success to the fact that, in his words, "I always put aside business when I went home, and always put aside literature when I went to business."[11] Cozzens took pride in his ability to balance his career as a merchant with his various literary pursuits, and despite his protestations to the contrary, frequently allowed the two spheres to overlap. In 1854 he founded and edited a monthly magazine dedicated to winemaking and suburban living, titled the *Wine Press,* and continued publication until the war broke out. Throughout his career he contributed regularly to *The Knickerbocker, Putnam's,* and *Hearth and Home,* among other periodicals. He was best known, however, for his best-selling country book *The Sparrowgrass Papers; or, Living in the Country* (1856), a book that drew on the businessman's understanding of the power of rhetoric and image to establish a mood and encourage a sale. In this country book, Cozzens presents readers with an extreme register of the established form, a literary outpost of domestic tourism that comically highlights the motley nature of suburban desire.

"Mr. Sparrowgrass" was Cozzens's pseudonym, and the account of his family's move from New York City to "Chestnut Cottage" in Yonkers became so well known that references to the character's foibles were not uncommon in works by other writers of the day. A feature on the author printed soon after the book's publication in *Ballou's Pictorial Drawing-Room Companion* praised "that happy compound of genial humor, acute observation and good-humored satire, cemented by eloquence, and even pathos" that endeared it to so many readers.[12] Mr. and Mrs. Sparrowgrass arrive in the suburbs with exquisitely detailed fictions in their heads that have been helped along by print culture. Even though they have never lived outside the metropolis, they intuit that the move will do them good, and they take pleasure in rehearsing the details of the life they have envisioned in their new home. After years of mentally caressing "a porch with honey-buds, and sweet-bells, a hive embroidered with nimble bees, a sun-dial mossed over, ivy up to the eaves, curtains of dimity, a tumbler of fresh flowers in your bedroom, a rooster on the roof, and a dog under a piazza," though, they are shocked to discover that "some preconceived notions had to be abandoned, and some departures made from the plans we had laid down in the little back-parlor in Avenue G."[13] The domestic existence they inhabit in actuality bears only a passing resemblance to the sort of life they had imagined took place in the vine-covered suburban cottages in pattern books.

Where they had pictured nouns, in other words, they unearthed verbs. Print culture had taught them to linger over finished products: just as the home outside the city was rhetorically framed as a reward for weekday labors and a mark of professional mastery, so too were the accoutrements that supported the dream's architectural frame ready-made. Because these products didn't have to exist beyond the plane of the page, writers, reformers, and advertisers were able to provide readers with an aura of the homespun and homegrown—a nostalgic, nationalist movement in itself, as Laurel Thatcher Ulrich has shown—without the work. Theirs were print harvests, and the labor involved in reaping the displayed fruit had been relegated to the margins. Mr. and Mrs. Sparrowgrass "moved into the country. . . [with] a looseness of calculation" (*SP,* 14). Once unpacked, they find themselves overwhelmed with things *to do,* rising early "to plant, prune, drill, transplant, graft, train, and sprinkle" (14) and investing in specialized tools and appliances for specific tasks. Mr. Sparrowgrass's domestic hijinks, some unwitting, some affected, constitute the bulk of the book, which moves forward on the premise that the would-be colonizer has been duly colonized—by the land, by consumer culture, and, most distressingly, by his own vision.

The Sparrowgrass Papers trades in naïve expectations and slapstick misjudgments. Whether he is recounting the fiasco that ensues when the couple sit down to plan their kitchen garden with bags of unlabeled seeds from the previous year, bemoaning the discovery that a local boy has stolen the only cherry their fruit tree ever produced, or reminiscing about the experience of drinking sherry with a Captain Bacon of the U.S. Navy while attempting to divert him from looking out the window at their unkempt lawn, Mr. Sparrowgrass's continual experience of bafflement serves to expose the quirks of suburban home life. However outlandish they appear in the many chapters of *The Sparrowgrass Papers,* Mr. Sparrowgrass's mishaps highlight some troubling by-products of new patterns of population and land use that previous articulations of masculine domesticity had overlooked or ignored.

The attraction of the book lay in Cozzens's ability to evoke the feelings of disorientation and disillusionment attendant upon any relocation from urban center to suburban outpost without angering or alienating his readers. By implicating himself in the very thoughts and behaviors he hoped to critique and by softening the blow through humor, Cozzens's narrator insinuates that he is simply one of many bumbling, slightly insane former urbanites trying to build the life of their dreams outside the city. Most chapters open with the pronouncement that it is a "good thing" to do or have something in the country, only to undercut those assertions as problems related to the given activity or commodity unfold. In the process, Cozzens prompts a more conscious awareness of the circulation and perpetuation of domestic trends and standards.

For instance, early in chapter 6, Sparrowgrass declares that "a dumb waiter is a good thing to have in the country, on account of its convenience," as it allows items to be delivered easily from a basement kitchen and an "unbearable" baby to be quickly dismissed to the help during dinner with company. He also remarks on the benefits of having one's floors "deafened" to muffle sound and details the family's fail-proof protection against potential burglars—iron bars on the lower windows and an agreement that the neighbor will appear with a revolver upon a signal rattle emanating from Chestnut Cottage. Thirsty for ice water one evening after everyone has retired, however, Mr. Sparrowgrass finds the kitchen door locked—for safety. Unwilling to awake the house servant to retrieve the key, he decides to descend into the kitchen by way of the dumbwaiter in the hope of accessing the country pump. His miscalculation of the distance of descent turns out to be the least of his worries when he finds himself trapped in a cage of his own making. His cries for help to his wife are of no avail, thanks to the sound-muffling floors, and when his escape attempts finally rouse the dogs, Mrs. Sparrowgrass alerts their neighbor to the perceived danger with the rattle signal. The man arrives with two dogs of his own, a lantern, and his gun, which he starts shooting immediately upon seeing movement through the window. Because Mr. Sparrowgrass can't remember the man's name, he finds himself unable to identify himself convincingly as the rightful owner of his own house. In the aftermath of his domestic trauma, an exasperated Mr. Sparrowgrass fumes over intrusive, demanding neighbors and local gossips who relish eccentric mishaps like the one from which he ultimately emerges unscathed.

In chapter 18, Mr. and Mrs. Sparrowgrass spend an evening reminiscing and contrasting their initial visions with the life they have found in Yonkers. Sifting through "a wilderness of scraps" that they have saved over the years, Mr. Sparrowgrass reflects: "Here are a few more scraps of anticipation, odds and ends of hope, minutes of dead-reckoning. Look now at that list of climbing plants! It was certainly my intention to get each and every one, and if I had, what a gorgeous show the cottage would have made by this time. . . . Then look here; another list! Rural ornaments for gardens, rustic vases, hanging flower-pots, urns, sun-dials, kiosks, arbors, terrace-work, rockwork, and as I live a fountain!" (239). It is not that he regrets their former plans; the evidence of their naïveté is—like his suburban theatrics—oddly endearing and surprisingly understandable. He also, however, finds the stack preposterous rather than visionary, exhausting rather than industrious, and spastic rather than focused. He soberly confesses that "the realization of a hope is sometimes not so beautiful as the hope itself," that "turnpike roads are not always avenues of happiness; that distance simply contemplated from a railroad depot, does not lend enchantment to the view of a load of furniture travelling up hill through a hearty rainstorm; that communion with the visible forms of nature, now and then, fails to supply us with the requisite amount of mild and healing sympathy; that a rustic cottage may be overflowing with love, and yet overflowed with water; that, in fine, living in the country rarely fulfills at once the idea of living in clover" (251–52). Like Cozzens, Sparrowgrass feels compelled to lay the whole picture on the table for the benefit of everyone involved.

Still, the couple agree that the new environment has its benefits, for both of them. Mr. Sparrowgrass is smitten with the physical effects of the country air on his wife's appearance. In a passage that echoes Mitchell's conjuration of "Irving's pretty picture of a wife," Cozzens can't help but take pleasure in the fact that she is turning into a fiction: "The roses again bloom in her cheeks, as well as freckles, big as butter-cups. When I come home in the evening from town, and see her with a dress of white dimity, set off by a dark silk apron, with tasteful pockets, and a little fly-away cap, on the back of her head, she does look bewitching" (27). Mrs. Sparrowgrass, in turn, remarks that suburban life has caused her husband to become "domestic," and he receives the assessment as a compliment (245). Indeed, when Mr. Sparrowgrass asks her if she thinks that "a domestic turn of mind can be better cultivated in the country than in the city" (246), and she replies that she feels it to be the case, he insists it is a fact worth publishing for the benefit of all. Cozzens's country book seeks to illustrate the truth of that claim in a way that combines humor with an honest account of the realities of home life. In *The Sparrowgrass Papers,* he speaks to the gap between imaginative visions and daily struggles—and he attempts to do justice to both extremes through his representations.

Despite all the unrealistic expectations, embarrassing snafus, and costly miscalculations, Mr. Sparrowgrass ultimately refuses to mock idealistic impulses. Dreams, he repeatedly insists, can act as powerful motivators and indices of individual priorities. More significantly, he views them as automatic, unavoidable by-products of a healthy, happy working mind. "Once [a relocation is] settled as a fixed fact, once established as a thing no longer debatable," he maintains, "the idea of living in the country speedily invests itself with its old and happiest colors, puts on cap and kirtle, and cottages the furniture in an Eden of lattice-work, and lawn. Thenceforth every glass-plat in the city becomes an object of interest, every tree a study, every market vegetable a vital topic. Anticipation can scarcely wait upon fluent time; weeks and months seem narrow and long, as the streets we traverse" (251). Mr. Sparrowgrass's dramatic reenactments of personal obsessions and domestic trials serve not to chastise readers for anticipatory imaginings but rather to remind them that, despite initial (or even repeated) setbacks and disappointments, their earliest heart's wishes *can* co-exist with suburban actualities. As inspirational sparks, they inform the final shape, even if they don't ensure it.

After he confesses to his wife that the "brightest and the cheerfullest" winter he spent with her in town prior to their move was "the winter of anticipations—when we were laying out our plans for living in the country" (236), she reminds him of the song he wrote during that time and used to sing to the children, "Oh, A Country Home for Me!". Mr. Sparrowgrass locates the lyrics in an old commonplace book. With the benefit of hindsight, the couple identify inaccurate images and phrases, such as the misinformed notion that swallows "soar" and "sing," but they decide to "let the lines remain, as they shadow forth the idea of what we thought of the country, when we lived in town" (238–39). Just as the song conjures impossible scenes, so too are there "many things which should have been thought of, and which one never does think of as accessories in the ideal picture" (254). Although the cottage life described in the song bears little resemblance to their suburban domesticity, and Mr. Sparrowgrass's "practical bundle of hints cut from newspapers" (240) are not as straightforwardly applicable as stopgap solutions to pressing problems as they pretended, both become valuable as artifacts of a time in their life that was full of longing and hope.

For Mr. Sparrowgrass, yearning occupies space and time. It offers a point of connection between individuals in a world that oftentimes feels isolatingly anonymous and frustratingly mundane. Picturing "the city school-boy and his mates" whom he imagines "pouring forth from the avenues of the town to revel in the ragged grass of the suburbs, to sit, haply, beneath the shadow of a tree, or to bathe in waters that dimple over beaches of sand, instead of beating against piers of weedy timber," he contends that such an instinct is not a preoccupation of youth or naïveté. To the contrary, "it is the prospect of some ideal home in the country that often binds the merchant to the town, in order that he may win a competency to retire with; binds him to the desk until his head begins to silver over, and habit has made the pursuit of wealth a necessity." This same anticipation of future domestic pleasures "haunts the statesman with pictures scarcely less seductive than ambition itself" and "passes like a vision before the eyes of the soldier in the solitary fortress; . . . lulls and cradles the mariner to sleep, in his oaken prison; . . . leads the angler into the depths of the solemn woods; . . . [and] depopulates cities in the sweet summer time" (248–49). Manifestations of that embodied state in print trace the beauty in groupthink and make plain the natural patterns and massive symmetries that continue to gestate even in the most manufactured of mental and physical environments.

In the end, after all, Mr. and Mrs. Sparrowgrass are content with how things turned out. The book itself stands as testament to pleasure in the public performance of suburban shenanigans, especially to an audience familiar with the outlines of the portrayal. For this sort of domestic humor, the more adept the writer at accessing unspoken but seemingly universal aspects of experience in tones that resonate with readers, the sharper and funnier the comedy. The object, Mr. Sparrowgrass soon comes to understand—in very practical ways, as in his interactions with the local carpenter—is not (as Thoreau would have it) to have "an original idea of your own" (*SP,* 51), but rather to don a cap, as it were, knowingly, with a wink. Sparrowgrass would have been pleased, rather than chagrined, to find his song title reproduced word for word in the advertisement displayed in figure 10. In *The Sparrowgrass Papers,* Cozzens embodies the stereotypes in a way that leaves no doubt as to his self-awareness of the doubleness in his representation. He covets suburban manhood ("Such is the idea and sentiment of every sensible man," the advertisement assures readers) at the same time that he points out its prefab failures of imagination (the assertion is mass-produced and ready-made for consumption).

Indeed, it is through the simultaneous vulnerability of the voice and bravado of the styling that he is able to make his critique *precious.* The goal of a smart man's domesticity, Cozzens gently insinuates, has always been to provide fodder for storytelling in the name of male bonding. In evoking the theatrics of everyday life, giving voice to the real ridiculousness and hilarity present in the intricate banalities of suburban routine, Cozzens—via Sparrowgrass, storyteller extraordinaire—forges a link with his readers through a shared realization of the extent to which modes of thinking imported from the business world govern manifestations of bourgeois desire. "Once understood that life in the country does not imply exemption from all the cares and business of ordinary life; that happiness, here as elsewhere, is only a glimpse between the clouds; that there are positive disadvantages incurred by living out of town; and that anticipation must succumb to the customary discount; once understood, and weighed in the balance," he advises, "life in the country becomes settled on a firm basis and puts on its pleasantest aspect" (254). Only upon reconciling self to stage and script can one assemble something new from set pieces.

Apart from what we learn about him in his own writings, there is little biographical information on Robert Barry Coffin. Born in the Hudson River Valley in 1826, he started writing anonymously for periodicals immediately after college. After a stint as a bookkeeper for a New York importing house between 1845 and 1849, he left for health reasons and opened a bookstore with his brother in Elmira, New York, in 1852. He briefly considered a career in the Episcopal clergy but returned to the city in 1857 and began to pursue writing in earnest. In 1858 he was named assistant editor at N. P. Willis's *Home Journal,* to which he had contributed anonymously since 1849. At the same time, he assumed the position of art critic for the *Evening Post.* From 1863 to 1869 and from 1875 until shortly before his death in 1886, while publishing his writing in book form and continuing to write for the periodical press, he also worked as an auditor's clerk in the New York Custom House. In his later years, he edited a monthly publication devoted to gastronomy called *The Table* (in 1873) and contributed culinary-themed articles to a Philadelphia magazine, *The Caterer* (from 1882 to 1886).[14]

At the height of Coffin's literary career in the mid-1860s, he was celebrated for the humorous sketches about domestic life that he wrote for various periodicals and eventually published as *My Married Life at Hillside* (1865), *Matrimonial Infelicities* (1865), *Out of Town* (1866), *Cakes and Ale at Woodbine* (1868), and *Castles in the Air and Other Phantoms* (1871).[15] These writings were received by readers as the poetic sketches of a man who had approached marriage with caution, only to become enamored of the routines of home life, especially upon discovering that he could retain elements of his former bachelor lifestyle in the suburbs. Like Frederic Cozzens, Robert Barry Coffin sought to take the lid off representations of connubial partnership in the country-book genre, but not everyone welcomed the realism. A review of *Matrimonial Infelicities* in *The Round Table* rejected Coffin's "commonplaces" as unfit for any venue more permanent than a story paper and chastised him for airing domestic squabbles in public company. "Married life has its ripples like all life," the reviewer wrote, "but it is no such inane humbug as this russet volume would lead us to believe. If a man and woman who have loved each other enough to be married are so foolish as to engage in petty disputes, it is certainly of no possible account to the outside world. And he who tries to catch the popular ear by lifting the curtain from private scenes, must submit to the verdict when called both common and unrefined."[16] Others, though, appreciated the revisionist approach: an advertising note from the publisher for *Out of Town* in the same periodical a year later suggested that both married and single men would find humor in Gray's account of his life story and quoted a *Brooklyn Eagle* review that praised its verisimilitude in relation to the lived experience of readers as a breath of fresh air.[17]

Like his fictional counterpart, Coffin moved to Fordham from New York City in the mid-1860s. At that time, the area now known as the Bronx had become a popular locale for raising a family outside the city. The completion of the New York and Harlem River Railroad in 1841, along with new road construction, had transformed a rural landscape into a suburban paradise over the course of two decades. As Lloyd Ultan and Barbara Unger recount in *Bronx Accent:* "Stations erected in the middle of nowhere attracted businesses and people, and new villages, such as Mott Haven, Tremont, and Williamsbridge, sprouted up around them seemingly overnight. These transformed the Bronx over time to a suburb, with residents commuting by railroad to their jobs in New York City. One of these new settlements was the village of Fordham."[18] Edgar Allan Poe had relocated to Fordham from Manhattan in 1846 in the hope of curing his wife's tuberculosis, and after his death in 1849 the town became especially attractive to the literati. The Irish poet John Savage moved there during the Civil War and soon talked Coffin into moving there as well.

Coffin published *Out of Town: A Rural Episode* in 1866, a text that opens with a fairly traditional (by country-book standards) discussion between Mr. Gray and his wife about whether they should seek "cheaper," "healthier," and "pleasanter" domestic accommodations beyond the city (iv). After visiting "a large number of 'suburban retreats'" (2) in search of a choice place to live, the narrator singles out a particular village about an hour away from his business, which he describes as a "quiet, unpretentious little place, nestled on and among the hills, with sundry picturesque houses, and an air of thrift pervading its people that was delightful to witness" (v). After they move, he designates his new home "Woodbine Cottage" after the vine that grows around the front veranda. The location offers urban and rural amenities of the sort advertised in *Woodward's Country Homes,* a popular architectural pattern book published in 1865 that encouraged "those who look to a full measure of comfort" to turn their attention to "a suburban life, ten to fifteen miles away from the unceasing noise of the city, where the business of the day is forgotten, and fresh air, fresh milk, butter, eggs, fruit, flowers, birds, etc. are luxuries unknown in town."[19]

The established mode of representation ends early, however. The author gives both his alter ego and his readers barely enough time to settle in to their surroundings before he fine-tunes the view. A sheepish admission that the vine covering Woodbine Cottage is not woodbine but honeysuckle signals Coffin's interest in manipulating romanticized norms. In *Out of Town* and its sequel, *Cakes and Ale at Woodbine,* Coffin represents Barry Gray embracing new domestic rhythms with unprecedented relish. As the man of the house transforms into a suburban epicure over the course of the series, readers witness an extreme example of a man discovering a passion for home economics. The scenes and situations are intended to provoke mirth in their over-the-top execution, but Gray's expertise is nothing to laugh about. Additionally, the level of detail included in Coffin's country books suggests a familiarity on the part of the author with the methods and recipes Gray shares with his wife and friends. Coffin presents readers with a breadwinner *and* bread maker, a man who—unapologetically and even with pride—finds his second calling in the artful preparation and combination of culinary flavors and textures and reshapes his family's understanding of domesticity in the process. In doing so, he seeks to develop Americans' literary and cultural palate for a more flexible definition of manhood.

Outside New York City, Mr. Gray can experiment with growing his own food while easily supplementing his produce with items from the urban market. In his half-acre garden, he allocates space for peas, beans, corn, potatoes, tomatoes, cucumbers, squash, pumpkins, melons, beets, lettuce, and radishes, in addition to an orchard with apple trees and grapevines. Although he eventually hires a gardener to help him maintain it, he takes pride in the fact that he can grow his vegetables in the country "for much less than I could purchase them in town,—besides having the advantage of getting them fresh from the garden" (*OT,* 14). With eggs from their chickens, his wife makes "custards, puddings, and cakes," and he concocts "noggs and mulls" (14). He buys milk from neighboring milkmaids, and every other day in warm weather an iceman delivers ice for the refrigerator, which in turn preserves their meats and "fancy dishes" (10). Barrels of ale are obtained in town or delivered by the brewers themselves. And all of it can be enjoyed in the company of good friends. He has room to grow mint for mint juleps, neighbors who provide fresh eggs and milk for the eggnog with strawberries and cream that he enjoys while reading, and plenty of space to store barrels of ale for gatherings of friends. At the same time, he doesn't have to abandon the amenities of New York City: the oyster soup, ice cream, brandied peaches, turkey, venison, raisins, almonds, and cakes that he loves can appear at a moment's notice.

The realization that his physical location allows him to experience the best of both culinary worlds awakens an unanticipated devotion to domesticity that temporarily threatens to interfere with his business obligations on Wall Street. Even though his job in the city is within easy commute, he finds himself "continually seeking reasonable excuses for not going into town every day" (12). In a more immediate way than his job as a clerk on Wall Street, domestic work produces material results, especially gastronomically. The effort expended in taking care of the chickens and gathering their eggs, for instance, yields the special reward of sharing fresh eggnog with his "savage literary friend" (14). While his novel respect for home duties would typically point, narratively, toward a recognition of his wife's efforts in that arena, Gray has no qualms about taking the reins from her, bypassing her focus on nutrition and economy in favor of beauty, taste, and conviviality. Even as the exasperated reactions of Mrs. Gray would imply that her husband's newfound commitment to food preparation is overzealous and certainly unnecessary, Coffin urges readers of both sexes to resist judgment, as men's unorthodox domestic regimens promised to reinvigorate the environment for the whole family. Beginning in *Out of Town,* Coffin's episodic narratives depict men who come to anticipate opportunities for personal expression and social fraternity in suburbs.

As Mr. Gray grows accustomed to life at Woodbine Cottage, he contemplates the foundations of good food. The availability of fresh produce and dairy products increases his interest in the taste of what he consumes, and he begins to think more about ingredients. His detailed description of the process of making and presenting the eggnog he enjoys with his artist friend John Savage reflect a new awareness: he relates how he locates the "freshest-laid eggs," brings out "the ancestral punch-bowl" and "a bottle of old Jamaica," and "a quart of pure milk, with the cream beginning to rise on the surface" (14–15), adding sugar and nutmeg to concoct "a drink worthy of being commemorated in verse . . . while conviviality and good-fellowship ruled the hour" (15). These sorts of moments, in which a culinary experience creates a mood that is conducive to conversation and reflection, become central to Mr. Gray's happiness. He jokes to his wife that the taste of eggnog made with fresh eggs and milk is reason enough to relocate away from the city. While he laughs at the extreme nature of his comment, his life in Fordham has given him a different understanding of the ends of domestic organization and labor. For the first time, he approaches food as a vehicle for community and sympathy as well as meditation and relaxation.

As Mr. Gray manifests increased involvement in domestic decision making, his wife does not know whether she should invite or resist his intrusions into her domain. By criticizing her suppers and her reluctance to host dinner parties, he calls into question her position as head of the realm. Remarking, for instance, that although her meal preparation "provided munificently for the family proper," she "had not laid in a sufficient store of the good things of this life to have satisfied, in a hospitable manner, the additional appetites which gathered around our mahogany" (50), he hints that their daily routine could benefit from a fresh male perspective. Mrs. Gray might understand that her husband's friends who are visiting for a few days would not be satisfied with "simple salt codfish and potatoes" (50), but she is too paralyzed to think of an adequate alternative. Even as he praises his wife's planning and labor, his masculine sensory awareness distinguishes his domestic efforts. Because of his ingenuity and foresight, he and his friends do not have to leave the home space in order to entertain themselves.

Mr. Gray's success at hosting prompts him to try his hand at planning Thanksgiving dinner in the hope of making it a more satisfying celebration for the whole family. Declaring that he would like a spread of the sort that he enjoyed at his grandmother's house as a child, he informs his wife that they have a duty to supply both quantity and quality for the table. On his menu list are "oysters, soup, fish, turkey, chicken-pie, vegetables innumerable, and pastry and dessert unlimited" as well as "a roasted pig, . . . a young, succulent, and crisply-cooked morsel, innocent of the sty, and stuffed with sweet smelling and savory herbs" (147–48). Mrs. Gray scoffs at his demands, proclaiming that meals like the ones provided by his grandmother are a thing of the past, but it soon becomes clear that her husband will not take no for an answer. Using their location as an excuse for his seeming extravagance, he argues that the country offers an opportunity to celebrate nature and family in ways that the city prevents. For men who live in the city, holidays like Thanksgiving offer little more than a day away from work, while their property in Fordham is naturally festive. After a magnificent dinner that celebrates the bounty of the earth, he could enjoy conversation with neighbors over tea and a game of whist accompanied by a pipe and a mug of ale or cider. In his vision, family prayers and a hymn would end the evening, rounding out a day of rejuvenation and celebration by all. His wife relinquishes control, and although she afterwards balks at the amount of brandy in the mince pies and wine in the pudding sauce, it is clear that both she and the children have enjoyed themselves.

After Thanksgiving, Mr. Gray is inspired to extend his repertoire from the aesthetics of consumption into the art of food preparation. He details the process of styling a dish and serving it to others. Declaring himself an expert on the subject of the country breakfast, with its "buckwheat cakes, country-made sausages, a delicate roll or two, and a cup of Mocha coffee, with cream" (206), he describes the shape and texture of a perfect pancake and lingers over the perfectly cooked sausage, which is "a little crispy, reminding one just a trifle of the cracklings of roasted pig" (206). His wife and servant become captive assistants to his plans as he decides to oversee the culinary production from start to finish. The sausage recipe he provides to his wife—and the reader—elevates the preparation of an everyday breakfast to the status of an art, wherein method makes all the difference when one is faced with a relatively fixed list of ingredients. "The mixing of these various ingredients," the recipe warns, "so that no one savor predominates—should be as carefully wrought as in making a salad. It is not everyone who can properly accomplish this, any more than can every one create a salad. It requires judgment in preparing the combinations, skill in putting them together, and an appreciative taste. Then it should be made into small cakes, and fried slowly and kindly in its own fat" (206–7).

While his servant does the actual frying, he supervises the entire procedure, recalling a failed attempt to fry the sausages in olive oil and a subsequent return to sausage fat. His opinions on and knowledge of the subject surprise his wife, who asks him if he has been surreptitiously attending a nearby French cooking academy in his spare time. Gray admits that he has not, then jokingly claims to have "serious intentions of visiting it" in order to "put the professor up to one or two ideas in the preparation of certain new dishes," such as green corn pudding (207). Although he takes pleasure in amusing his wife with this retort, his instructions are earnest in their suggestion that the true cook combines discernment, talent, and patience. In this sort of moment, Coffin employs humor to disarm the reader's knee-jerk reaction to a character like Mr. Gray by making Mrs. Gray a representative of a more traditional, female-centered domesticity. At the same time, he allows the denigration of women's capacity to create a meal that feeds the soul in addition to the body to stand unchallenged. Although his wife might please him with her pies or simple meals, he unseats her as the practical, as well as titular, head of the household.

Coffin's next country book, *Cakes and Ale at Woodbine; From Twelfth Night to New Year's Day*, centers almost exclusively on food, and more specifically, on Mr. Gray's resolution toward the end of *Out of Town* to celebrate gastronomically as many holidays as possible. With an additional year's experience of country living under his belt, the types of dishes that Gray describes and serves to his family and friends are increasingly exotic and complicated. He and his male friends, who have similar culinary interests, begin exchanging recipes, which he in turn shares with his wife and the reader. A conversation with his friend Tomaso, for example, convinces him that an omelet is the most delicate breakfast one could serve to a houseguest.

He explains the proper preparation and presentation essential to the dish's success: the pan should be continually agitated during the frying, as " 'Ships at Sea,' to and fro," and the omelet served on a warm plate, garnished with a sprig of parsley (*CAW,* 73–74). It is Tomaso, fresh from cooking classes with an Italian opera-singer-turned-cook, who recommends that Mr. Gray travel to New York City to obtain ostrich eggs for the ultimate omelet. Armed with the food options available to him in the country and an understanding of and appreciation for meal preparation and taste combinations, he turns to the city market for new flavors and techniques.

Whereas accounts of variations on ham and eggs in La Mancha, Spain, and other parts of the world fascinate Mr. Gray, Mrs. Gray tries to slip out of the room whenever he starts talking about food. In the opening pages of *Cakes and Ale at Woodbine,* she declares that she has lost interest in his " 'deep quaffings' and 'hobnobbings' " and fears that "[his] mind runs too much upon eating and drinking" (10). She complains to him that the pleasant accounts of their domestic life made public in his earlier country books and periodical contributions have been replaced by endless recountings of "breakfasts, dinners, and suppers with your bachelor friends." She takes particular offense at the title *Cakes and Ale at Woodbine,* as it makes it seem as though their entire domestic existence revolves around food, laying forth their home as a consumable, "just for all the world as if our little cottage were a restaurant or a red-latticed ale-house, and you were going to publish the bill of fare" (10). Family time, religious holidays, social gatherings with friends, and domestic labor, she implies derogatorily, have all come to revolve around culinary efforts and the pursuit of particular tastes and sensations. It seems unrepentantly self-centered, inexcusably self-indulgent.

Mr. Gray defends himself against his wife's charges by arguing that writing about cakes and ale cannot help but illustrate larger home felicities. To help her reframe her reading of his suburban enthusiasms, he reveals the title of his newest book and its subject:

> "Instead of being everlastingly occupied in talking, as you surmise, about stuffing myself and the children"—I purposely left my wife's name out of the list—"with sweet cakes, pan-cakes, plum-cakes, short-cakes, johnny-cakes, and indeed, every other kind of cakes under the sun, and pouring

down their throats and my own, countless mugs of sparkling, foaming, creamy, October, imperial, pale, X, XX, XXX, old, and new ales, I intend to treat the subject aesthetically; regarding the title simply as meaning the good things of this life, the joys and blessings, the comforts and delights, the smiles and laughter, the soft answer that turneth away wrath, and the soothing word that drieth up tears, the bright glance of the eye, the gentle pressure of the hand, the kiss of love, and, in short, a reflex of the sunny hours and days which you and I, my dear, together with these little ones, and all who may dwell under this roof-tree with us, may pass in Woodbine Cottage." (13)

Eccentric and exclusionary as it might appear at first glance, the relentless pursuit of gustatory pleasures, when facilitated by the ideal mix of market amenities and homegrown bounty, demonstrates a deep commitment to one's surroundings and the ingenuity to turn its "raw materials," whether tillable soil or ingredients brought home from the city via railroad, into creative expressions of selfhood. If he can make food speak through careful attention to its growth patterns, taste affinities, and methods of preparation, there is no reason why he can't then unhinge the vocabulary from its native scaffolding to enable it to do more work for him.

Following this conversation with his wife, Mr. Gray arrives at a radical understanding of the role of food in the domestic environment. When he suggests that they celebrate his sister's birthday with a pie and his wife replies that she doesn't have time to make one, he proclaims that the mere invocation of pie is enough, that "it is not necessary to actually have a pie on these occasions,—the spirit of the thing is all that is required" (30). Memories of past pies, he insists, can provide the sought-for gratification. To illustrate his point, he tells his wife that he always thinks about delicious pies from his past when he is "participating in some unusually delightful festivity," so much so that he conceives of a particularly memorable event or moment as an "extra slice of pie of my boyhood" (30–31). Referring to any pleasurable experience as "cutting a pie," he claims both that a good meal can influence a person's thoughts and emotions, and, less obviously, that certain experiences and feelings can trigger memories or sensations associated with particular foods. As he declares to Mrs. Gray on a picnic with their children, the outing itself is the very best cake and ale he could ever ask for. While Mr. Gray certainly appreciates the taste and appearance of dishes and drinks, he also values the opportunities for conversation, education, culture, relaxation, celebration, and meditation that food provides. For him, the pleasures of good eating do not come at the expense of other domestic obligations or experiences. Rather, they help mark important moments as well as create occasions for them—the essence of domesticity.

Manifesting a domestic goodwill that transcends categorical boundaries, Gray freely borrows from his surroundings and expertise to suit his needs and desires. Using intuition as a guide, he welcomes serendipitous and eclectic exchanges and interminglings, all in the name of palate cultivation. Firm in his belief in the overlap between sensory experiences and aesthetic vocabularies, he understands his voice in terms of his role as host. Whether finalizing the details of a holiday menu, leading a family picnic excursion, or drafting a country book, he prides himself on transforming an otherwise humdrum existence into an occasion worthy of commemoration. Originality, in Gray's suburban routine, literarily or otherwise, materializes via the internalization of passion-borne intimacies and a tinkerer's hankering for a better way. While his wife may view his behavior as exploitative and cavalier, he labels it generous and thoughtful.

Toward the end of *Out of Town,* Gray gathers his wife, children, and live-in writer-apprentice/governess/sometimes-love-interest Miss Floy in the library on Christmas Eve to read them a story he claims to have written during his bachelor years, titled "My Family in Utopia." Initially his tale seems to be a relatively simple representation of a bachelor longing for a wife and children, along the lines of Mitchell's *Reveries of a Bachelor,* with a fictional Mr. Gray sitting in his easy chair in his study before a blazing fire, "lost in a golden reverie" of an ideal vision of married life (*OT,* 221). This Mr. Gray lives in a Manhattan boardinghouse and works as a bank clerk, but manages to visit his family in Utopia several times a year, traveling by balloon "to the vine-clad cottage in which they live." He admits, however, "I have never been able to learn exactly where Utopia is situated, though I have made diligent search for it on many maps, at various times" (221).

Apparently the Mr. Gray who narrates the story is the incarnation of a redeemed bachelor as he sits with his family in the library on Christmas

Eve, but there are aspects of his tale that push against that characterization. Within the story, Mr. Gray continually insists that his Utopian family is *not* simply the product of reverie. Whenever distance causes him to question "whether, after all, I am really a husband and father; or, if it be not simply a dream,—well defined, indeed, and like reality; but still only a dream, a very myth" (250), he checks his Bible and finds the marriage and childbirths recorded there. As if to corroborate this evidence, he refers to his bachelor days in the past tense, and the children of the story share the names of his real children. Moreover, the language and imagery Mr. Gray uses to describe Utopia, with its "woodbine-covered cottages" and "picture[s] of loveliness" seen "in the soft sunshine and roseate light, nestled between green hill-sides" (243), are strikingly similar to his descriptions of the suburban home and community that open *Out of Town.*

To make matters more puzzling, even as he romanticizes his suburban netherworld, the Mr. Gray of "My Family in Utopia" does not profess any desire to relinquish his ties to Manhattan. As much as he treasures his family in Utopia, he takes pride, he claims, in the fact that "few persons of my acquaintance suspect my being at the head of a family." By playing the part of a bachelor while in the city, he has been able to avoid the "signs" that "denote either the husband or father," such as wrinkles, gray hair, and care-worn sighs. "There is much to convince my friends that I am unmarried," he remarks. "I am well preserved; my constitution is unimpaired; my step as elastic as it was twenty years ago; and, I am gratified to be able to say it, I whistle as I walk" (222). While he celebrates his capacity to change modes effortlessly, to, he says, "put off, as I would a garment, the mildewed air of a bank clerk, and assume the sunshiny lounge of a man of leisure," for example, he makes no attempt to conceal the staged nature of the act: "I do not, however, suppose that my assumed character imposes on any one. I feel the disguise is altogether too feeble. I can detect such in another as quickly as I do a counterfeit bill" (224).

The performance, like its literary corollary in "My Family in Utopia," is self-generated and self-motivated, a commentary on the status quo rather than an attempt to subvert it. "I take the character simply to please myself," he remarks, "and, as I stroll up Broadway, among gaily attired ladies and well-dressed men, I forget that I am nailed, like a spurious coin, to a bank desk, while I revel for a time in the brief Arcadian dream of happiness I conjure up" (224). Although he blames financial constraints for his decision to keep his family life—imagined or realized—a secret, he seems to be glad that his employers and friends, he reports, "regard me as a single man." The geographic separation between his work and home life affords him variety and spice, allowing him the freedom to try on various roles without feeling bound to any of them. Moreover, such physical gaps facilitate the illusion of self-sufficiency and the glorification of private desire that comes along with it. Within the story, Gray assures himself that it is better "for [his family] to be here in Utopia, with its delightful climate and sunny skies, than in the unhealthy city, with its noise and dust" (224).

Despite the fact that the Mr. Gray who is telling the story wants to cast his current situation as a realization of his utopian bachelor dreams, in another sense it reflects the author's current situation. After all, Mr. Gray still considers himself a businessman. He commutes to and from Wall Street on a daily basis and adjusts his speech, dress, and thought patterns to fit the exigencies of each environment. In a very real way, the narrator's family still resides in Utopia and his moments of storytelling in the library are nothing more than "visits" from a husband and father whose professional obligations in the city control the fate of the very dream they purport to serve. As a meditation on the machinations of suburban romanticization and a recognition of his own complicity in its production as a writer of country books, Gray's story highlights the slipperiness of the view presented and of the protagonist doing the telling.

Coffin and Cozzens know they cannot refrain from embellishment and flourish, even as they hope to intervene in the genre's genealogy by demanding a level of realism and accountability. Like the other authors treated in this book, they are in search of a locale where reverie and physical reality are not in conflict, where domestic space is as much mental as material, where it is not a matter of "either/or" but instead one of "both/and." They trace the roots of the dream alongside their readers to an urban garret and a man beset by business concerns and deep-seated longings. On some level, everyone knows the longings will never be appeased. And so the writer asks the reader (and himself) to make do with what he has, to take his "wilderness of scraps" and his hours of "book farming" and indulge the play. As his is a desire propagated in print, it is only right that its flowering take place on the page as well. In any case, in the course of the telling, a curious and unanticipated occurrence takes place. The teller finds the identity he was looking for in moveable type—the ultimate suburb—in the set pieces that can be rearranged and combined at will, each combination a little different, channeling a simple but beautiful wish and broadcasting a self-conscious incantation over an otherwise anonymous, ubiquitous, unremarkable domestic drama.

AFTERWORD
Suburban Nostalgia, Then and Now

If the recent critical success of *Mad Men* is any indication, suburban nostalgia is alive and well. The surprise-hit television drama, which aired its first season on AMC in the summer of 2007, follows a group of 1960s advertising executives as they shuttle between their day jobs on Madison Avenue and their evenings and weekends in the New York and New Jersey suburbs. The main character, Don Draper, is a brilliant, mysterious adman struggling to come to terms with his identity and life purpose, all the while juggling a secret history and city mistresses with his suburban domestic routine. In early seasons, as viewers learn more about Don (played by Jon Hamm) and his wife, Betty (January Jones), as well as members of the supporting cast, characters who initially appeared to be stock cutouts are revealed to be complexly driven, committed, questioning, and conflicted individuals who sense the ways in which their work and home lives define and constrict them even as they experience moments of desire, pleasure, happiness, love, and creative fulfillment in their drab offices and manicured suburban boxes. The fact that the rise of *Mad Men*'s cult following coincided with public conversations about the impending "death of suburbia" as a combined result of a new urbanism and the "greening" of America, rising gas prices, the subprime mortgage crisis, and a tanking economy raises questions about the show's success. More specifically, why were so many people able to embrace the 1960s aesthetic that *Mad Men* embodied at the same time they were decrying the shells of communities that had been left to rot, or worse, to be occupied by ethnic minorities and working-class families who suddenly could not afford to go anywhere else?

In the last episode of season one, Don presents an ad campaign for a new Kodak slide projector, and his pitch takes on surprisingly personal overtones as he stocks the mechanism with slides of family photos. When the Kodak representatives ask if he has found a way to "work the wheel" into his ad, Don replies: "Technology is a glittering lure, but there is the rare occasion when the public can be engaged on a level beyond flash—if they have a sentimental bond with the product. My first job—I was in-house at a fur company, with this old-pro copywriter, a Greek named Teddy. And Teddy told me the most important idea in advertising is 'NEW'—it creates an itch. You simply put your product in there as a kind of calamine lotion. But he also talked about a deeper bond with the product: nostalgia. It's delicate, but potent." The carousel starts up; photos of the Draper family appear, one after another, as Don continues: "Teddy told me that in Greek, *nostalgia* literally means 'the pain from an old wound.' It's a twinge in your heart, far more powerful than memory alone. This device isn't a spaceship; it's a time machine. It goes backwards, forwards, takes us to a place where we ache to go again. It's not called the wheel; it's called the carousel. It lets us travel the way a child travels, around and around and back home again to a place where we know we are loved."[1] The clip ends with a mock-up ad for the "Kodak Carousel."

While Don's presentation is intended to market a specific product, the juxtaposition of his words with candid snapshots from his suburban home life links nostalgia to the domestic sphere. As Don self-consciously voices his desire for a past that never really was, he reflects on the decisions he has made and the paths he has taken. His presentation takes on the quality of metanarrative when viewers of the clip interrogate their own investment in a show that invites a similar sense of nostalgia through the invocation of a ritualized, historically situated suburban lifestyle.

Don never mentions manhood in his monologue; on the surface, nothing appears to be further from his mind than concerns about what it means to be a man in America—and yet his vision is inflected by this unvoiced, unrecognized referent. Indeed, his recognition of nostalgia as a powerful motivating impulse—one that can be harnessed by others, in turn, for their own purposes—has much to tell us about the nature of both domesticity and masculinity, the slippery way in which known—if imagined—geographic, historical, and ideological landscapes silently impress themselves on the memory, taxing its contents, informing its dreams, and determining its limits. Collectively enfranchised (in many instances through print culture), specific modes of thinking and doing are reborn and purified in the built environment, rights and privileges made manifest in the structures and objects that surround us in our everyday lives.

In *The Past Is a Foreign Country*, the geographer David Lowenthal describes nostalgia as "the foreign country with the healthiest tourist trade of all."[2] If we apply this notion to the concept of suburbia on the one hand, as the "Carousel" clip from *Mad Men* overtly invites us to do, and masculinity on the other, which it does so less obviously but no less insistently, we gain a new perspective on the content I have discussed in *Suburban Plots*. Even the earliest suburban developments, after all, were both forward- and backward-looking in orientation—fundamentally nostalgic attempts to infuse utopian hopes for the future with rosy visions of the past. Fueled by desires for the distance associated with travel to foreign parts and accompanying experiences of touristic play, they functioned simultaneously as places of escape and embrace. These carefully situated and appointed enclaves enabled their male inhabitants to structure participation in domestic rites and ends as nothing more (nor less) than a series of immersive visits to the sites they claimed to value most. So too did acts of appropriation and exclusion take place in the formation of suburbs, as it was only a certain type of person who could plan and enjoy these particular domestic vacations, often at the expense of the individuals who buttressed the paradisiacal view.

White-collar, upper-middle-class white Americans groomed a new vision of manhood as they dug and built, razed and reshaped the land on which they and others resided. Visible boundary formation and invisible, J. B. Jackson reminds us, go hand in hand.[3] At the same time, they were forced to acquiesce to the notion that what the suburbs did best, perhaps, was teach them how to be citizens, husbands, fathers, and friends in absentia. While we often start from the premise that the built environment seeks to house or protect known entities and freedoms, the evidence I have presented suggests that the process is not unidirectional.

As much as the male authors treated in this book called readers' attention to new opportunities for identity formation and creative expression in cottages located outside but within reach of cities along the northeastern seaboard, their articulations of masculine domesticity initially were driven by certain modes of behavior and types of people that should *not* constitute it. "Safe" in their suburban homes, they continually surveyed the threat from a distance, the mystery and unmappedness of what existed beyond the carefully constructed fence and door, wall and window, which haunted them with the suggestion that it was *they* who were removed and disenfranchised, that somewhere along the path of industry they had lost the essence of the dream that had motivated it in the first place. They found themselves, in other words, simultaneously hinged and unhinged, architects of their own undoing. The violence (to land, to people, to self) that enabled their freedoms stubbornly refused complete erasure, clean lines and orderly grids acting, mockingly, as monuments to control and mastery gone awry. What they claimed as their birthright materialized differently than they had imagined: they found themselves bound together in a shared inheritance that did not require their presence, let alone their assent or action, in order to stand and deliver. They were only (and by choice) de facto citizens, the ultimate suburbanites, tourists to their own constitutions.

After all, what is the suburban landscape if not alien and infinitely unknowable? Popular movies like *The 'Burbs* and *American Beauty,* television series including *Weeds, The Sopranos,* and *Desperate Housewives,* and books such as Sinclair Lewis's *Babbitt* and Don DeLillo's *White Noise* testify to the weirdness of clipped lawns and prefab houses, not to mention the people who live in them. In the words of Thomas Harris in *The Silence of the Lambs,* "This was somebody's environment, chosen and created, a thousand light-years across the mind from the traffic crawling down Route 301."[4] Artist Sarah McKenzie's aerial paintings of suburbs similarly highlight the disembodied quality of suburban neighborhoods, the unnerving results of human efforts to dig patterns into the earth with economy, rapidity, precision, and consummate reproducibility. Whether in the middle decades of the nineteenth century or of the twentieth, suburban nostalgia helped American men make peace with masculinity's precondition: estrangement. At once saving grace and Achilles' heel, it promised a blueprint to something better in "the pain from an old wound," a path out of the wilderness and into it all at once. Even in the most banal, fake suburban communities, where every house looks staged and every family seems mass-produced from some mold that we can no longer locate, nostalgia assures us that serious work is afoot. Agency locates itself somewhere, after all. Long after its denizens are dead, its furnishings sold, and appointments scattered, the structure housing mind and body remains as archive, pointing homeward. Perhaps, returning to David Lowenthal's association of nostalgia with tourism, we would do well to heed his warning that "like other tourists, those to the past imperil the object of their quest."[5] That's a truth we already know, though. One we love, even.

HOWELLS'S ANAESTHETIZED LANDSCAPES

Although nineteenth-century suburbs looked very different from the suburbs of today, representations by the writers discussed in this book established the groundwork for popular conceptions of suburban domestic life that remain with us today. By the late 1860s, the businessman had become a recognizable figure in American culture, in large part as a result of the midcentury literature that depicted men shuttling between their paperwork in the city and family life in the suburbs. Asserting the necessity of helping those who had little knowledge and even less time to improve the appearance of their yards, suburban "idea books" like Frank J. Scott's *Art of Beautifying Suburban Home Grounds of Small Extent* (1870) employed tactical details to cement and legitimize what they insisted was a complementary dreamy view of self-realization in the suburbs. Advising that "a velvety lawn, flecked with sunlight and the shadows of common trees, is a very inexpensive, and may be a very elegant refreshment for the business-wearied eye," Scott urged readers to approach their domestic desires in an organized, businesslike fashion.[6] Reinforcing the notion that a satisfying domestic life is the universal reason for labor, these lifestyle manuals, in turn, extended the courtesy of professionalism to their readers, promising the pleasurable perusal of facts and figures that, in the businessman's mind anyhow, constructed the romantic ideal.

By articulating goals, acquiring financial capital, drawing up plans, and executing them in a timely fashion, publishers suggested, readers could (with the help of a book) apply themselves (productively!) to the fulfilling art of suburban home ownership. The author of *Atwood's Country and Suburban Homes* (1871) dedicated the volume "to the seeking millions / whose faith in, and love for a home lightens / every toil and self-denial / exerted in its behalf."[7] Associating the place of work with "self-denial," Atwood urged his readers to embrace customized pleasures at home. Proceeding from the implicit understanding that every workingman had the same goal in mind, suburban planners were able to produce cookie-cutter designs while also

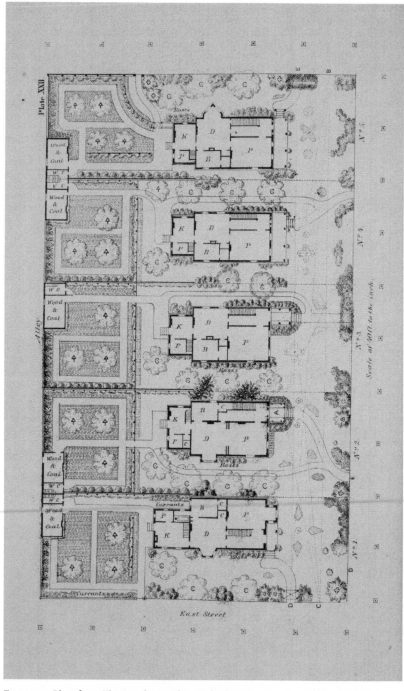

FIGURE 11. Plate from *The Art of Beautifying Suburban Home Grounds of Small Extent* (1870). Courtesy American Antiquarian Society.

reifying a sense of individualism (fig. 11). As Scott remarks in chapter 15, "Plans of Residences and Grounds":

> Every intelligent reader knows that no two building lots are often exactly alike in any respect. Not only in size and form, but in elevation, in shape of surface, in the exposure of the front to the north, east, south, or west, or intermediate points; in the presence and location of growing trees, large or small; in the nature of the improvements to the right or left, in front or rear; in the aspect of the surrounding country or city; in the connections with adjacent streets or roads; in the prospective changes that time is likely to bring which will affect their improvement for good or ill;—all these things are external conditions as similar in the main as the colors of the kaleidoscope, *and as invariably different from each other in their combinations.* Not only these external conditions, but an equally numerous throng of circumstantial conditions connected with the tastes, the means, the number, and the business of the occupants, tend to render the diversities of our homes and home-grounds still more innumerable. . . . We furnish them as a good musical professor does his instrumental studies, not to be used as show-pieces, but to be studied as steps and *points-d'appuis* for one's own culture.[8]

Armed with a basic plan (fig. 12), suburban male readers could apply the work world's method and efficiency to the blank page of the home and, in so doing, mitigate and even erase anxieties about their own mediocrity, replaceability, and liminality. It was as simple as planning before planting.

As streetcars forged "metropolitan corridors" and "bedroom communities" throughout the Northeast and suburbanization spread south and west in the late 1860s and early 1870s, though, the negative impacts of endless construction and massive population shifts became more visible and therefore harder to ignore. Social critics such as Edward Everett Hale and Frederick Law Olmsted, for example, praised suburban development but called for a more comprehensive consideration of the fate of lower-class Americans in the new domestic order. While early proponents of suburban domesticity frequently overlooked ethnic and class issues in their representations, magnified poverty and discrimination in the post–Civil War period demanded recognition and response in print. William Dean Howells situated his *Suburban Sketches* (1871) within this corrective vision by calling attention to the

CHAPTER IX.

FAULTS TO AVOID—PLAN BEFORE PLANTING.

FIGURE 12. Chapter heading from *The Art of Beautifying Suburban Home Grounds of Small Extent.* Courtesy American Antiquarian Society.

individuals whose labor supported early suburban growth and problematizing the position of the white male suburban home owner.

Suburban Sketches rarely appears in Howells criticism, typically deemed significant only as an early trial of what would soon become more consciously realist theories and techniques. When it *is* mentioned, scholars traditionally associate it with the author's *Venetian Life* (1866) and the genre of the travel book more generally. As Susan Goodman and Carl Dawson note in their biography, Howells himself (as is often the case for this author, who carefully combed through his papers and arranged an image) encouraged the linkage stylistically. Writing to his daughter Mildred in 1913, he praised Bayard Taylor's *Views Afoot* (1846) as "very simple and natural" but insisted that he himself had "invented the modern travel [book]."[9] The legitimacy of Howells's puffery, of course, is debatable; his insertion of the qualifier "modern," in this case, makes all the difference, as his word choice deftly commands respect by making a claim that can't be evaluated objectively, much less contradicted. And though his impulse to provoke questions of tourism, nostalgia, and appropriation in a series of vignettes about life in suburban Cambridge in the late 1860s certainly can be read as an innovative inversion of the travel book, by characterizing the volume as unsentimental or unembellished, we perpetuate a narrative that Howells himself helped institute, one that is only partially true. More troublingly, though, we simultaneously obscure the process of seduction through storytelling, the literary business of "turning to account" which Howells thematizes in *Suburban Sketches* and which has been the subject of this book. For while it is true that Howells's vignettes offered a model for local-color fiction published in the *Atlantic Monthly* and elsewhere in the later nineteenth century, the volume also harkened back to an earlier moment and performed homage to "romantic" authors such as Nathaniel Hawthorne, whose stature he admired and from whom he sought approval.

Howells first published *Suburban Sketches* in installments between 1868 and 1870 in the *Atlantic*. Although the narrator remains unnamed throughout the volume, the setting and circumstances parallel Howells's own experiences in suburban Cambridge while living on Sacramento Street, where he and his wife moved in 1866. Over the course of the collection's ten sketches, the speaker tours various neighborhoods in Cambridge and beyond, commenting on what he sees and hears. While clearly a resident himself—the entire first story, "Mrs. Johnson," centers on his family's quest for a replacement maid after their Irish "girl" leaves them—for the most part he moves through the narratives as a knowledgeable, slightly amused hidden observer of the suburban landscape.

In the early sketches especially, some of his proclamations replicate the language of country books almost exactly. In "Mrs. Johnson," for example, the narrator describes his neighborhood in Charlesbridge as "a frontier between city and country" and the suburb more generally as "appear[ing] to us a kind of Paradise" in that it allowed his family to "[live] in the country with the conveniences of the city about us."[10] Horsecars bound for Boston passed along the head of their street, while, he says, "two minutes' walk would take us into a wood so wild and thick that no roof was visible through the trees" (14). In addition to what had become rather hackneyed verbal representations of suburban amenities, he reproduces standard accounts of domestic rhythms that revolve around commuting, as men leave each morning for work in Boston and return every evening to their wives and children.

Such descriptions become mere truisms, though, as the plots move forward, and readers are left wondering at the impulse to describe a space fraught with ethnic and class tensions as a paradisiacal dreamscape. At the closing of the rosy passage just cited, for example, Howells toys with the stereotype: "All round us carpenters were at work building new houses; but so far from troubling us, the strokes of their hammers fell softly upon the senses, like one's heart-beats upon one's own consciousness in the lapse from all fear of pain under the blessed charm of an anaesthetic" (14). Perhaps most immediately, by making palpable the noise of construction, he reminds readers that the suburbs did not simply appear; they were built by laborers. Yet the passage also implies that the suburbs themselves were intended to operate as a "blessed charm," as an "anaesthetic" against some sort of "fear" or threat. Over the span of the stories, it becomes clear that people are dreaming in the sense that they are asleep to the realities of other people's lives, and to the effects of their words and actions on the world around them.

Throughout *Suburban Sketches,* Howells attempts to reproduce the carpenters' hammering through the voice of his speaker, anaesthetizing his representation of the suburban experience. At the same time that he lulls readers with diction that mirrors popular accounts from the 1850s and early 1860s, though, he begs them to stop and read more carefully, as if the process of consciously reproducing the apparatus that perpetuates the "blessed charm" that defines suburban life will enable the erstwhile invisible elements of the landscape to attain the status of visibility. In Howells's hands, the sights and sounds are meant to trouble the seduction; they serve to expose the unfinished nature of the dream itself. While everything is moving forward as though the end points were predestined, Howells interrogates the manufacturing processes that undergird a landscape shaped by the desire to escape from the work world and ruminates on the tension between men's plans and nature's purposes. Histories of the space and of its previous (oftentimes displaced) inhabitants remain, even as they are systematically erased by new construction and new families. Rummaging through cast-off assemblages of silent objects at local shops, the narrator designates them as "all old and equally pathetic . . . whether they are things that have never had a home and have been on sale ever since they were made, or things that have been associated with every phase of human life" (78). Faced with the silence of objects and materials, a "strange assemblage of incongruities" (83), Howells's speaker insists, "I think I know a part of your story" (80).

As the narrator ambulates around Charlesbridge, he approaches the landscape as a body of evidence or symptoms and diagnoses it linguistically. He excavates and digs, exposing innards in almost a bodily way, refusing to obfuscate the physical detritus that stubbornly remains around the edges of the dream. Vacant lots become gaping, untended wounds calling for attention; descriptions of "half-finished wooden houses, empty mortar-beds, and bits and lath and slate strewn over the scarred and mutilated ground" (11) resound with echoes of recent military casualties impressed into the public consciousness by photographers such as Mathew Brady. These sorts of depictions are reinforced on the human level by his careful attention to the large number of itinerants and beggars who traverse the suburban environment in search of work. And while the narrator claims to eschew romanticization, there is sympathy in his accounts of the individuals who populate his theater—not simply curiosity. He often bemoans his own literary failure to depict more than the "black and white" (49) of someone's personal history, calling attention to the inevitable loss of "the color and atmosphere which his manner as well as his words bestowed upon it" (49).

Frederic Cozzens and Robert Barry Coffin used semiautobiographical narrators to call attention to gaps between castles in the air and earthy realities, but one could also argue that they and other country-book authors employed humor and theatricality to soften critiques and keep threats at arm's length. By trading in what were assumed to be shared experiences of misjudgment and naïveté, they still cultivated a fiction of middle-class domestic life through print culture, one that enabled uncomfortable questions related to race, class, and gender to circulate lightly without settling on any concrete philosophy or practice as culpable. Howells turns humor to account in *Suburban Sketches* as well, but in his case erstwhile foibles become, for attuned readers, moments of uncomfortable consciousness rather than opportunities for collective absolution.

On an unseasonably warm spring day, for instance, the narrator and his wife head to Boston in search of a replacement house servant. As if gently joking with friends, he soliloquizes that their "hearts sang of Africa and golden joys" as a result of the weather, with the effect that "a Libyan longing took us, and we would have chosen, if we could, to bear a strand of grotesque beads, or a handful of brazen gauds, and traffic them for some sable maid with crisped locks, whom, uncoffling [unchaining] from the captive train beside the desert, we should make to do our general housework forever, through the right of lawful purchase. But we knew that this was impossible, and that, if we desired colored help, we must seek it at the intelligence office, which is in one of those streets chiefly inhabited by the orphaned children and grandchildren of slavery" (18). Here and in the rest of the passage, although the narrator clearly recognizes and mocks his own domestic acts of objectification, he seems reluctant to relinquish the ethnic fetish. Even as he notes that the African American children he watches "subtly remind us that we have yet to redeem a whole race, pawned in our reckless national youth" (18), he feels compelled to remark upon the dress of the young women among them, calling them "the black pansies and marigolds and dark-blooded dahlias among womankind." Tripping the "blessed charm" of the narrator's desires and the suburbs more generally, these sorts of passages put readers in the awkward position of not knowing how to react to the "joke" and therefore force them to reassess the narrator's position, motives, and ethics as he turns people into specimens to be seen and used despite manifesting an awareness of the irreparable folly of doing so.

As reminders of the flip side of experiences of fraternity and enfranchisement, lines referencing our "national youth" compound the uneasy mood by essentially collapsing any pretense of distance between the narrator and Howells himself. Indeed, in *Suburban Sketches,* Howells refuses to extricate either himself or his readers from textual experiences of discomfort and culpability related to the marginalization and colonization of others. While his retellings of their narratives fill page after page with sympathetic, sometimes pathetic histories, the narrator intermittently admits that he "lov[es] to trace the intricate yet often transparent operations" of others' minds, that he takes aesthetic pleasure in analyzing, calculating, inferring, and imagining. More than simply a listener, he employs them for his own work, even if he is "merely touched as a human being . . . [with] little desire to turn the scene to literary account" (66). Implicitly recognizing his scope and influence, he also occasionally manifests regret or embarrassment about his portrayals, as when he "vainly seek[s] to atone" for reproducing stereotypes about Italians upon meeting a particularly generous Italian woman who, he says, "makes me ashamed of things I have written about the sordidness of her race" (46); but he nonetheless persists in the very depictions he claims to regret.

In the end, it is difficult to locate Howells, to see where he stands in relation to the anaesthetization he presents. Although he certainly seeks to revise earlier depictions of suburban life, it becomes almost impossible to ignore the ways in which the structure of the stories themselves enables him to slip out of our grasp, hinting at real anxieties without resolving them. Sometimes the act of writing itself seems to function as a defense mechanism. Certain characters bring the narrator trepidation; every so often he admits to feeling "a little uncertain how to regard" (31) people, but he lets them go, narratively, by simply remarking that their "presence" has "unaccountably oppressed our imaginations" (32). Despite his ostensible purpose, he fails to move beyond voicing the fear, to flesh out his critique in any detail.

Faced with the arrival at his door of a one-armed Irish Civil War veteran turned peddler in "Doorstep Acquaintance," the narrator provides refreshment and listens to the man "tell of the fight before Vicksburg," even as he ashamedly remarks that he "suspects [the peddler] was very probably an impostor" (53). Such articulations of caution and claims to disaffectedness remain unresolved throughout *Suburban Sketches,* and suggest that the author suffers from the same lack of foresight he hopes to expose. He obviously feels a need to confess the shortcomings in his own perspective, but ultimately rehearsals of his inability to "turn to account" in the way he had hoped become somewhat frustrating dead ends in themselves. The narrator soon becomes sickened by this amputee, whom he lets weed his strawberry bed. In the final lines of the essay, when the man asks when he can return to "work out this dollar," the speaker casts him out of his mental vision: "A sudden and unreasonable disgust for the character which had given me so much entertainment succeeded to my past delight. I felt, moreover, that I had bought the right to use some frankness with the veteran, and I said to him: 'Do you know now, I shouldn't care if I *never* saw you again?'" (59). The essay ends with an announcement that the man never returned, but the story is unsettling. The narrator's willingness to expose his own meanness doesn't make matters any better, and he knows it.

For all the "telling" in *Suburban Sketches,* perhaps the central anxiety is that the act of "turning to account" is automatic and unavoidable, that domestic fraternizing through storytelling is always appropriative. Like suburbanization, which itself is both a glorification of the transformative power of narrative and a recognition of the ultimate predictability of its arc, the process absorbs and redeploys otherness in the name of selfhood in a way that imperils the quest, despite any "good intentions." The speaker in "A Day's Pleasure" contemplates his surroundings on a train:

> It is noticeable how many people there are in the world that seem bent always upon the same purpose of amusement or business as one's self. If you keep quietly about your accustomed affairs, there are all your neighbors and acquaintances hard at it too; if you go on a journey, choose what train you will, the cars are filled with travellers in your direction. You take a day's pleasure, and everybody abandons his usual occupation to crowd upon your boat, whether it is to Gloucester, or Nahant, or to Nantasket Beach you go. It is very hard to believe that, from whatever channel of life you abstract yourself, still the great sum of it presses forward as before: that business is carried on though you are idle, that men amuse themselves though you toil, that every train is as crowded as that you travel on, that the theatre or church fills its boxes or pews without you perfectly well. I suppose it would not be flattering; for if each one of us did not take the world with him now at every turn, should he not have to leave it behind him when he died? And that, it must be owned, would not be agreeable, nor is the fact quite conceivable, though ever so many myriads in so many million years have proved it. (135)

The passage invokes the sense of desperation that Thoreau warns against in *Walden:* the possibility that, despite the relocation, the home improvements, the endless paper-pushing, the tasty dinners, and the time spent with family and friends, it is all for naught—that the effort to locate and enshrine selfhood in the suburban landscape or on the printed page, to "take the world with you," is impossible, and that the very problem the suburb promised to resolve is reproduced endlessly, street after street, neighborhood after neighborhood, defining the space itself and the people who live there.

As the suburbs promised to "turn to account" men's lives in myriad ways, and as that promise acted as an anaesthetic for individuals who themselves felt increasingly marginalized, undervalued, and uninspired, Howells depicts himself inadvertently instrumentalizing these people he wants to "make real" to readers in the act of writing them. He knows, moreover, that there is something unaccountable in the process of "turning to account," and that the thing that always seems to elude him is what he wants to capture. In that sense, the country book—a literary form composed of previously published "sketches" produced for other purposes at earlier times and now peddled in new form for new profits—becomes perhaps the only adequate genre for the type of work he finds himself doing.

Comparing his work to that of the storekeeper in "A Pedestrian Tour," he recognizes that "I am in the trade and have a secondhand shop of my own, full of poetical rubbish, and every sort of literary odds and ends, picked up at random, and all cast higgledy-piggledy into the same chaotic receptacle" (84). Continuing the parallel, he notes that "it is surprising to find how much business can be transacted, and how many sharp bargains struck without the help of a common language. I am in the belief, which may be erroneous, that nobody is wronged in these trades" (84). Despite the hesitancy in his tone that his sketches might be the literary equivalent of "walking for walking's sake," which he claims to dislike, he nonetheless revels in the process by which "the whole suburb of Charlesbridge stretches about me,—a vast space upon which I can embroider any fancy I like as I saunter along" (61), even if he recognizes that he doesn't share the language of the people or objects he hopes to voice. For a writer such as himself, he hints, some sort of intangible richness exists in the in-betweenness, the attempted evocation, as it is sometimes "sufficient to give me a slight heart-ache for I know not what" (62). And he holds out hope that business and the writerly life might not be so inimical as they initially seem. Recognizing himself as a suburban collector *and* inhabitant, he casts himself among his subjects, however motley, "naturally look[ing] for many unprosaic aspects of humanity" (92), professing even in these places to "have beheld for the most part only mysteries" (92).

NOTES

Introduction

1. Ralph Waldo Emerson, "The Fugitive Slave Law" (1854), in *Emerson's Antislavery Writings*, ed. Len Gougeon and Joel Myerson (New Haven: Yale University Press, 1995), 74.
2. Ibid., 74, 73.
3. Ralph Waldo Emerson, "Domestic Life" (1843), in *The Collected Works of Ralph Waldo Emerson: Society and Solitude*, vol. 7 (Cambridge: Harvard University Press, 2007), 54.
4. Ibid., 56–57, 59.
5. Both "Private Theatricals" and "Wives and Weathercocks" originally appeared in periodicals and were reprinted in a posthumous volume prepared by Donald Grant Mitchell, *Sayings, Wise and Otherwise* (New York: United States Book Company, 1870).
6. Part 1 of Mary Chapman and Glenn Hendler's edited collection *Sentimental Men: Masculinity and the Politics of Affect* (Berkeley: University of California Press, 1999) recognizes this critical lacuna, even if it does not address it in a comprehensive way. Katherine V. Snyder's *Bachelors, Manhood, and the Novel, 1850–1925* (Cambridge: Cambridge University Press, 1999), Howard P. Chudacoff's *The Age of the Bachelor: Creating an American Subculture* (Princeton: Princeton University Press, 1999), and Margaret Marsh's essay "Suburban Men and Masculine Domesticity, 1870–1915," in *Meanings for Manhood: Constructions of Masculinity in Victorian America,* ed. Mark C. Carnes and Clyde Griffen (Chicago: University of Chicago Press, 1990), 111–27, address men's domestic lives later in the century. For more general studies of the influence of architectural and environmental trends on antebellum literature, see Adam Sweeting, *Reading Houses and Building Books: Andrew Jackson Downing and the Architecture of Popular Antebellum Literature, 1835–1855* (Hanover, N.H.: University Press of New England, 1996); and Edward Halsey Foster, *The Civilized Wilderness: Backgrounds to American Romantic Literature, 1817–1860* (New York: Free Press, 1975).
7. See, for example, Chapman and Hendler, *Sentimental Men;* Lora Romero, *Home Fronts: Domesticity and Its Critics in the Antebellum United States* (Durham: Duke University Press, 1997); and Milette Shamir, *Inexpressible Privacy: The Interior Life of Antebellum American Literature* (Philadelphia: University of Pennsylvania Press, 2006).
8. For relevant analyses of Irving in relation to the history of bachelorhood and masculinity, see David Grevin, "Troubling Our Heads about Ichabod: 'The Legend of Sleepy Hollow,' Classic American Literature, and the Sexual Politics of Homosocial Brotherhood," *American Quarterly* 56, no. 1 (March 2004), 83–110; Bryce Traister, "The

Wandering Bachelor: Irving, Masculinity, and Authorship," *American Literature* 74, no. 1 (March 2002), 111–37; Michael Warner, "Irving's Posterity," *ELH* 67, no. 3 (Fall 2000), 773–99; and Jenifer S. Banks, "Washington Irving: The Nineteenth-Century American Bachelor," *Critical Essays on Washington Irving*, ed. Ralph M. Aderman (Boston: G. K. Hall, 1990), 253–65.

9. Washington Irving, *The Sketch Book of Geoffrey Crayon, Gent.* (1819–20; repr., Charlottesville: University of Virginia Press, 2000), 57. Further references will be cited in text.

10. Leslie Fiedler, *Love and Death in the American Novel* (1960; repr., Urbana-Champaign: Dalkey Archive Press, 2003), 343.

11. "Rural Tales and Sketches of Long Island, No. 1—The Kushow Property: A Tale of Crow-Hill," *Knickerbocker*, September 1838, 191–95.

12. Kenneth T. Jackson, *Crabgrass Frontier: The Suburbanization of the United States* (New York: Oxford University Press, 1985), 20. Even Jackson, however, admits that "transportation change is not a sufficient explanation for the initial development of the suburban trend" and suggests that "for the underlying causes of the increasingly stratified and segregated social geography of great American cities, as well as their relatively low density as compared to Europe, we must look not just to transportation technology and the powerful mechanical forces unleashed by the Industrial Revolution but to the development of new cultural values" (42, 44).

13. The interests of the gentlemen farmers conflicted with those of the rural farmers who lived nearby. As Dolores Hayden observes, the initial clash between farmers whose livelihood was based on agriculture and the wealthy families whose breadwinners worked in the cities "became a sustained economic conflict between those who viewed the landscape as a place to rest from profiting elsewhere and those who viewed it as a place to make a profit." Dolores Hayden, *Building Suburbia: Green Fields and Urban Growth, 1820–2000* (New York: Pantheon Books, 2003), 22. This new, distinctly urban man approached any farming as a hobby rather than a career and typically limited agricultural pursuits to a kitchen garden, a fruit orchard, possibly a vineyard, and an ornamental landscape of attractive trees, shrubs, and flowers. Characterizing the transition in landownership as an exercise in progressive nation building, books and magazines encouraged the distinction between the farmers who previously lived on the land and the gentlemen farmers who had begun to settle it as they outlined the process whereby new residents could buy a run-down farm from the lazy, lower-class rural people and transform it into a "country seat" within ten years.

14. A. J. Downing, *A Treatise on the Theory and Practice of Landscape Gardening* (1841; repr., New York: John Wiley & Sons, 1921), 185. According to at least one architectural historian, because Sunnyside prompted Downing to devote more thought to the small-scale residence, it can be regarded as an important "precursor of American suburban design." Robert M. Toole, "An American Cottage Ornee: Washington Irving's Sunnyside, 1835–1859," *Journal of Garden History* 12, no. 1 (January–March 1992): 69.

15. Washington Irving to Mrs. Sarah Van Wart, November 25, 1840, quoted in Joseph T. Butler, *Washington Irving's Sunnyside* (1967; repr., Tarrytown, N.Y.: Sleepy Hollow Restorations, 1974), 31.

16. John Archer, *Architecture and Suburbia: From English Villa to American Dream House, 1690–2000* (Minneapolis: University of Minnesota Press, 2005), 183.

17. Washington Irving to Mrs. John P. Kennedy, November 11, 1853, quoted in Harold Dean Cater, *Washington Irving and Sunnyside* (Tarrytown, N.Y.: Sleepy Hollow Restorations, 1957), 26.

18. A. J. Downing, *Cottage Residences; or, A Series of Designs for Rural Cottages and Cottage-Villas, and Their Gardens and Grounds: Adapted to North America* (New York: Wiley and Putnam, 1842), 15–16.

19. Washington Irving to Mrs. Catharine Paris, June 21, 1843, quoted in Cater, *Washington Irving and Sunnyside*, 23.

20. *Sketches of Distinguished American Authors, Represented in Darley's New National Picture Entitled Washington Irving and His Literary Friends, at Sunnyside* (New York: Irving Publishing Company, 1864). All quotations are from the text accessed through the Princeton University Library's blog Graphic Arts: Exhibitions, Acquisitions, and Other Highlights from the Graphic Arts Collection, http://blogs.princeton.edu.

21. Nathaniel Parker Willis, "Willis at Sunnyside," *Home Journal*, August 15, 1857, 2.

1. Thoreau's Unreal Estate

1. Letter, *The Country Gentleman*, January 4, 1855, 61–62.

2. Henry David Thoreau, *Walden* (1852; repr., Princeton: Princeton University Press, 1989), 324. Further references will be cited in text.

3. Robert A. Gross, "Transcendentalism and Urbanism: Concord, Boston, and the Wider World," *Journal of American Studies* 18 (1984): 363.

4. Thoreau quoted ibid., 378.

5. *Journal of Henry D. Thoreau*, ed. Bradford Torrey and Francis H. Allen, 14 vols. (Boston: Houghton Mifflin, 1949), 4:478–79.

6. Charles P. Dwyer, *The Economic Cottage Builder: or, Cottages for Men of Small Means* (Buffalo: Wanzer, McKim & Co., 1856), 7.

7. Gervase Wheeler, *Homes for the People, in Suburb and Country* (New York: Charles Scribner, 1855), 56.

8. Ibid., 315.

9. *The Economic Cottage Builder* explains the process, as did many newspapers of the day: "Let a small club or association of such men put into one common fund sufficient to make the first payment on a piece of land a few miles from the city. Let them keep a conveyance for their special use, if they do not locate near a railroad or canal, or public conveyance of some description, and they will derive ten fold benefit." Dwyer, *Economic Cottage Builder*, 56–57.

10. Ibid., 11.

11. T. Thomas, *The Working-Man's Cottage Architecture, containing Plans, Elevations, and Details, for the erection of Cheap, Comfortable, and Neat Cottages* (New York: R. Martin, 1848), 4.

12. On midcentury clerks and white-collar labor, see Thomas Augst, *A Clerk's Tale: Young*

Men and Moral Life in Nineteenth-Century America (Chicago: University of Chicago Press, 2003); and Brian Luskey, *On the Make: Clerks and the Quest for Capital in Nineteenth-Century America* (New York: New York University Press, 2010).

13. For ecocritical perspectives on midcentury changes taking place in Concord and around Walden Pond, see the essays by Robert Fanuzzi and Robert Sattelmeyer in *Thoreau's Sense of Place: Essays in American Environmental Writing,* ed. Richard J. Schneider (Iowa City: University of Iowa Press, 2000).

14. *The Journals of Ralph Waldo Emerson, with Annotations,* vol. 6 (1841–1844), ed. Edward Waldo Emerson and Waldo Emerson Forbes (New York: Houghton Mifflin, 1911), 496.

15. Quoted in Walter Harding, *The Days of Henry Thoreau: A Biography* (1962; repr., Princeton: Princeton University Press, 1992), 220.

16. A. J. Downing, "Hints to Rural Improvers," *Horticulturalist,* July 1848, 11–12.

17. Sarah Ann Wider, "'And What Became of Your Philosophy Then?': Women Reading *Walden,*" in *More Day to Dawn: Thoreau's "Walden" for the Twenty-first Century,* ed. Sandra Harbert Petrulionis and Laura Dassow Walls (Amherst: University of Massachusetts Press, 2007), 162.

18. For *Walden's* engagement with domestic treatises written by and for nineteenth-century women, see Cecelia Tichi, "Domesticity on Walden Pond," in *A Historical Guide to Henry David Thoreau,* ed. William E. Cain (New York: Oxford University Press, 2000), 95–121, and Etsuko Taketani, "Thoreau's Domestic Economy: Double Accounts in *Walden,*" *Concord Saunterer* 2 (Fall 1994): 65–78.

19. Henry David Thoreau, "The Landlord," *United States Magazine, and Democratic Review* 13, no. 64 (October 1843): 427. I am grateful to Steven Fink's article "Building America: Henry David Thoreau and the American Home," *Prospects* 11 (1986): 327–65, for alerting me to this piece.

20. Milette Shamir, *Inexpressible Privacy: The Interior Life of Antebellum American Literature* (Philadelphia: University of Pennsylvania Press, 2006), 210.

2. "To Build, as Trees Grow, Season by Season"

1. Henry Ward Beecher, *Star Papers; or, Experiences of Art and Nature* (New York: J. C. Derby, 1855), 286. The volume consisted of a collection of articles previously published in the *New York Independent.* Further references will be abbreviated *SP* and cited in text.

2. William Stowe, "'A Minister of Happiness': Nature in Beecher's America," *Interdisciplinary Studies in Literature and Environment* 13, no. 1 (Winter 2006): 45.

3. Henry Ward Beecher, *Seven Lectures to Young Men on Various Important Subjects: delivered before the young men of Indianapolis, Indiana, during the winter of 1843–4* (Indianapolis: Thomas B. Culter, 1844), 171–72. Further references will be abbreviated *SL* and cited in text.

4. Andrew Lawson, "Men of Small Property: Henry Franco and Henry Ward Beecher in the Antebellum Market," *Common-Place* 10, no. 4 (July 2010), www.common-place.org.

5. Henry Ward Beecher, *Journal,* October 17, 1835, quoted in Clifford E. Clark Jr., "The Changing Nature of Protestantism in Mid-Nineteenth Century America: Henry Ward Beecher's Seven Lectures to Young Men," *Journal of American History* 57, no. 4 (March 1971): 834.

6. Debby Applegate, *The Most Famous Man in America: The Biography of Henry Ward Beecher* (New York: Doubleday, 2006), 291.

7. Milton Rugoff, *The Beechers: An American Family in the Nineteenth Century* (New York: Harper & Row, 1981), 367.

8. Henry Ward Beecher, *Eyes and Ears* (Boston: Ticknor and Fields, 1862), 87. The volume consisted of a collection of articles previously published in the *New York Independent.* Further references will be abbreviated *EE* and cited in text.

9. Henry Ward Beecher, *Plain and Pleasant Talk about Fruits, Flowers and Farming* (New York: Derby & Jackson, 1859), iv. Further references will be abbreviated *PPT* and cited in text.

10. Henry Ward Beecher quoted in Applegate, *The Most Famous Man in America,* 167.

3. "A Man's Sense of Domesticity"

1. Donald Grant Mitchell, *Rural Studies, with Hints for Country Places* (New York: C. Scribner & Co., 1867), 293–94. The volume consisted of a collection of essays previously published in *The Horticulturalist* and *Hours at Home* between 1866 and 1867. Further references will be abbreviated *RS* and cited in text.

2. For statistics, see Waldo H. Dunn, *The Life of Donald G. Mitchell* (New York: Charles Scribner's Sons, 1922), 225; Paul Gutjahr's anthology *Popular American Literature of the Nineteenth Century* (New York: Oxford University Press, 2001), 473; and Lisa Spiro's "historical commentary" " 'Smoke, Flame, and Ashes': A 'Reverie' from Ik Marvel's (Donald Grant Mitchell) *Reveries of a Bachelor* (1850)," http://etext.lib.virginia.edu.

3. "Literary Notices," *Harper's New Monthly Magazine* 2, no. 8 (January 1851): 281.

4. On this topic, see G. J. Barker-Benfield, *The Horrors of the Half-Known Life: Male Attitudes toward Women and Sexuality in Nineteenth-Century America* (New York: Harper & Row, 1976); Stephen Nissenbaum, *Sex, Diet, and Debility in Jacksonian America: Sylvester Graham and Health Reform* (Westport, Conn.: Greenwood Press, 1980); and Thomas Laqueur, *Solitary Sex: A Cultural History of Masturbation* (New York: Zone Books, 2003).

5. Ik Marvel [Donald Grant Mitchell], *Reveries of a Bachelor, or, A Book of the Heart* (New York: Baker & Scribner, 1850), 16. Further references will be abbreviated *RB* and cited in text.

6. Catharine Beecher, *Treatise on Domestic Economy* (Boston: T. H. Webb & Co., 1842), 244.

7. Ibid., 199.

8. Samuel Otter theorizes this process in relation to Mitchell in *Melville's Anatomies* (Berkeley: University of California Press, 1999).

9. Waldo Dunn, *The Life of Donald G. Mitchell* (New York: Charles Scribner's Sons, 1922), 34.

10. For a full list of correspondences, see ibid., 29.

11. Donald Grant Mitchell to Mary Goddard, December 8, 1848, quoted ibid., 204–5.

12. Mitchell authored the columns until 1855 and was succeeded by George William Curtis and William Dean Howells.

13. Donald Grant Mitchell to Mary Pringle, quoted in Dunn, *Life of Donald Grant Mitchell,* 252.

14. Donald Grant Mitchell to Mary Pringle, March 28, 1853, quoted ibid., 254.

15. Ibid., 253.

16. Andrew Jackson Downing, preface to *Architecture of Country Houses* (New York: D. Appleton & Company, 1850), xix.

17. Ibid., 27.

18. Donald Grant Mitchell, "Landscape Gardening and Rural Architecture," *New Englander* 1 (April 1843): 205.

19. Donald Grant Mitchell, "Landscape Gardening," *American Review* 5 (March 1847): 295–306.

20. Downing, *Architecture of Country Houses,* 40.

21. Eager for advice on various aspects of home building as he searched for a plot, he conversed with the aging Washington Irving about domestic architecture and ornament as they vacationed together first in the Hudson River Valley and then at Saratoga, and he even toured Downing's house in 1853. After the visit, he wrote to Mary that Downing's house demonstrated "what taste can accomplish upon a very common-place landscape" but recognized that it was best to build moderately and within one's means. Donald Grant Mitchell to Mary Pringle, April 10, 1853, quoted in Dunn, *Life of Donald Grant Mitchell,* 254. Downing had notoriously left his family deep in debt at his death; everything, including their house, had to be sold.

22. Donald Grant Mitchell, *Pictures of Edgewood* (New York: Charles Scribner and Company, 1869), 16, 17.

23. Donald Grant Mitchell, *My Farm of Edgewood: A Country Book* (New York: C. Scribner, 1863), hereafter abbreviated *MFE* and cited in text; Donald Grant Mitchell, *Wet Days at Edgewood: With Old Farmers, Old Gardeners, and Old Pastorals* (New York: C. Scribner, 1865); and Donald Grant Mitchell, *Rural Studies, with Hints for Country Places* (New York: C. Scribner & Co., 1867). *Rural Studies* was eventually republished with illustrations as Donald Grant Mitchell, *Out-of-Town Places: With Hints for Their Improvement* (New York: C. Scribner's Sons, 1884).

24. On rhetorics of and outlets for leisure in the nineteenth century, see William A. Gleason, *The Leisure Ethic: Work and Play in American Literature, 1840–1940* (Stanford: Stanford University Press, 1999); Donna R. Braden, *Leisure and Entertainment in America* (Dearborn, Mich.: Henry Ford Museum & Greenfield Village, 1988); and Foster Rhea Dulles, *A History of Recreation: America Learns to Play* (1940; New York: Appleton-Century-Crofts, 1965).

25. Braden, *Leisure and Entertainment in America,* 9.

26. Jennifer Jensen, "Teaching Success: American Board and Table Games, 1840–1900," *Antiques* (December 2001): 815.

27. Kenneth T. Jackson, foreword to Margaret Hofer, *The Games We Played: The Golden Age of Board and Table Games* (New York: Princeton Architectural Press, 2003), 6.

28. Gleason, *The Leisure Ethic*, 23.

29. Steven Fink, "Building America: Henry David Thoreau and the American Home," *Prospects* 11 (1986): 337.

30. Downing, *Architecture of Country Houses*, 27.

31. Beecher, *Treatise*, 247.

4. Advancement and Association, Nostalgia and Exclusion

1. Albert Brisbane, "Association; or, Principles of a True Organization of Society," *New York Tribune*, March 2, 1842.

2. Ibid.

3. Ralph Waldo Emerson to Thomas Carlyle, 1840, in *The Letters of Ralph Waldo Emerson*, ed. Ralph L. Rusk, 5 vols. (New York: Columbia University Press, 1939), 2:353.

4. D. H. Lawrence, *Studies in Classic American Literature* (1923; repr., New York: Viking Press, 1969), 9–10.

5. Lewis Mumford, *The Culture of Cities* (New York: Harcourt, Brace, and Co., 1938), 216.

6. Carl J. Guarneri, *The Utopian Alternative: Fourierism in Nineteenth-Century America* (Ithaca: Cornell University Press, 1991), 126.

7. Dolores Hayden, *Seven American Utopias: The Architecture of Communitarian Socialism, 1790–1975* (Cambridge: MIT Press, 1976), 15.

8. Arthur Brisbane, *Social Destiny of Man: or, Association and Reorganization of Industry* (1840; repr., New York: Augustus M. Kelley, 1969), 1. Further references will be abbreviated *SDM* and cited in text.

9. Arthur Brisbane, *Association; or, A Concise Exposition of the Practical Part of Fourier's Social Science* (1843; repr., New York: AMS Press, 1975), 31. Further references will be abbreviated *A* and cited in text.

10. In the March 29, 1842, issue of the *Tribune*, Brisbane claimed that these private rooms would "vary in price from $30 to $500 per annum" and would be selected on the basis of individual "tastes and pecuniary means."

11. He expanded his reasoning in *Associationism* (16), designating the ideal spot as within twenty to thirty miles of a major urban area.

12. Hayden, *Seven American Utopias*, 156.

13. The original "Articles of Confederation of the North American Phalanx" stipulated in article 1, section 2, that "its location shall be as near to the city of New York or Philadelphia as may be practicable." Brisbane, *Associationism*, 79.

14. Guarneri, *Utopian Alternative*, 2.

15. Hayden, *Building Suburbia*, 52. Hayden reports that by 1852, approximately three hundred families were in residence. By the 1860s, though, many members had sold their lots to outsiders, creating a secularized community that nonetheless had been planned along Associationist principles.

16. Quoted in Sterling F. Delano, *Brook Farm: The Dark Side of Utopia* (Cambridge: Belknap Press of Harvard University Press, 2004), 39.

17. Guarneri writes extensively on the decision at Brook Farm to adopt Fourierism, and the latter incarnation's relationship to original Transcendentalist philosophies, in *Utopian Alternative*.

18. George Ripley to Ralph Waldo Emerson, November 9, 1840, in Octavius Brooks Frothingham, *George Ripley* (Boston: Houghton Mifflin, 1882), 307–8.

19. Guarneri, *Utopian Alternative*, 77.

20. Nathaniel Hawthorne, *The Blithedale Romance* (1852; repr., New York: Penguin Classics, 1986), 2. Further references will be abbreviated *BR* and cited in text.

21. Mumford, *Culture of Cities*, 214–15.

22. Ibid., 216.

23. N. P. Willis, *Home Journal*, May 14, 1853, 3.

24. Nathaniel Hawthorne to William B. Pike, July 24, 1851, in *The Letters, 1843–1853*, ed. Thomas Woodsen, L. Neal Smith, and Norman Holmes Pearson, vol. 16 of *The Centenary Edition of the Works of Nathaniel Hawthorne* (Columbus: Ohio State University Press, 1985), 464–67.

25. Brenda Wineapple, *Hawthorne: A Life* (New York: Knopf, 2003), 147.

26. Nathaniel Hawthorne to Sophia Peabody, Brook Farm, April 28, 1841, in *The Letters, 1813–1843*, ed. Thomas Woodsen, L. Neal Smith, and Norman Holmes Pearson, vol. 15 of *The Centenary Edition of the Works of Nathaniel Hawthorne* (Columbus: Ohio State University Press, 1984), 535.

27. Nathaniel Hawthorne to Sophia Peabody, May 1, 1841, ibid., 538.

28. Ibid.

29. Benedict Anderson, *Imagined Communities: Reflections on the Origin and Spread of Nationalism* (London: Verso, 1983), 15.

30. George Ripley quoted in Edward K. Spann, *Brotherly Tomorrows: Movements for a Cooperative Society in America, 1820–1920* (New York: Columbia University Press, 1989), 62.

31. Wineapple, *Hawthorne: A Life*, 333.

32. Nathaniel Hawthorne to Charles Ticknor, quoted ibid., 333.

5. A Networked Wilderness of Print

1. Nathaniel Parker Willis, *Out-doors at Idlewild; or, The Shaping of a Home on the Banks of the Hudson* (New York: C. Scribner, 1855), 65.

2. In this stance, he was part of a broad cultural shift that has been discussed and debated by historians such as Jack Larkin in *The Reshaping of Everyday Life, 1790–1840* (New York: Harper and Row, 1988), Stuart M. Blumin in *The Emergence of the Middle Class: Social Experience in the American City, 1760–1900* (New York: Cambridge University Press, 1989), and Richard L. Bushman in *The Refinement of America: Persons, Houses, Cities* (New York: Alfred A. Knopf, 1992).

3. *Home Journal*, July 7, 1855, 2, quoted in Cortland P. Auser, *Nathaniel P. Willis* (New York: Twayne, 1969), 128.

4. Willis, *Out-doors at Idlewild*, 134.

5. Sandra Tomc, *Industry and the Creative Mind: The Eccentric Writer in American Literature and Entertainment, 1790–1860* (Ann Arbor: University of Michigan Press, 2012), 170. For Tomc, Willis's pose of leisure functions as another manifestation of the "close remotenesses" I discuss here.

6. Freeman Hunt, *Letters about the Hudson River, and Its Vicinity* (New York: Freeman Hunt, 1836), 3. The letters were originally written for the *American Traveller* magazine between 1835 and 1836.

7. Nathaniel Parker Willis, "The Catskill Mountains," *New Mirror,* September 9, 1843, 353. See also N. P. Willis, *American Scenery,* 7 vols. (London: George Virtue, 1840).

8. Fredrika Bremer, *Homes of the New World,* 2 vols. (New York: Harper and Brothers, 1854), 1:49.

9. Tom Lewis, *The Hudson: A History* (New Haven: Yale University Press, 2005), provides an excellent overview of the ways in which travel by steamship and railroad transformed the landscape along the Hudson River in the nineteenth century.

10. Nathaniel Parker Willis, *Letters from Under a Bridge* (1840; repr., New York: Morris, 1844), 13.

11. In his biography *Nathaniel Parker Willis* (Boston: Houghton Mifflin, 1885), Henry Beers states that Harriet Jacobs was a servant in the Willis household between 1842 and 1861. After her escape north, she "was engaged by Willis as a house servant when he went to Glenmary" and stayed with him intermittently until the beginning of the Civil War, when, according to Beers, Willis "bought her freedom out and out" as a result of the frustrations he experienced when she "had to leave the Willises and go into hiding at Boston and elsewhere" to avoid capture by her former owners (285).

12. According to Fred Lewis Pattee in *The Development of the American Short Story* (New York: Bilbo and Tannen, 1966), Willis "was the best paid magazinist of his generation: in 1842 he was receiving from four magazines $100 a month each for tales and sketches and he had other literary income nearly as large" (80). For biographies of Willis, see Thomas Nelson Baker, *Sentiment and Celebrity: Nathaniel Parker Willis and the Trials of Literary Fame* (New York: Oxford University Press, 1999); Cortland Auser, *Nathaniel P. Willis* (New York: Twayne, 1969); and Beers, *Nathaniel Parker Willis.*

13. For many historians, the Astor Place Riot has come to represent the divide that developed between the "Codfish Aristocracy" of Whiggish political leanings and the "Broadway B'hoys" of the immigrant-heavy American working class. The English actor William Charles Macready and his New York rival Edwin Forrest became symbolic of the two sides, as Forrest's supporters descended on the Astor Place Opera House on May 7, 1849, where Macready was starring in *Macbeth* (Forrest was playing Macbeth at the Bowery Theater on the same night), throwing food and objects at Macready onstage. By the afternoon of the May 10 performance, more than twenty thousand people had gathered outside Astor Place. Rioting quickly broke out, and the National Guard responded; the melee left eighteen dead and many wounded. Willis had become friendly with Forrest when they were introduced at the Tremont Hotel in 1830, and he and his second wife, Cornelia, became especially close friends with Forrest's wife, Catherine. Even in response to the riot, Willis was sympathetic to Forrest,

asserting that "WEALTH IN REPUBLIC SHOULD BE MINDFUL WHERE ITS LUXURIES OFFEND" (*Home Journal,* May 26, 1849, 2). Nonetheless, when news of the impending Forrest divorce broke in early 1850, Willis chose to defend Catherine's honor, both in society and in print. Thomas Baker discusses this event and the divorce scandal as a whole in his Willis biography, *Sentiment and Celebrity.*

14. Calvert Vaux, *Villas and Cottages* (1857; repr., New York: Da Capo Press, 1968).

15. Addison Richards, "Idlewild: The Home of N. P. Willis," *Harper's New Monthly Magazine,* January 1858, 152.

16. Willis, *Out-doors at Idlewild,* 50; *Home Journal,* April 23, 1853, 2.

17. Willis, *Out-doors at Idlewild,* 519; *Home Journal,* October 7, 1854, 2.

18. Willis, preface to *Out-doors at Idlewild,* v. According to Beers, in the 1850s "his disease finally declared itself as epilepsy, and resulted at the last in paralysis and softening of the brain. He was subject for years to epileptic fits, occurring periodically, usually on the tenth day [after a prior attack]. . . . After Willis's death, one of his physicians, Dr. J. B. F. Walker, printed some 'Medical Reminiscences of N. P. Willis,' in the course of which he said: 'Not only was he a martyr to the agonies of sharp and sudden attacks, but he suffered all the languors of chronic disease. . . . There has hardly been a man of letters doomed to such protracted torments from bodily disease.'" Beers, *Nathaniel Parker Willis,* 348–49.

19. Beers, *Nathaniel Parker Willis,* 328.

20. *Home Journal,* January 1, 1853, 2.

21. Willis, *Out-doors at Idlewild,* 193–94; *Home Journal,* October 22, 1853, 2.

22. Willis, *Out-doors at Idlewild,* 17; Nathaniel P. Willis, "The Highland Terrace above West Point," in *The Home Book of the Picturesque: or American Scenery, Art, and Literature,* ed. George P. Putnam (1852; repr., Gainesville: Scholars' Facsimiles and Reprints, 1967), 111.

23. Willis, *Out-doors at Idlewild,* 513–14; *Home Journal,* October 7, 1854, 2.

24. Willis, *Out-doors at Idlewild,* 193–94; *Home Journal,* October 22, 1853, 2.

25. Willis, *Out-doors at Idlewild,* 62–63; *Home Journal,* May 14, 1853, 2.

26. Nathaniel Parker Willis, "Ephemera," in the *Complete Works of Nathaniel Parker Willis* (New York: J. S. Redfield, 1846), 650, quoted in Baker, *Sentiment and Celebrity,* 92.

27. *National Press,* February 14, 1846, 2.

28. *Home Journal,* November 21, 1846, 2.

29. Ibid.

30. "Society and Manners in New York," undated *Home Journal* column reprinted in Nathaniel Parker Willis, *Hurry-Graphs; or, Sketches of Scenery, Celebrity, and Society, Taken from Life* (New York: Charles Scribner, 1851), 285.

31. Ibid., 286.

32. *Home Journal,* February 15, 1851, 2. A month earlier, in the January 4, 1851, issue, Willis had marveled that there were three subterranean telegraph lines in operation across the Hudson River (2).

33. *Home Journal,* February 15, 1851, 2.

34. *Home Journal,* March 15, 1851, 2.

35. Ibid. The "Perfecting the Home" series ran on the second page of the *Home Journal* each week from March 1 to April 19, 1851, and was signed by an architect, "G.W.,"

presumably Gervase Wheeler, who would publish *Homes for the People, in Suburb and Country* four years later.

36. *Home Journal,* March 1, 1851, 2.

37. Willis, *Out-doors at Idlewild,* 385–86; *Home Journal,* May 7, 1854, 2.

38. *Home Journal,* May 31, 1851, 2.

39. *Home Journal,* March 15, 1851, 2.

40. *Home Journal,* March 1, 1851, 2.

41. Willis, *Out-doors at Idlewild,* 45; *Home Journal,* April 23, 1853, 2.

42. Willis, *Out-doors at Idlewild,* 47; *Home Journal,* April 23, 1853, 2.

43. John Nerone, "Newspapers and the Public Sphere," in *The Industrial Book, 1840–1880,* ed. Scott E. Casper et al., vol. 3 of *A History of the Book in America* (Chapel Hill: University of North Carolina Press, 2007), 231–32.

44. "The Relation of an Author to the Public," *Circular,* March 4, 1858, 24.

45. Willis, *Out-doors at Idlewild,* 48; *Home Journal,* April 23, 1853, 2.

46. *Home Journal,* January 31, 1952, 2.

47. *Home Journal,* November 26, 1853, 2.

48. Willis, *Out-doors at Idlewild,* 66; *Home Journal,* May 14, 1853, 2.

49. Basil Rauch, "The First Hundred Years," special centennial issue of *Town and Country,* December 1946, 62.

6. Speculative Manhood

1. Barry Gray [Robert Barry Coffin], *Out of Town: A Rural Episode* (New York: Hurd and Houghton, 1866), 50. Further references will be abbreviated *OT* and cited in text.

2. For supplemental information on this nineteenth-century literary genre, see John Stilgoe, *Borderland: Origins of the American Suburb, 1820–1939* (New Haven: Yale University Press, 1988), esp. chap. 4, "Borderland Life and Popular Literature." Adam Sweeting and Loren C. Owings also write on the country book in *Reading Houses and Building Books: Andrew Jackson Downing and the Architecture of Popular Antebellum Literature, 1835–1855* (Hanover: University Press of New England, 1996), and *Quest for Walden: A Study of the "Country Book" in American Popular Literature with an Annotated Bibliography, 1863–1995* (Jefferson, N.C.: McFarland, 1997), respectively.

3. Fredrika Bremer, *Homes of the New World,* 2 vols. (New York: Harper and Brothers, 1854), 1:52.

4. *Dwight's American Magazine, and Family Newspaper, for the Diffusion of Useful Knowledge and Moral and Religious Principles,* October 11, 1845, 576.

5. "Shade Trees in Cities," *Horticulturalist,* August 1, 1852, 345.

6. F. W. Shelton, *Up the River* (New York: Charles Scribner, 1853), xiii.

7. Ibid., xviii–xix.

8. Ibid., xiv.

9. Ibid., 1–2.

10. See L. W. Mansfield, *Up-Country Letters* (New York: D. Appleton & Co., 1852); as well as S. H. Hammond and L. W. Mansfield, *Country Margins and Rambles of a Journalist* (New York: J. C. Derby, 1855).

11. F. S. Cozzens, *Sayings, Wise and Otherwise* (New York: United States Book Company, 1870), xx. Most of the essays contained in the volume had been published previously in the periodical *Hearth and Home.*

12. "Frederick S. Cozzens, Esq.," *Ballou's Pictorial Drawing-Room Companion,* August 30, 1856, 140.

13. Frederic S. Cozzens, *The Sparrowgrass Papers: or, Living in the Country* (New York: Derby & Jackson, 1856), 13–14. Further references will be abbreviated *SP* and cited in text.

14. John Fiske and J. G. Wilson, eds., *Appleton's Cyclopaedia of American Biography* (New York: D. Appleton and Company, 1887–1889), 626.

15. Robert Barry Coffin, *Cakes and Ale at Woodbine; From Twelfth Night to New Year's Day* (New York: Hurd and Houghton, 1868), abbreviated *CAW* and cited in text; *Castles in the Air, and Other Phantoms* (New York: Hurd and Houghton, 1871); *Matrimonial Infelicities: With an Occasional Felicity, By Way of Contrast* (New York: Hurd and Houghton, 1865); *My Married Life at Hillside* (New York: Hurd and Houghton, 1865); and *Out of Town: A Rural Episode* (New York: Hurd and Houghton, 1866).

16. Review of *Matrimonial Infelicities, The Round Table: A Saturday Review of Politics, Finance, Literature, Society,* October 14, 1865, 85.

17. Advertisement for *Out of Town, The Round Table,* December 15, 1866, 332.

18. Lloyd Ultan and Barbara Unger, "Out of Town: The Suburban Bronx, 1800–1898," in *Bronx Accent: A Literary and Pictorial History of the Borough* (New Brunswick: Rutgers University Press, 2000), 25.

19. George E. Woodward and F. W. Woodward, *Woodward's Country Homes* (New York: Geo. E. Woodward, 1865), 38.

Afterword

1. Transcribed from *Mad Men,* season 1, episode 13 (Santa Monica: Lionsgate, 2008).

2. David Lowenthal, *The Past Is a Foreign Country* (1985; repr., New York: Cambridge University Press, 1988), 4.

3. J. B. Jackson, *Discovering the Vernacular Landscape* (New Haven: Yale University Press, 1984), 12.

4. Thomas Harris, *The Silence of the Lambs* (1988; repr., New York: St. Martin's Press, 1989), 53.

5. Lowenthal, *The Past Is a Foreign Country,* 4.

6. Frank J. Scott, *The Art of Beautifying Suburban Home Grounds of Small Extent* (New York: D. Appleton & Co., 1870), 22.

7. Daniel Atwood, *Atwood's Country and Suburban Homes* (New York: Orange Judd & Co., 1871), dedication page.

8. Scott, *The Art of Beautifying Suburban Home Grounds,* 132.

9. Quoted in Susan Goodman and Carl Dawson, *William Dean Howells: A Writer's Life* (Berkeley: University of California Press, 2005), 94.

10. William Dean Howells, *Suburban Sketches* (New York: Hurd and Houghton, 1871), 12. Further references will be cited in text.

INDEX

MAURA D'AMORE was born in Tulsa, Oklahoma. She earned a PhD in English from the University of North Carolina at Chapel Hill, where she specialized in American literature to 1900 and minored in American studies. She is an assistant professor of English at Saint Michael's College in Colchester, Vermont. She resides in Shelburne, Vermont, with her husband, Jonathan D'Amore, and their sons, Frank and Rufus.